READING
ESSENTIALS

P9-BBP-620

READING
ESSENTIALS

The Specifics You Need to Teach Reading Well

REGIE ROUTMAN

HEINEMANN
Portsmouth, NH

Heinemann
A division of Reed Elsevier Inc.
361 Hanover Street
Portsmouth, NH 03801–3912
www.heinemann.com

Offices and agents throughout the world

© 2003 by Regie Routman

All rights reserved. No part of this book may be reproduced in any form or by any electronic or mechanical means, including information storage and retrieval systems, without permission in writing from the publisher, except by a reviewer, who may quote brief passages in a review, with the following exceptions: Appendices A–J may be photocopied for classroom use only.

The author and publisher wish to thank those who have generously given permission to reprint borrowed material:

Excerpt from *Better Than Life* by Daniel Pennac. Copyright © 1999. Reprinted with permission of Stenhouse Publishers, simultaneously published by Pembroke Publishers in Canada and Stenhouse Publishers in the United States.

Excerpt from *Keepers* by Jeri Hanel Watts. Text Copyright © 1997 by Jeri Hanel Watts. Permission arranged with Lee & Low Books, Inc., New York, NY 10016.

Making a Hat by Kate McGough. Originally published by Reed International Books, Australia. Reprinted by permission.

Library of Congress Cataloging-in-Publication Data
Routman, Regie.
    Reading essentials : the specifics you need to teach reading well / Regie Routman.
       p. cm.
    Includes bibliographical references and index.
    ISBN 0-325-00492-7 (alk. paper)
    1. Reading (Elementary)—United States. I. Title.

    LB1573 .R66 2003
    372.4—dc21   2002011704

Editor: Lois Bridges
Production: Patricia Adams
Production coordination: Abigail M. Heim
Typesetting: Gina Poirier; David Stirling, Black Dog Graphics
Interior design: Judy Arisman, Arisman Design; Robert Torrens contributed the Optimal Learning Model and scripted lessons
Cover design: Ellen Korey-Lie
Cover photography: Regie Routman
Manufacturing: Louise Richardson

About the Cover: Regie Routman took this photograph of Matt, engrossed in some essential reading, during a weeklong residency in his classroom.

Printed in the United States of America on acid-free paper
06   05   04   03   RRD   3   4   5

To Don Holdaway

In appreciation of your enormous contribution to literacy, and especially for bringing joy into learning

Contents

Optimal Learning Model	
Who *Holds Book/Pen*	*Degree of Support*
Teacher /Student	DEMONSTRATION
Teacher /Student	SHARED DEMONSTRATION
gradual handover of responsibility	
Teacher /Student	GUIDED PRACTICE
Teacher /Student	INDEPENDENT PRACTICE

Optimal Learning Model	
Degree of Support	*Learning Context*
Demonstration	
Shared Demonstration	
gradual handover of responsibility	
Guided Practice	
INDEPENDENT PRACTICE	**INDEPENDENT READING**

Three Teaching Essentials

Optimal Learning Model	
Degree of Support	*Learning Context*
Demonstration	
SHARED DEMONSTRATION	**SHARED READING**
gradual handover of responsibility	
Guided Practice	
Independent Practice	

Four Advocacy Is Also Essential

Optimal Learning Model	
Degree of Support	*Learning Context*
Demonstration	
Shared Demonstration	
gradual handover of responsibility	
GUIDED PRACTICE	**GUIDED READING**
Independent Practice	

Appendices

Brief Definitions of Terms A-12

Notes A-17

A Note About Notes

To keep the text clean and unencumbered, all references to research, ideas, authors, and quotations are listed in a notes section on page A-17 in the end matter. The notes are divided by chapter and sequenced consecutively by page number. Sources and/or elaboration, including bibliographic information to help you find referenced material easily, are presented after a brief identifying phrase or statement linked to the text. Any statement or concept not attributed is based on my own teacher-research, observations, and thirty-five years of teaching experience. To keep the book itself to a manageable length, the notes also provide additional recommended resources and references for information and self-study. Brief definitions of terms that may not be fully explained in the text are included beginning on page A-12.

Acknowledgments

As with my previous books, this work is a true collaboration. Although the words are mine, I have been deeply influenced by the children, teachers, and administrators I work with in schools around the country. In particular, many talented educators have generously shared ideas and materials for which I am most grateful: Karen Anderson, Gerry Coles, Pat Dragan, Melanie Fry, Diane Gillespie, Deb Greenwood, Bonnie Campbell Hill, Linda Hoyt, Marilyn Jerde, Nancy Johnson, Jane Jones, Rebecca Kimberly, Stephen Krashen, Gloria Norton, Jeri Ozbun, Thommie Piercy, Kathy Struck, and Lindy Vizyak. A special heartfelt thanks to Bob Torrens for his computer genius in creating the visual for the optimal learning model and for formatting the reading lessons.

I always depend on trusted reader/responders to ensure that my writing is clear, sensible, and helpful to teachers. The following distinguished educators have generously given their time and talents, and the book is richer because of their honesty and expertise. I am greatly indebted to Mark Andrews, Angela Beland, Monica Carrera-Wilburn, Marnie Danielski, Don Holdaway, Devon Isherwood, Nicole Luthy, Mike Marinello, Jana McPherson, Mike Oliver, Kari Oosterveen, Susan Thaney, and Robin Woods. And a special note of gratitude to Richard Allington and Elaine Garan for their thoughtful, expert review of my research section.

My publisher, Heinemann, has been devoted to publishing a book that is timely, accurate, and beautiful. I especially thank my beloved friend and editor Lois Bridges for her brilliant insights, superb editing, and willingness to do whatever is necessary to support my efforts. Alan Huisman, stellar copy editor, is the best gift an author can have. He makes my life easier by deftly editing the manuscript with exceptional care, all the while maintaining my voice and intended meaning. Abby Heim has been an extraordinary production manager. I am appreciative of her flexibility, patience, and amazing skills and for hiring terrific Patty Adams to support the production process. The book is stronger because of

Patty's meticulous line-by-line editing and vigilant attention to details great and small. Special thanks to Diane Brenner for her fine work on the index. Talented editorial assistant Kären Clausen has been tireless in her efforts, tracking down everything from an errant student release to a hot-off-the-press research citation. Others at Heinemann deserve special mention for their fabulous efforts and continuing support: Lesa Scott, Leigh Peake, Mike Gibbons, Tracy Heine, Cherie Bartlett, and Charlene Morris. And Maura Sullivan, an insightful marketer with a creative flair, has also become a dear friend.

Reading Essentials was written in the midst of daily living and working while also dealing with important life issues. Without the love and understanding of friends and family, I could not have completed this book. I continue to rely on the professional judgment of cherished colleagues and friends. Diane Levin, Judie Thelen, and Judy Wallis are always available for lively conversation, ideas, and support. I treasure Linda Cooper, Loretta Martin, and Karen Sher not only for being terrific reader/responders to major portions of this text, but as my life-long trusted friends and colleagues who never fail to inspire my thinking. I am thankful for my dear sister Amy Bushman—and her husband Earl as well. They are devoted lifetime supporters of my work. Harriet Cooper, my best friend for forty years, always adds clear perspectives, humor, and unconditional love. My son Peter, wife Claudine, and granddaughter Katie continue to add much joy to my life. Most of all, I am happy and grateful to have Frank as my loving husband and lifetime partner.

July 2002

READING
ESSENTIALS

One

The Essential Reading Life

If we want our students to be excited about literacy, they need to have teachers who love coming to work, who are literacy learners themselves, who find ways to make curriculum relevant to children's lives, and who can put high-stakes testing in perspective.

1. Simplify Your Teaching Life

My husband and I were out for a Saturday breakfast when I bumped into a teacher I used to work with. "How's your teaching going?" I asked. "I'm overwhelmed" were the first words out of her mouth. "We've got too much to cover with the kids and never enough time to do it." These days, of course, that's a very common response. But it's not just the feeling of having too much put upon us that worries me. The joy seems to have gone out of teaching.

Let me illustrate. It was the first day of a new school residency. I was spending a week at an elementary school in the Southwest, working with the teachers and principal to strengthen and refine their school's literacy instruction. I had just finished working with a group of students in a grade 1–2 class, with twenty teachers looking on. The students and I had spent the last hour happily reading, writing, chanting, singing, and rereading texts, some of which we'd written ourselves. Each activity was purposeful and carefully thought out to introduce students to high-quality materials, guarantee success for all, provide possibilities for differentiated instruction, and teach skills and strategies explicitly. The host-classroom teacher's comments (sentiments that were echoed throughout the week) surprised and saddened me:

> I'd forgotten what it's like to enjoy teaching. You were having fun with my students, and, at the same time you were teaching them a lot. We're under huge pressure to cover so much material and for kids to do well on the tests. We're told exactly what and how to teach. I'm just so exhausted and burned out.

If we want our students to be excited about literacy, they need to have teachers who love coming to work, who are literacy learners themselves, who find ways to make curriculum relevant to children's lives, and who can put high-stakes testing in perspective. None of this is possible if we're constantly exhausted from an overstuffed curriculum and have no time to collaborate, reflect, and renew ourselves.

Why Reading Essentials?

My purpose in writing this book is to make your life easier, to put some fun back into your teaching, to clarify difficult issues, and to rethink what's truly essential for students to become lifelong readers and thinkers. By understanding the essentials for teaching children to read well, I hope to build on your confidence and knowledge so you can and will make the best decisions for your students—regardless of the reading program you use. By getting at what's really important and focusing on essentials, we can accelerate instruction, especially for our readers and writers who struggle.

In my present role as a visiting literacy teacher, I provide demonstration teaching in schools around the country in weeklong residencies. The first things I am struck by are the demands on teachers' time, how hard teachers are working, and how little time they have for reflection. The teacher's life is that of a juggler, trying to keep all the balls in the air; inevitably, one or more fall to the ground.

Teachers are working way too hard. We're overburdened with too much to do and too little time in which to do it. Many of us teach in schools without adequate resources and support. Often, our students' needs extend beyond what we can comfortably provide. Still, we're held responsible for "closing the achievement gap" by increasing students' test scores.

Along with this push for more accountability come the accompanying "packages" to "fix" the schools, the teachers, and the kids. Too many of us have adopted questionable practices and materials because we've been told to do so, and, mostly, we're too tired—and sometimes too scared—to protest. Increasingly, programs and curriculum are mandated without our input, and we remain at the mercy of politicians and others outside our profession.

As a profession, we suffer from a collective lack of self-confidence. We devalue our own knowledge and experiences while overrelying on scientific research. We fail to see teacher research as credible, and we ignore decades of literacy research from around the world. We've made teaching and learning more difficult than it needs to be (see "Ways We Complicate Our Teaching Lives" on page 7). It's time for a change—a return to the basics of relying on professional common sense, credible classroom research as well as scientifically based research, teachers as decision makers, and reading as a meaning-making process right from the start.

Our teaching lives need to become saner, smarter, more manageable. One of the first things I say to teachers during a new school residency is this:

> My aim this week is to make your teaching life easier, more efficient, more meaningful, and more fun. If I leave at the end of the week and you feel you have more demands on you, I have failed. I hope to lift a burden. You're working way too hard.

My goal is the same for you, dear reader. Use this book to reflect on your practices and think about what you might try, alter, or adjust to increase students' learning, maintain sensible and rigorous practices, and make your teaching life easier and more enjoyable.

Be as Knowledgeable as You Can Be

In order to make the best teaching decisions for our students, we must be fully informed about credible research, exemplary teaching practices, the social aspects of learning, how children develop as learners, and much more.

One of the best ways I know to be knowledgeable is to engage in ongoing professional conversations. Otherwise, every time something new comes along, we are quick to get "on board" without knowing whether the new program, material, or procedure is really applicable and beneficial. We don't know the questions to ask, we lack the confidence to voice objections, we feel powerless and alone. Without ongoing professional conversations in our schools, we are at the mercy of politicians and publishers who think they should determine how and what we should be teaching.

I no longer return to a school beyond a second visit unless the administration and faculty commit to holding weekly professional conversations. These meetings are voluntary, but the majority of the teaching staff, including the principal, attend them. Educators come to value these meetings for the increased collegiality and knowledge that ensue, which eventually translate into higher student achievement.

There Is No One "Right" or Best Way

Teachers ask two related questions all the time:

☐   What's the best way to do such-and-such?
☐   What should I be doing relative to thus-and-so?

The answer depends on your students, your teaching contexts, your beliefs, your curriculum, and your standards. Only you can decide, but you have to be highly knowledgeable to make these decisions.

This book shares my thinking right now. My beliefs and practices are based on reading widely, examining research, collaborating with colleagues, listening to and interacting with literacy leaders, and reflecting on my thirty-plus years of teaching experience and my current weeklong school residencies around the country. Instead of focusing on "Is it right?" or "What's the best way?" let's think about and focus on what's right and best for a particular student or group of students at this point in time as indicated by what we've read, the conversations we've had with our colleagues, valid research we've consulted, our teaching experiences, and our students' needs and interests.

Throughout this text I give my informed opinion, but it is up to you as another informed teacher to decide what works for you and your students in your particular school and classroom. Our decisions cannot be based on a "gut feel," what the teachers down the hall are doing, the newest program, or pressure from "above." We have the responsibility to act each day as knowledgeable professionals.

Adapt ideas to fit your particular school, students, beliefs, and contexts. Accept the fact that someone else's idea or form never quite works the way you want it to. Your students are unique. Only you know them well enough to meet their needs and build on their interests and competencies. Use this book as a springboard for your own thinking and teaching practice. Start new conversations with yourself and your colleagues. Keep questioning everything you do.

Question Research

"Research" is driving reading instruction; federal funding is now linked to "scientifically proven methods," and in some cases, the approved research is of questionable value. How can we as teachers know what research we should pay attention to and what research we should ignore?

The irony in "scientific research" being given such credence and weight with regard to how we teach reading is that true scientists rarely reach a "forever" conclusion. They continue to question, hypothesize, speculate, and come to new conclusions. Just because there's research doesn't mean we shouldn't question it. In fact, when it flies in the face of everything we know, we *must* question it. For example, questioning the value of voluntary reading in the classroom has led some schools to abandon this critical reading essential. (See Chapter 11 for some guidelines on how to evaluate, interpret, and use research in your teaching practice.)

Teach What's Essential to the Well-Being of the Child as a Learner and a Developing Person

We need to get back to the basics of what really matters in teaching and learning:

FOCUS ON WHAT MATTERS MOST

- ☐ Inspiring ongoing curiosity and a love of learning.
- ☐ Acquiring the skills and tools to learn and go on learning.
- ☐ Guaranteeing immediate and continued success.
- ☐ Ensuring that learners become thinking, probing users of language.
- ☐ Implementing challenging and relevant curriculum.
- ☐ Establishing and sustaining collaborative and caring communities.

I see these as goals for both teachers and students. If schools are not nurturing, exciting, and safe places for teachers, we teachers cannot create those environments for our students.

WAYS WE COMPLICATE OUR TEACHING LIVES

- ☐ Focusing first on procedures rather than on learning.
- ☐ Concentrating on programs instead of students (relying on a "one size fits all" program rather than on the knowledgeable teacher).
- ☐ Focusing on strategies instead of comprehension.
- ☐ Creating elaborate, time-consuming management systems rather than simple, effective ones.
- ☐ Overrelying on commercial assessments when classroom-based assessments (for example, assessing reading comprehension using

the book the child has picked out herself and is reading) are by far the most reliable.

- ☐ Relying on phonics to the exclusion of other reading strategies.
- ☐ Overrelying on scientific research while ignoring classroom-based research and experiences.
- ☐ Going along with practices without knowing why (for example, creating a word wall because "everyone" else is and "we're supposed to").
- ☐ Ignoring kids' interests and feedback instead of negotiating with them (for example, putting together our classroom libraries and rooms without consulting our students).
- ☐ Working mostly in isolation instead of with colleagues.
- ☐ Focusing on test-taking skills rather than on engaging kids in challenging, meaningful curriculum.
- ☐ Breaking learning into bits and pieces instead of centering learning on meaningful wholes.
- ☐ Relying on experts while ignoring and devaluing our own literacy knowledge.

What About Learners with Special Needs?

Teachers always ask, "But how do I teach my readers who struggle, the students with learning disabilities, those with emotional and behavioral problems, the growing number of EAL [English as an additional language] students?" (And that's just for starters.) You teach them the way you teach all students. You respect them as individuals. You hold high expectations for each one of them. You build on their strengths. You find out what their interests are. You make sure they experience immediate success. You give them the best instruction, first-rate materials, real books, challenging curriculum, and you continually evaluate their progress so you know what to teach next. All the teaching strategies I describe in this book can be used or adapted for your learners with different needs.

This may sound simplistic, but it works. If we recognize that we all learn at different rates and that progress may be very slow for some, we can still celebrate the learning that does occur. Have the courage to use the best teaching practices you know with all students, not just "the stars."

Teach to the Child, Not the Label

Teaching a child on the basis of his label rather than his uniqueness inhibits best practice and limits our expectations. One of the big advantages I have when I work in classrooms as a visiting literacy teacher is that I don't know who the supposed slow ones are, who have been identified as gifted, who have behavior problems. Very often teachers tell me they are surprised by what a student has accomplished: usually (but not always, of course) this is a struggling student.

In a recent school residency, I was demonstrating how to conduct an informal reading evaluation during independent reading (see Chapter 7). I asked the host-classroom teacher (lots of other teachers were observing) whom she wanted me to evaluate first. Joey, a fourth grader, came to the table with the chapter book he was reading. While he had a good grasp of the story and did an adequate retelling, he was not able to read between the lines, to talk about character motivation and behavior. "You know he's gifted," his teacher told me after the conference. That came as a surprise to me, and I was glad I had not known that ahead of time. Inadvertently, I might not have evaluated his comprehension as thoroughly as I did. Because I didn't know anything about his abilities, I made no assumptions.

Every type of special needs student is in most of the classes we teach. If I can't find books a student can read, we write one (or more) together. If she can't read words, I make sure I have an activity that will allow her to participate by being able to identify a letter (I have never yet had a student who couldn't at least identify one letter matching a letter in her name). If students don't know enough letters to be able to write in their journals independently, I gather that group and we write, and then read, an interactive story together. Learning magic begins only when children believe they can succeed. And children believe they can succeed when they connect the unknown to the known. (There are examples of how to capitalize on each child's level so they experience success on pages 13–15 and 57–62.)

View Teaching as an Art Supported by Science

Teachers need to gain back the confidence to trust their own professional knowledge. There is enormous pressure these days to trust only so-called scientifically based research and to ignore the idiosyncratic world of the classroom containing real kids with different abilities, needs, and interests.

The federal endorsement of teaching reading by emphasizing science and systematic instruction over all else is troubling. While science is necessary and important in deciding which teaching approaches to use, it is insufficient. We educators must ultimately make the teaching/learning decisions for the students in our classroom, because we know them best. Scientific knowledge and professional experience and judgment must go hand in hand.

A personal story here. Throughout the time I was writing this book, my husband and I were caretaking an elderly, cherished friend in the final months of her life. Juliette carefully followed the "prescriptions" medical science offered, including myriad tests using sophisticated technology. But there was no one authority to monitor her condition and make adjustments based on her needs as an individual. The lack of coordination and customization made her treatment haphazard and inadequate, and in some cases recommended procedures exacerbated her illness. Without a caring expert who knows the patient and can tailor "science" to the person receiving treatment, medical procedures can go awry. This is no less true for teaching.

Without devoted teachers to individualize instruction for the students in their classroom, any program—even a scientifically proven one—will be, at best, minimally effective. Art and science must always work together. It is our professional responsibility to ensure that they do and that, always, above all, we honor the human element—teacher to child, child to child, person to person.

2. Bond with Your Students

The modeling by people that we love is what changes us.
—Don Holdaway

Several years ago, my mentor and dear colleague, Don Holdaway, was visiting Frank and me at our home. I invited a group of teachers to join us for an evening of literacy conversations. Don told a story that had a profound effect on many of us.

In the late 1980s, when Don was working in Cambridge, Massachusetts, setting up a demonstration literacy school, his daughter Rebecca was enrolled in kindergarten. Several months into the school year, she was resisting going to school and complaining about not liking her teacher. Don and his wife, Frances, scheduled a conference with the teacher during which Don boomed, "Look, you don't have to like my child, but you must bond with her if she's to learn anything at all! That's your job as a teacher."

During the week after this discussion, Rebecca's teacher bonded not only with Rebecca but with all of her students. Don said the most critical step the teacher took was to look Rebecca in the eye with interest, acceptance, and curiosity. Rebecca received the response she had never received before from her teacher, and her shyness and fear dropped away. They talked and began a genuine friendship. "It happened in less than a minute during regular lessons without any need to take the child aside or make a special case of her."

I think of that story and those words—"You must bond with her if she's to learn anything at all"—every time I go into a classroom to work with kids. We've been told as teachers that we must fall in love with each of our students. Yet we've all had students who, for whatever reasons, are difficult for us to love. But bonding is quite another matter. We can and must bond with them all. This is not a choice but a duty and responsibility.

Bonding with our students means that we:

☐   Treat them and their families with respect.

☐   Act kindly toward them.

☐   Show that we care about them.

☐   Listen to them.

☐   Keep them safe.

☐   Celebrate their efforts and accomplishments.

☐   Know their interests and incorporate those interests
     into the curriculum.

☐   Provide optimal learning conditions.

☐   Make sure they succeed from the very first day.

☐   Have faith in them as learners.

☐   Value them as individuals.

No one talks about bonding, and we need to. Curriculum and standards must first connect with the lives and spirits of our children if we're to have any lasting success. Unless we reach into our students' hearts, we have no entry into their minds. Through drill and memorization, we can get students to complete assignments and pass tests. But there is a price to pay for such short-term accomplishment. We will never inspire our students to learn for their own sake and to love coming to school.

Bonding with our students is the "human essential," the intimately personal connection that is the core of responsive, excellent teaching. We simply cannot teach our students well until we show them we know them, care about them, and connect with them.

How Does Bonding Work?

Bonding depends on teaching that incorporates a learning model that assures success for all children (see the inside front cover and pages 43–49). That is, through demonstrations, invited participation, guided and independent practice, in an accepting and encouraging social and academic environment, students gradually become confident learners. But bonding involves much more. Don Holdaway explains it best, and the next two paragraphs are in his own words.

Bonding rests in the first place on what the teacher *gives* rather than what she *demands* or seeks to induce from the children—her own behavior must be emulative, attracting attention and admiration. *She* must be liked rather than her liking them. This can be achieved in so many ways by powerful demonstrations of reading aloud, writing with punch, and exposing secrets in texts and stories. She shares her love of words and intonations, expresses meanings frontally through facial expression, body language, and voice. Once she has caught the fascination of each child—perhaps at different times—the situation is ripe for bonding. She may be invitational—"Would you like to read like that? Would you like some more stories as good as this one? Would you like to read this story again with me?" etc. As the children respond with ideas and perceptions of their own, she affirms and celebrates their ideas. From here on it's a cinch!

For those children who for one reason or other are not captured by those first invitational exchanges it is simply a matter of waiting. As they observe the enthusiasm and interaction of other children they begin to pick up interest. As shared activities become more lively, they feel a need to be part of the processes and make tentative or hesitant stabs at participation. This is a critical moment. The teacher may react immediately, or wait now for an appropriate chance to intervene. She uses the child's name, catches his or her eye with approval and interest and delight, and commends the response—"Oh, Damion, you said that so well!" or "Helen, you enjoyed that, didn't you!"

We need to pay attention to bonding and the power of emotional commitment to our students. Worldwide, the strongest predictor of reading achievement is the quality of student-teacher relations.

Work Your Magic with Students

One recent September, I initiated the school year with a weeklong school residency in a wonderful public school with a terrific principal and teachers. The student population was an enthusiastic group of mostly Hispanic, economically very poor, transient girls and boys. On that first Monday morning, I began by introducing myself to the eager group of first graders gathered on the floor in front of me. As I began telling them about all the reading and writing we'd be doing together that week, a student blurted out, "But I can't read." That was followed by a resounding chorus of "I can't read."

I was taken aback because at every school I work in, including this one, kindergarten teachers do a marvelous job convincing their charges that they can read, whether or not they've actually mastered the act of reading. Kindergarten teachers have always known that kids have to believe they can read before they actually do it.

Realizing I had a crisis on my hands—that is, if I was to teach these children to read—I immediately had to win their trust and convince them they were readers. So, right on the spot, I boasted:

> I'm a magician of sorts. I guarantee by the end of this week every single
> one of you will be able to read. I'm a terrific reading teacher. I've never
> had a student I couldn't teach how to read. I promise you by Friday you
> will be able to read. I never make a promise I can't keep.

They looked back at me with wide, astonished eyes, and I scrapped my lesson plan and started afresh.

> Here's what we're going to do. We're going to write a book together
> right now. And by the end of the week, you'll be able to read it all by
> yourself. Let's call our book "We Can." Let's make it about all the things
> you know how to do. How about if we start it this way: We can *play*.

We wrote the story on large chart paper, bound it into a big book, and also word-processed small copies for each student. As promised, on Friday every single child could read the "We Can" book, even the many who didn't know all their letters and sounds. It was not just that the book was written in their own words, that they had read and reread the book, that they had drawn their own illustrations, that they had practiced reading and writing the words in isolation. It was that they believed my promise—that I could teach them and they could learn.

We teachers have the power to make magic happen in our classrooms. Once our students bond with us and trust us, anything is possible. This is true in our relationships with other teachers too. We learn more, and learning is easier, when we trust our mentors and colleagues. This was brought home to me recently in a letter I received from principal Diane Gillespie after I had completed a second weeklong school residency in her school: "The first visit was wonderful, but there was something special about that second visit. It must have been because we already knew you and trusted you."

Ensure Early Success for Every Child

When I am working with children—whether it's the whole class, a small group, or one at a time—I look for ways for students to shine. I am especially alert for the quiet child, the withdrawn one, the one whose hand never goes up, the disruptive child. I have learned from years of teaching that if a child experiences immediate and early success as a reader and writer, that child willingly engages in reading and writing with a spirit of "I can do this." If, on the other hand, the child experiences years, or even months, of frustration and failure, it is unlikely he will become a successful reader and writer. Success breeds more success; repeated failure leads to the feeling "I can't do this." Often, students just give up.

Every year we have a new group of students. Regardless of their past experiences, we must find ways to have them experience and build on immediate successes. Sometimes, it's writing down a child's language and creating a text he or she can read, as with the "We Can" book. Or it may be finding the one sentence in a piece of writing that makes sense, affirming it, and helping the child move on from there. Or perhaps it's finding out what the child knows a lot about and recognizing and celebrating their expertise. Or it might be calling on a student to respond and collaborating with him so that success is guaranteed. All these are ways we work our magic with students. Reprimands, which distract from teaching and break the lesson focus and pace, become unnecessary when each child believes he is a valued and successful literacy contributor. I continually look for ways to create moments in which children who are not used to success can be successful. One way I keep students engaged is to make the curriculum relevant and challenging and to keep a fast pace (more on this in Chapter 12).

Model Respect

You can't bond with someone you don't know. I'll never forget reading Don Graves's *Writing: Teachers and Children at Work* in the 1980s and being jolted by his statement about knowing our students. I was embarrassed to admit that there were several students in my room I knew little about. Today when I work in classrooms with students and teachers, I make an effort to know them—not just as learners but as unique human beings. It works. I was surprised but pleased when a principal told me, "You didn't just model lessons. You modeled respect by the way you treated each student and teacher."

The tragic events of September 11, 2001, make clear how desperately important it is to model and practice—through our own behavior—respect, tolerance, compassion, and courtesy as we work to know our students and bond with them. We need to make our classrooms not only learning communities but also safe havens. Life seems more fragile than ever before.

<table>
<tr><td>

*Teacher
Talk*

</td><td>

Use the language of encouragement and respect

☐ *You can do it.*
☐ *You did it.*
☐ *You knew it.*
☐ *You figured that out.*
☐ *You thought about it before you answered.*
☐ *I can tell you were thinking. Tell me how you knew that/figured it out.*
☐ *You didn't give up. You kept trying.*

</td></tr>
</table>

Encourage Shared Decision Making

When we make all decisions and choices for students, we disenfranchise them. When we seek input from students and value what they say, we demonstrate respect for their thinking. Even more, we are telling them, "We are a partnership. Our collaboration will result in the best product or decision or format." As teachers, we must involve students in establishing classroom rules and procedures, determining room and library organization, developing formats for projects and reading records, creating rubrics, and much more.

One easy way to demonstrate your collaborative intent from the first day of school is to leave the classroom partly undone; that is, leave some decisions about bulletin boards and room arrangement to the students. When students enter classrooms in which we have decorated and planned every inch of space, the message we are sending is: "This is my classroom. You are welcome to be tenants here this year." However, when we say to students, "Let's talk about how we want to use the spaces in our classroom. Do we want to . . . ?" the message is very different. Then we are saying to them: "Welcome to *our* classroom. Let's decide together how we want it all to look and work."

teaching tip

*Value Students'
Literacy and
Culture*

Celebrate the everyday literacy kids bring to school with them. I cringe when I hear teachers say that a child has no literacy or language experiences. Ridiculous! All children have literacy and language experiences, and we need to value them. Do everything you can to find out about and celebrate students' lives and backgrounds.

Take a Look at Your Classroom

Honestly examine how your classroom is set up:

☐ Who's doing most of the talking? Is every child's voice encouraged and respected? Can students respond to one another as well as the teacher?
☐ Do displays and materials motivate and celebrate children's writing?
☐ Are kids' favorite books and authors available and accessible?
☐ Have the library corner and reading materials been organized with students' input? (See Chapter 5.)
☐ Are responsibilities for keeping the room orderly, well functioning, and beautiful shared with students?

teaching tip

Comfortable Classroom

Look at your classroom through the eyes of your students. Would you feel comfortable and welcome spending six or eight hours a day in this room? Think of your classroom as a living room. Make it as beautiful and inviting as you can.

By giving students some choice within the structures we set up, we make it possible for them to feel more comfortable with us. Such faith in students shows our respect for them; in turn, they are likely to feel empowered knowing that their voices and opinions matter. Sharing the power with students establishes a collaborative, congenial tone and helps students bond with us and engage more deeply in learning. When Jane Jones, a third-grade teacher in Westminster, Colorado, reorganized her extensive book collection to include students' suggestions, interest and enjoyment in reading dramatically increased, even for her lowest-performing readers (see page 76). She says,

> Allowing the children to reorganize our classroom library turned out to be one of the most rewarding experiences of the year. In fact, the hardest thing I had to do during this whole process was give up my adult preconception that I was the only one who could organize the library in a meaningful way. Through this experience *my* library truly became *ours*.

Bring in Stories

Stories of our lives are powerful because they humanize and personalize us. It's hard to trust and relate to someone you don't know. When we bring our lives into the classroom, students get to know what we love and what we struggle with, our ups and downs, our hopes and accomplishments. We become "real" to our students, and they come to trust us. And our stories help us make sense of our own lives as well. Stories are how we connect with others.

Tell the Stories of Your Life

When I am meeting students for the first time, I always gather them close around me and begin by telling them about myself and my family. I may talk about my plane trip and packing up to leave, how I had difficulty sleeping last night, how I miss my husband when I'm away, how I made a batch of chocolate chip cookies for him before I left and how he loves them straight out of the freezer. I often show some recent photos of my family. Here's part of a story I told recently:

> I'm so happy to meet all of you. Whew! I came a long way on a plane to get here. In fact, I had to get up at four A.M. this morning. I set two alarm clocks in case one didn't work. And you know what? I still didn't sleep well. I never sleep well the night before a trip. I guess I'm always a little bit nervous. I worry about how the week will go, because of course I want everything to go just right. I worry about my husband, Frank, because I'm not sure he eats properly when I'm away.

Speaking of my husband, you won't believe what he did this morning. He made me pancakes with bananas, blueberries, and pecans. Can you imagine, at that hour of the morning! It was a good thing, too, because they didn't serve any breakfast on the plane.

When I am working with a group of teachers for the first time, I start the same way, telling stories about my life, my teaching experiences, my husband, my grandchild, my dad, what I'm currently reading and thinking, how I hope the week will go. I also emphasize that I'm available every day after school for informal conversations. I bond with most students on the first day. It always takes at least three days and often longer to win teachers' trust.

Value Children's Stories

When we celebrate the stories of children's lives, we blur the lines between home and school and let students know that their lives matter. I always publish the writing of the most struggling students first. Jessica was the lowest-performing student in her kindergarten class. When her journal story (see page 19) about her fish (written over three consecutive days) was published, Jessica proudly read it to everyone who would listen. Her teacher, Melanie Fry, notes that after that success, Jessica was less withdrawn and more willing to attempt new tasks: "Her self-esteem blossomed."

Students are also very motivated to read the texts they have written together as a class—journals of classroom experiences and daily happenings, little books for guided reading, letters, and much more. (For some examples, see "What We're Really Good At" and "Connect Reading with Writing" on pages 53–61.) One of the reasons I always do a shared writing when I am meeting with new students is that it's a way for me not only to get to know them but also to value what they know and love.

Read Stories Aloud

I always read aloud, in my most dramatic voice, when I first meet students. It's the fastest way I know to bond with kids. It says to them, "I have a favorite story that I love, and I want to share it with you." There is nothing like enjoying a good story together to begin to build a trusting relationship and classroom community.

Reading aloud enables children to hear the rich language of stories and texts they cannot yet read on their own or might never have chosen to read. Our students learn vocabulary, grammar, new information, and how stories and

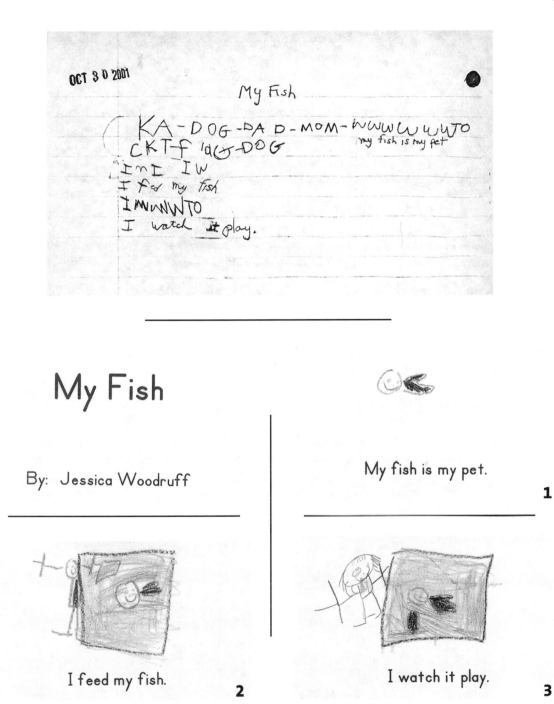

Jessica's published journal story becomes her first successful reading

teaching tip

*Choosing
Read-Alouds*

Choose excellent literature, in various genres, with which students can identify. Listening comprehension comes before reading, so choose books that provide an opportunity to expand the background knowledge necessary for comprehension.

written language work, especially when we talk about the background of the piece of writing and encourage active participation and discussion. Reading aloud—in all grades—has long been viewed as a critical factor in producing successful readers as well as learners who are interested in reading.

When I am working in a school where a majority of the students are African American or Hispanic, I make sure many of the books I read reflect and value that culture, so that the students can see themselves in the characters, can make connections to their own lives. I also use great read-alouds as a springboard to discussion, writing, and further reading. But mostly we just enjoy and savor the language of a well-told story in a relaxed, congenial environment.

In a recent school visit where the overwhelming majority of students were African American, I chose a wonderful story that students could relate to and that reflected the student body. I read *Jump Rope Magic* by Afi Scruggs to the group of first graders I'd be working with all week. They loved the rhythm and beat of the fanciful jump-rope story and easily began to fill in the rhyming words when I paused at the end of some sentences. Days later, after they had heard and chanted the book many times, they could choose to write their own jump-rope chants, first as a class shared-writing task, later as an option with a partner or on their own.

Get to Know Your Students as Readers

For years, I used a written survey to find out about students as readers. However, I found that the form itself and the required writing greatly limited the information I received. These days I much prefer interviewing students one at a time while they are reading independently and making brief notes. An informal interview encourages both the student and teacher to speak freely about reading habits, attitudes, and preferences in a natural, relaxed way. The information helps teachers choose specific reading materials for the classroom library, make future instructional decisions, discern their students' reading attitudes, and get to know each student as a reader.

The following questions will help you guide a reading interview:

- ☐ Tell me about yourself as a reader.
- ☐ Do you have a favorite author?
- ☐ What was your last favorite book and why?
- ☐ What kinds of things do you like to read?
- ☐ How do you decide what to read?
- ☐ What kinds of reading materials would you like to have in our classroom library?
- ☐ Where do you like to read?
- ☐ Do you have a special place at home where you keep your books and reading materials?

☐ What are you reading right now? Do you know what you will read next?
☐ Are you a good reader? Why or why not?
☐ How would you like me to help you as a reader?

Learn About Students' Reading Lives at Home

Based on what we observe in the classroom, we sometimes make assumptions about our students as readers that may or may not be completely accurate. It's important that we find ways to acknowledge our students' reading lives outside school.

On a recent progress report, Justin's fifth-grade teacher remarked that he needed to broaden his selection of books. His mother was surprised, because her ten-year-old son was reading a broad range of texts:

> We have a family Saturday morning routine that Justin picks up the pile of books that have collected around his bed during the week. As we raked books from under the bed, I thought about his teacher's comments and decided to make a list of the books and send her a note about Justin's *real* reading life.

The remarkable list she sent demonstrated Justin's wide interests, passion, humor, curiosity, and love of learning. It included challenging literature (fiction and nonfiction), sports books, magazines, and joke books. Unfortunately, his teacher had no such picture of Justin's rich reading life. Here, I'm as guilty as the next teacher. While I check that each student is reading an appropriate book independently and monitor her or his comprehension (see Chapter 7), I am less likely to invite information about and validate students' home reading. Justin's story reminds me of the importance of the home-school connection with regard to both optimal learning and respect for all parts of the reading life.

teaching tip

Wide-ranging Selections

Be sure to include picture books for older readers and chapter books for younger readers. I often bring in a picture book or a poetry book to read to older students because too many of them believe that if it's not a chapter book, it's not acceptable. A favorite read-aloud for upper elementary students is *Jorge: On Both Sides of the River* by Jane Median, a touching book of poems in English and Spanish that deals with respect for one's culture.

Enjoy Your Students

I always return from a weeklong school residency exhausted but exhilarated. I feel privileged to be doing the best work in the world. I love working with students. I love getting to know them, watching their enthusiasm grow, seeing them excited and confident about learning. And I love the weeklong conversations with teachers about teaching, learning, and living.

Sadly, joy is missing from too many of our schools and classrooms. In a recent school residency, I can recall only one teacher who talked about her students—how delightful they were, how curious they were, how much she enjoyed them. Other teachers talked about all the work they had to do, the drudgery, the pressures of teaching. It was no surprise to find that the joyous teacher's students were drawn to her like a magnet and that they were eager and accomplished readers and writers. The burdened teachers' students reflected their teachers' demeanor; work was getting done, but there seemed to be no enjoyment in doing it and little pride of accomplishment.

Celebrate Your Life

Recently I was asked to speak at the memorial service of our dearest friend in Cleveland, Juliette Hamelecourt. She was the wisest person I have ever known, and I spoke of her wisdom. One of the things she used to say to me was, "Celebrate your life." Hearing that Frank and I planned to stay home one New Year's Eve, she said, "Get dressed up. Go dancing. Celebrate your life."

She certainly knew how to celebrate hers. She was the richest person we knew, and it had nothing to do with money. She lived in a small apartment and, at eighty-nine, still worked as an artist, writer, lecturer, and gardener to support herself. She took pleasure in small things—feeding the birds, preparing a meal, delighting in the bloom of a flower, having a friend in for tea, getting the color right in a painting.

On one of my many visits, I found her stretched out on her sofa with a book. (It would be just days before she would need to enter a hospice.) "I still have quality of life. I can read," she told me. Her curiosity was insatiable. She had spent her life reading widely and savoring lively conversations about history, philosophy, art, religion, cooking, literature. Even in the last days of her life, reading was a joy for her.

Juliette reminds me how important it is to celebrate our learning lives, not just to show up for school and get bogged down by the standards and testing and added curriculum. If we want our students to be excited about learning, they need to have teachers who relish learning, who are passionate about reading and other interests, and who find the classroom an inspiring and thrilling place to be.

Yes. Celebrate your life! In school and everywhere else. Thank you, Juliette, my very wise friend.

3. Share Your Reading Life

When I introduce myself to a new group of students, I always talk about myself as a reader. My reading life is a huge part of who I am, both as a literate person who is always seeking to learn more and as a pleasure-seeking person who reads for fun, relaxation, and diversion. Reading is integral to my well-being. I deliberately use my influence as a teacher and role model to foster a love of reading along with excellent reading habits.

A great way to begin a school year is to examine your own reading life, make it visible to your students, and connect world reading with school reading. Many students will not see and feel the power of reading without your enthusiasm and modeling. While excellent teaching is essential, without time to practice and read extensively, students will not become readers. More than any other factor, reading success for students depends on a carefully monitored independent reading program connected to an excellent classroom library. (See Chapters 5 and 6 for research and specifics.)

Tell Students Why You Read

I often start off by saying something like this:

> All the time you've been in school, your teachers have devoted a lot of
> time to reading. They give you time to read in school, and they expect
> you to read each day at home. So reading must be pretty important.
> Why do you think you're expected to spend so much time reading?

These are the typical answers I receive, regardless of the age of the students:

- ☐ It makes you smarter.
- ☐ You learn new words.
- ☐ You'll do better in the next grade.
- ☐ You can move on to harder books.
- ☐ To learn more.

Typically, I respond along these lines:

> All of this is true. But over the weekend I spent several hours reading
> my book. I ignored everything going on around me and just read for
> hours. Why do you think I did that?

Finally, someone will say, "Because you liked it." Sadly, reading for pleasure rarely comes up without some prodding. While it is true that we want our students to be able to read and comprehend well in all curriculum areas, including required high-stakes tests, let's not lose sight of the fact that if they don't read for pleasure they are not likely to make reading a lifelong habit or goal.

Perhaps even more important, I want students to know I am compelled to read. It is almost impossible for me *not* to read. It's much more than enjoying a well-told story, increasing my knowledge about the world, following directions, or, say, understanding philosophy. Reading pervades my life and sustains me the same way friendship and love do. Reading gives me joy, comfort, perspective, new ideas, questions to ponder, and connections to other lives. I want nothing less for my students.

I let students know that I:

- ☐ Love owning books.
- ☐ Have an extensive home library.
- ☐ Talk about books with friends (often as a member of a book club).
- ☐ Keep a reading record.
- ☐ Get most of my reading recommendations from friends.
- ☐ Know what I am going to read next.
- ☐ Read more than one book at a time.
- ☐ Read what interests me.

teaching tip

Examine your own reading life and use it to determine what's important for your students and your classroom practices. Trust yourself as a reader. If you are not an avid reader, think about becoming one. It's hard to model something that is unfamiliar to you.

- ☐ Am influenced by book reviews.
- ☐ Read every day in many genres, mostly nonfiction (including plenty of functional reading like newspapers, magazines, recipes, and information on the Internet).
- ☐ Love browsing in bookstores.
- ☐ Need to read to continue working as a writer.
- ☐ Read professional books and journals to "keep up" in my field.
- ☐ Use reading to expand my thinking.
- ☐ Record memorable passages in a notebook.

Share Your Reading Habits

As teachers we need to examine what we do as a reader and make our thinking and practices visible to our students. Our students admire us and seek to emulate us. When we make our reading lives explicit to our students, their reading lives expand in many directions.

Let Students Know What You Are Reading and What You Will Read Next

When I introduce myself to students, I always bring the current book(s) I am reading as well as the books I intend to read next. I gather the students close around me as I hold up each book and tell the students such things as why I chose it, what it's about, how I'm enjoying it, what I'm learning, what I hope to learn. For example, during a recent school visit, I gathered the students close by on the floor in front of me, showed them my pile of books, and said something like this:

> I'm going to be working with you all week to help you become the best readers you can be. One of the most important things good readers do is to read a lot and to choose the books they want to read. I've brought the books I've been reading and am about to read. I can't wait to show them to you and tell you about them.

Then I talked about each book in the pile:

- ☐ *Sailing Alone Around the Room* by Billy Collins, a book of poems I was just starting.
- ☐ *Picnic, Lightning* by Billy Collins, a book of poems I'd just completed.
- ☐ *Literature Circles: Voice and Choice in Book Clubs and Reading Groups* by Harvey Daniels, a professional book I was in the middle of reading.
- ☐ *Is That a Fact? Teaching Nonfiction Writing K–3* by Tony Stead, another professional book I was reading.

☐   *Still Waters* by Jennifer Lauck, a memoir I'd just finished.
☐   *Witness* by Karen Hesse, a young adult novel that's more like a prose poem, the latest book by one of my favorite authors, which I'm planning to read.
☐   *Any Small Goodness: A Novel of the Barrio* by Tony Johnston, a short novel I want to read because it might be appropriate for literature conversations.
☐   *Captain Underpants and the Wrath of the Wicked Woman* by Dav Pilkey, an entry in a humorous children's fiction series that I'm curious about and plan to read.

I was reading two professional books and a book of poetry. I had just completed a memoir and book of poetry, and I planned to read three works of children's fiction. I also let students know that I usually read more than one book at a time. Often, I am reading at least one professional book and one work of fiction or nonfiction.

We need to let our students in on the fact that we often know what we will read next and encourage them to be thinking ahead about their own reading choices. To promote such thinking, one principal I know frequently asks students and teachers:

☐   What is your "now" book?
☐   What is your "next" book?

To that I might add:

☐   What is your "last favorite" book?

Even if the books you are reading are not appropriate to share with students, talk about what you are reading. Students don't have to see us read each day (although it's wonderful when they do), but they do need to know we read and value reading.

Share Your Passion for Reading

Teachers ask all the time, "What about the student who just won't read or can never find a book he likes?" Help that student find a book that interests him. Is the student interested in snakes, cars, sports, history, stamp collecting? Find out; go the library with him; put a book in his hands; read the beginning aloud to him; do whatever it takes to get him started. Even students with reading disabilities can become proficient readers if their interest in the subject is great enough. Many teachers find that when they and their students work together to establish rich and diverse classroom libraries, finding a book to read ceases to be a problem (see Chapter 5).

I let students know that most of the books I read are related to literacy and children's literature, that as soon as a new professional book comes out I want to know about it, that I depend on colleagues to tell be about the latest and best children's literature, that I am always reading about my profession. I read an education newspaper (*Education Week*) and at least half a dozen journals devoted to news, views, and research related to reading and literacy. I explain that this is what people do when they are passionate about a subject and want to increase their knowledge. "What are you passionate about?" I ask. "I will help you find a book."

Discuss the Importance and Pleasure of Having a Personal Library

I have a large library in my home office, and I show the students a full-color picture of it (see page 28). My library is precious to me. It reflects my reading history, interests, and knowledge. I confess that my husband is always saying, "Why can't you just get it at the public library?" But I love owning the book, holding it in my hand, arranging it on a shelf, referring to it, taking it out and flipping through the pages, admiring the cover, just looking at it and knowing it's there. I like having my books with me all the time, and I let students know that. Students are always amazed that I have so many books.

When I ask, "Who has a library or shelf at home for your own books?" typically just a few hands go up. We need to encourage students to establish their own home libraries. (This is not really an option. Kindergarten students who do well in school own more than fifty books, at a minimum! Well-stocked and well-used libraries, in school and at home, are positively associated with reading achievement. In fact, students in communities that have higher numbers of books per student in school and public libraries typically score higher on a national reading test.) Our talk about libraries moves on to classroom libraries. We discuss possibilities, and begin to make a plan. (For a full discussion on establishing and maintaining wonderful classroom libraries, see Chapter 5.)

Talk About Favorite Authors and Favorite Books

Avid readers talk about their favorite authors and books. Sadly, many of our students are hard pressed to cite even one author they know and like. When I ask fourth graders to name their favorite authors, I usually get two responses: J. K. Rowling and Roald Dahl.

My home library

I let students know that I have favorite authors and that when a new book of theirs comes out, I want to have it. For example, I love the short stories of Canadian writer Alice Munro. When I heard about her latest release, *Hateship, Friendship, Courtship, Loveship, Marriage* and then read the glowing review in *The New York Times Book Review*, I rushed out to the bookstore and bought two copies, one for myself and one as a gift for a dear friend. I showed students the full-page review and noted the words and phrases the reviewer used to describe the collection of stories: "powerful," "impressive," "extremely moving autographical resonance," "best yet," "lovely," "wise." Book reviews influence me, and I let students know I depend on reviewer's comments in selecting books.

Also, so that I can remember, cherish, and reread striking quotes and passages I have read, I keep a writing notebook. I record memorable sayings along with unique and beautiful use of language. I revisit these quotations often, both for inspiration when I am writing and for pleasure when I want to recall favorite books. I share my notebook with students and read some examples aloud. (See the sample on page 29.) There are always several students who begin to keep similar writing notebooks to recall their own prized books and passages.

11/00   Writers on Writing series
The Living Arts, NY Times, B1+2, 11-20-00
"To See your Story Clearly, Start by
Pulling the Wool Over your Own Eyes,"
by Kent Haruf (au of Plainsong)

The holy trinity in the art of fiction writing –
spontaneity, simplicity, clarity   (B2)

"Ring the bells that still can ring.
Forget your perfect offering.
There is a crack in everything
That's how the light gets in."

                    poet, Leonard Cohen

8/01 From Still Life with Oysters & Lemon
by Mark Doty   memoir, 2001

"Not that grief vanishes – far from it –
but that it begins in time to coexist
with pleasure; sorrow sits right
beside the rediscovery of what is to
be cherished in experience. Just
when you think you're done."

                            p. 47

A page from my writing notebook

*Talk About
Favorite
Authors and
Favorite Books*

✐ Begin a class chart listing favorite authors, and keep adding to it. Save lists to share with future classes. Promote talk about books and authors. (See the photos on pages 71–72.)

✎ Have students bring in books by favorite authors, on loan to the classroom library.

✐ Have students make yearly timelines of their favorite books, by age or grade in school. Have them share and discuss these timelines with other students.

✐ Create with the students a "favorite author" area that includes books by the author and information about the author, including the publisher's (and perhaps the author's) website to log on to for more information.

✎ Combine classes at your grade level to compare and discuss favorite authors.

✐ Do occasional "author talks" along with weekly book talks to recommend books and to "sell" an author.

✐ Consult school and public librarians for suggestions about authors to study.

✎ Have baskets of recommended books: "Mrs. Sher's Favorite Books," "Mrs. Sher's New Books."

✐ Have blank "writing notebooks" available in which students can record quotes or reactions to favorite books and passages.

Talk About How Book Clubs Work

Most of my adult life I have belonged to a book club. I bring literature conversations modeled on these experiences into the classroom. Students read a great book, raise important questions, take brief notes to prepare for a discussion, and meet together in self-directed, small groups—after all these steps have first been carefully demonstrated and practiced, of course. These literature conversations are powerful for enriching reading lives and extending texts' meaning.

Explain How You Choose Books to Read

I let students know how I choose books and other texts:

☐ Recommendations from friends, colleagues, and students.

☐ Book reviews.

☐   Best-seller lists in newspapers and magazines.

☐   Award winners.

☐   Browsing at a local bookstore.

Recommendations from friends and book reviews are my main sources for deciding what to read. I read *The New York Times Book Review* every Sunday, clip book reviews, and earmark books I want to read. But mostly, I rely on friends for trusted recommendations. One friend in particular, Toby Gordon, is my literary soul mate. I know that if she loves a book, I will probably love it too, and the same is true for her. She lives in another state, and we keep in touch by letter and email. We almost always end our letters and notes by telling about what we are reading. When we occasionally talk by phone, we always ask each other, "What are you reading? Have you found a book you love?"

I also keep a folder of "Books I Want to Read." When I hear or read about a book I might want to read or clip an intriguing book review, I place it inside the folder. Then, when I'm off to the library or bookstore, I grab the folder. That way, I always have a reliable source for future reading.

Students, too, influence what I read. When I am meeting with students in one-on-one reading conferences (see pages 101–109), a student's excitement about a book often compels me to read it. For example, *Esperanza Rising* was sitting in the middle of a large pile of books I wanted to read. Hearing a student's enthusiasm for the book, I moved it to the top of the pile.

TRY IT APPLY IT

teaching tip

Save book jackets from new, quality hardcover books, and use them as models for how to write flap copy and back-cover blurbs.

- Have kids recommend books to one another. Making time for students to "sell" books to peers (in a weekly "Critic's Corner" or "Book Talks" session, for example) is crucial. A peer's enthusiasm for a book will do more to entice a student reader than anything else. Kindergarten teacher Karen Sher does book talks once a week. Instead of bringing in an object to share, students bring in a book.

- Ask kids to share a favorite book, or part of a book, with a partner.

- Create a class book or bulletin board highlighting favorite books and authors. (See the photo on page 72.)

- Demonstrate browsing through books and guide kids in the art of browsing. (Before we can expect students to read or write well in a genre, they need time to get familiar with how the genre works.)

- Create "top-ten" or "best-seller" classroom book lists based on what students are reading. Model these, including the one-sentence summary for each book, on lists in *The New York Times Book Review*, *USA Today*, or your local newspaper (see the example on pages 71–72).

- Establish your own classroom "book awards" ceremony. Include the nominees and announce the winners and runner-ups.

- Ask kids to give book talks or write book reviews. Book reviews can be:

  - ☐ Compiled into a class book or file that becomes part of the classroom library or a reference for next year's students or other classes.

  - ☐ Displayed on a bulletin board in the classroom or school hallway.

  - ☐ Posted on a school or classroom website.

  - ☐ Used as benchmark writing samples.

- Teach students the purposes of and differences between book reviews and book blurbs. (The latter are written by the publisher to sell the books.)

- Have kids design covers and write book-jacket copy that will entice readers.

- Have kids write promotional book blurbs and advertisements meant to help sell a book (a fifth grader's ad for the *Replica* series is shown on page 73).

- Promote "top-ten" picture books, even with older students.

- Read lots of great books aloud in class.

- Encourage students to keep their own list of "Books I Want to Read."

(See also Choosing a "Just-Right" Book, pages 93–96.)

teaching tip

Book Review and Book Talk Guidelines

Briefly include:

☐ Title and author.
☐ Genre (type of book).
☐ Subject of book or plot summary.
☐ Best features of the book.
☐ Interesting words that describe the book.
☐ Who should read the book.

Read a Variety of Genres

When I ask students what *genre* means, they often don't know. When I explain that I read many kinds of books and show them poetry, nonfiction, and fiction, someone volunteers that a genre is a "type" of book or reading material. I let students know I prefer reading well-written realistic fiction and memoir because I love reading about other lives.

Then we begin to list, usually on large chart paper, genres the students know. I take what they give me. As their knowledge increases, our draft evolves and changes. For a while we revisit it daily and talk about what we might add, change, cross out. When our chart is complete, I word-process it and each student pastes a copy into the inside front or back cover of his or her reading record. On page 33 is an example of a genre list in process.

GENRES BRAINSTORMED BY A FIFTH-GRADE CLASS

Autobiography	Historical Fiction
Biography	Humor
Horror	Memoir
Realistic Fiction	Informational Books
Mystery	Picture Books
Poetry	Sports
Fantasy	Classics
Adventure	Legends
Science Fiction	Fables
	Fairy Tales

Maintain a Reading Record

Since 1992, I have maintained a monthly record of the books I read (a page from it is shown on page 34). I let students know that while I read the daily newspaper, magazines, professional journals, catalogues, and information on the Internet, what I value most are the books I read. I proudly show them my current and past reading records, saying something like this:

> Kids, my reading record is one of my most prized possessions. It is my history as a reader. I would be very upset if I ever lost this record, because who I am as a reader is so important to me. I go back and look at my record all the time, and I often carry it with me. My reading record makes me feel proud of my reading accomplishments.
>
> Each month I begin a new page where I list the title, author, and genre of every book I complete that month. As soon as I finish a book, I enter it into my record. If I think the book is one of the best I've ever read, I give it an asterisk. Today we're going to begin to think about how we want our reading record to look and what we want to include.

I have also shared my reading record with thousands of teachers, and many have written me to say that they have happily begun keeping their own. Until I began keeping a record, my reading diet was unbalanced. I was reading mostly professional books about teaching. I would talk about wanting to read great fiction but was not following through. Once I began examining what I was actually reading, I was able to change my reading choices. Keeping a record also encourages me to read more. When it's the middle of the month and the page is still blank, I push myself to turn off the television or put aside some other distraction and get started on a book. I try to read at least two books a month.

When I started my first reading record, I felt I needed to model one I thought would be appropriate for students. Daily, I listed my book title, how many pages I read, how many minutes I read. I found doing this so tedious and inauthentic

A page from my reading record

that I abandoned it after a few weeks. I then thought about what *I* wanted to do as a reader and created my present system, which I also use with students.

We teachers have to be readers if we are to teach reading and writing well. Keeping a reading record is a great way to begin to keep track of our own reading. When teachers begin to keep their own reading records, they stop worrying about book levels and the number of pages and number of minutes students read each day. That carries over to students, who also stop focusing on how many pages they've read. We need always to ask ourselves: *What kinds of messages am I sending with the work I am structuring?*

TRY IT
APPLY IT

Maintain a Reading Record

- Use shared writing to set expectations for daily reading. Start with a draft. Final copy can be a wall chart or word-processed sheets that become part of the reading record.
- Negotiate the record-keeping form with the students.
- Simplify the record keeping students do.
- Trust your students.
- Instill a sense of, "This record is primarily for you, not for me."
- Minimize the writing students do.

Even kindergartners can keep a reading record. Some teachers will photocopy the cover of one favorite title a month for each student, and the student rates the book in some agreed-on manner. (Appendices H, I, and J contain examples of reading-record forms. See also page 36.)

Carefully Model How to Keep a Reading Record

Using a projected transparency of a blank record form, I spend at least twenty minutes on one or more days showing students, one line at a time, what to include:

- ☐ Title—underlined, correctly spelled, first letter of each word (except short prepositions) capitalized.
- ☐ Author (and illustrator)—correctly spelled, first letters capitalized.
- ☐ Genre—type of book. (A number of genres are listed on page 33.)

I also stress:

- ☐ Skipping lines between entries.
- ☐ Using careful, legible handwriting.
- ☐ Having the book right next to me so I can check my spelling.

Reading Log

Title: *The Landry News*

Author: *Andrew Clements*

Genre: *realistic fiction* Finished Date: *October 2001*

Rate the Book: *two thumbs up*

fantastic   marvelous

Using a projected transparency to model how to keep a reading log/record
(partial transparency shown)

I cannot overemphasize how important this initial modeling is. It sets expectations for neatness, accuracy, and pride in work. Otherwise, students' records tend to be messy, inaccurate, and filled with misspellings. Check records regularly. You can also have a student "checker" at each table or in some other grouping look over peers' work.

Also show students what you expect the cover of their reading record to look like. Examples of covers created by previous students are your best bet here. Until you have those, set some guidelines: creating illustrations that show a meaningful connection to reading, using colored pencils, adding careful details. Think about laminating these covers to ensure durability.

Respect Parents' Busy Lives

While many teachers require parents to sign off on the reading students do at home or be part of the required record keeping in some other way, I don't agree with this practice, even for young children. When procedures and expectations are clear, modeled, and negotiated, students can take charge of simple record keeping. When we shift this expectation onto parents, we create extra work and pressure for some overburdened families. I much prefer that students assume this responsibility and share their reading accomplishments with their families in a relaxed, enjoyable manner. Such a process saves us teachers time and energy, too, as we no longer have to "check" the home monitoring system.

Show Your Students How You Read

Students need to know not only *that* we read but *how* we read. Many of our students are superficial readers; that is, they read the words but don't think much about what they're reading. We need to show our students that reading means making meaning.

TRY IT
APPLY IT

- Use read-alouds, shared reading experiences, guided reading, and reading conferences with students to demonstrate your thinking as you read.

- Think aloud as you read. Don't worry about doing it "right." Let students in on how you think and problem solve.

- Go beyond just showing students what you do. Explain the *why* of your thinking and actions. (See the examples on pages 49 and 57–61.)

Demonstrate Your Pleasure in Reading

Too many of our students are reading because they have to, not because they want to. A first-year principal told me, "Kids take no pleasure in reading in this school." Students had so many requirements for each book—daily recording of pages and minutes read, having parents verify their child's nightly reading by signing a form, writing a summary about the completed book (all of which were tied into students' grades on report cards)—that reading had become a chore, something they dreaded.

Think about what gives you pleasure as a reader, and bring that into the classroom. When you have a book you love, let students know it. When you've talked with a friend about a book you're both enjoying, tell your students. If our students are to become readers, they have to enjoy reading and find it satisfying. Only then will they choose to read, read for their own purposes—and get high test scores too.

Two

The Essential
Reading Day

*WE NEED TO KEEP OUR
EXPECTATIONS HIGH . . .
INTRODUCING STUDENTS TO
COMPLEX AND RELEVANT
TEXTS AND CURRICULUM VIA
HIGH-LEVEL THINKING,
PROBLEM SOLVING, AND
QUESTIONING. WE NEED TO
SUPPORT STUDENTS IN
BECOMING MORE SELF-
SUSTAINING, THOUGHTFUL,
INDEPENDENT READERS AND
WRITERS.*

4. Teach with a Sense of Urgency

Deep down I now see the importance and the need to teach with urgency. I see how much more effective my teaching has become and, most important, I see my kids and myself having fun and enjoying ourselves.

—Darcy Ballentine (fourth-grade teacher, Westminster, Colorado)

When I suggest that we need to "teach with a sense of urgency" I'm not talking about teaching prompted by anxiety but rather about making every moment in the classroom count, about ensuring that our instruction engages students and moves them ahead, about using daily evaluation and reflection to make wise teaching decisions. Complacency will not get our students where they need to be. I am relaxed and happy when I am working with students, but I am also mindful of where I need to get them and how little time I have in which to do it. I teach each day with a sense of urgency. Specifically, that means that I am very aware of the students in front of me, the opportunities for teaching and evaluating on the spot, the skills and strategies I need to be teaching, the materials I need, the amount of time available, and the optimal contexts and curriculum.

> We need to get down to the essence of what we believe and what we do to ensure our students become excellent readers who choose to read. If we don't know how to teach reading and move students forward, we must take responsibility for learning how. We must jumpstart our own professional development.

We need to keep our expectations high. I am constantly amazed at how little we require of students. Here I am not talking about assigning and completing more activities but rather of introducing students to complex and relevant texts and curriculum via high-level thinking, problem solving, and questioning. We need to support students in becoming more self-sustaining, thoughtful, independent readers and writers.

Do More Teaching

In workshops for teachers, I often ask, *What are the top five things you do to ensure that your students become excellent readers? Write down what you actually do, not what you think you should be doing. What you do reflects your beliefs about teaching children to read whether you articulate those beliefs or not.* Then, after a few minutes of reflection, teachers talk among themselves, usually with colleagues at their respective grade levels. Next, we reconvene as a group, and I write down what they consider their top priorities. Here is a typical list:

TOP FIVE THINGS WE DO TO ENSURE STUDENTS BECOME EXCELLENT READERS

- ☐ Introduce students to all kinds of genres.
- ☐ Have lots of books they like to read and that are at their level.
- ☐ Read good literature to them.
- ☐ Share our love of literature.
- ☐ Give students time to talk about their reading.
- ☐ Set aside significant blocks of time for reading.
- ☐ Give children choice in what they read.
- ☐ Tell kids, "You are a reader."

☐ Make reading fun.

☐ Model.

☐ Link reading to the curriculum.

These responses are telling. Intentional teaching is rarely on the list. Assessment/evaluation almost never comes up either, and if it does, it doesn't include using evaluation to move students forward. When I conduct the same exercise relative to excellent writing, the results are similar. Teaching and evaluation are barely mentioned.

Here's my list:

TOP FIVE THINGS I DO TO ENSURE STUDENTS BECOME EXCELLENT READERS

☐ Demonstrate that I am a reader.

☐ Provide an excellent classroom library.

☐ Let students choose books they want to read and give them time to read them.

☐ Teach strategies students need to know to process and understand text.

☐ Evaluate students regularly, giving them feedback and helping them set goals.

This list is not the "right" list or even a permanent list. It reflects my current thinking, which is always evolving. Teaching and moving students forward are priorities. So is my belief, carried out in my practice, that we as teachers need to incorporate our own reading lives and model how we behave, think, and talk as readers. Independent reading supported by a well-stocked classroom library is another strong part of my reading program.

Rely on an Optimal Learning Model

Everything I do with teachers and students is based on an optimal learning model (see the inside front cover and the schematic shown on page 44). When teachers understand and internalize this model, teaching and learning become more effective, efficient, and enjoyable. Teachers increase the time they allot to shared and independent reading and spend a little less time on guided reading. They begin to base instruction on what kids need rather than on the components of a literacy program.

The optimal learning model relies heavily on Don Holdaway's principles of developmental and social learning. With expert assistance and encouragement, learners gradually move from dependence to independence. The degree and intensity of assistance the learner requires to be successful determines how we structure our teaching. Inherent in the model is the engagement of the learner, which becomes likely because of the appropriateness and probable success of the task and the admiration the learner has for the teacher. Also inherent in the model is a relaxed, collaborative, accepting environment that encourages and supports the learner in trying out what is being demonstrated, taking risks, monitoring himself or herself, and setting goals while moving toward independence.

The model helps us understand and determine the levels of support students need in learning a new skill, strategy, or task rather than focus first on the specific teaching context (such as shared reading and guided reading). The teaching context is significant only because it provides the level of support and explicitness the learner requires.

This model applies across all disciplines and to all language learning. Implicit in the model is:

- ☐ Students who have bonded with their teacher.
- ☐ A knowledgeable teacher who models the values of literacy as she demonstrates, supports, encourages, and affirms.
- ☐ A collaborative learning environment.
- ☐ Tasks and skills that are worth knowing and doing.
- ☐ Successful engagement with the task.
- ☐ Enjoyment and pride in learning.

The four phases of learning—demonstration, shared demonstration, guided practice, and independent practice—appear distinct but in fact are seamlessly integrated.

Who Holds Book/Pen	Degree of Explicitness/Support
Teacher /Student	DEMONSTRATION
Teacher /Student	SHARED DEMONSTRATION
gradual handover of responsibility	
Student /Teacher	GUIDED PRACTICE
Student /Teacher	INDEPENDENT PRACTICE

The Optimal Learning Model

Demonstration

The teacher or expert shows—precisely—"how to do it" by initiating, modeling, explaining, thinking aloud. The teacher's demonstrations and explanations make the task—in this case reading, to include thinking, using strategies, reading fluently, working through confusions, rereading, monitoring, correcting—visible, explicit, and clear. Learners listen and observe carefully; although they may be invited to participate in a limited way, there is no pressure to perform. The task or skill being modeled is authentic; that is, it has meaning for and is useful to the learners and its purpose is explained and understood. The teacher is also modeling her pleasure in doing the activity. Demonstration teaching is always explicit and intentional.

Shared Demonstration

The teacher still demonstrates and leads (and holds the book or pen), but now the children are encouraged to participate and collaborate in the activity and discussion as much as they are able. There is no expectation for mastery, and the teacher adjusts the pace to accommodate the learners. As the learners interact and respond, the teacher acknowledges and affirms while observing what additional supports they may need. This is the "hand holding" stage; the teacher invites participation while providing explicit demonstrations of and scaffolds for the skills or tasks being employed. The teacher also observes what each learner is able to do; this assessment is ongoing, and the teacher makes adjustments based on what a learner needs.

Students—working with a partner, in a small group, or as a whole class—share their thinking with one another and the teacher gives feedback. The social interaction between the teacher and students is integral to the learning. In fact, "teaching and learning are seen as inseparable components of the same process." Because the learners admire the teacher and find the task interesting and worth doing, they may become fully engaged.

Shared demonstration is routinely ignored as a rich teaching context. Yet it is here that I do the bulk of my teaching (see pages 57–61, and 132–149 for examples). Holdaway says:

> In the instructionally rich sharing situations of participation or hand-in-hand learning lie the most fruitful situations for powerful teaching.
> Here it is the intuitive skill of the "teacher" in initiating, guiding, suggesting, questioning, supporting, backing off, acknowledging—and

a host of other facilitating interventions or withdrawings—that mediate the efficiency of the situation. These complex interactions, which have variously been called *scaffolding, prompting, hinting,* and *cueing,* form the foundation skills of effective instruction.

The scaffold of shared reading, for example, makes it possible for the teacher to choose challenging material, above the independent reading level of the children:

> Because of the cooperative support of class members and the powerful techniques available to the teacher, the children may successfully enter challenging and satisfying literature well beyond their current level of difficulty or their ability to persist on their own.

Guided Practice

Students practice thinking and acting like readers (or writers or whatever). The learners now hold the book or pen and are expected to take charge of their learning, using and applying what was previously demonstrated and practiced with the direct support of the teacher and the group. The teacher or mentor is on hand (or close by) to validate, support, teach, provide scaffolds, encourage, help, and give feedback as needed. The teacher may also talk through, think, and question to show students how to read and interpret the text. However, there may be occasions when applied practice does not include direct supervision and may even occur out of sight of the teacher. In these cases, the knowledgeable teacher builds in an evaluation (see the examples on pages 170–171, and 175–182) to monitor student understanding and help determine what further support/teaching is needed.

Making errors and approximations are expected as a normal part of the learning process. At the same time, the students are also attempting to correct and monitor their behavior and strategies. Trial and error, supported by judicious teacher feedback, allows the learners to develop a "self-improving system":

> To become dependent on being corrected by someone else is to remain at an inefficient level of learning and to be cheated of the opportunity for rapid independent self-improvement.

Independent Practice

The learners have developed a level of competence and confidence enabling them to do the task successfully with minimal assistance. The teacher or expert is available to offer limited assistance if necessary but mostly to affirm, appreciate, and celebrate the learners' efforts. Primarily, the learners are using what they have already learned and practiced to problem solve successfully on their own. If there is intervention, it is just as likely to be to help move a student to the next level of skill development as to support the task at hand. Teacher feedback builds on the learners' competence and strengths. (Learners may benefit from reminders to support them in their independent efforts—using bookmarks or note cards when reading independently, for example.)

The learners are proud of their ability, aware of their progress, and involved in setting new learning goals for themselves. Their reward for their successful learning is intrinsic, personal pride and pleasure in their accomplishments. In a noncompetitive manner, they enjoy demonstrating small improvements and achievements, often to "the bonded skill user who has shared and introduced the skill" as well as to peers and significant others (parents, for example) for approval and affirmation. They are also able to apply what they know to new learning contexts and to direct their own learning.

Understand and Apply the Learning Model

When we teachers understand the learning model, we begin to make different decisions. We recognize teaching as "a powerful, invitational relationship that pulls the learner in." We no longer follow a lock-step program, framework, or teacher's guide with little modification. Instead, we think about teaching in terms of our students' needs and interests. Additionally, we no longer jump right in to provide the expected word or response but now give children an opportunity to problem solve on their own. "The idea that children achieve mastery of the conventional forms of literacy through gradual and successive approximations is one of the most important concepts in the emergent literacy model."

Every action teachers take involves treating each student respectfully and moving him or her closer to independence as a learner. In a congenial atmosphere of interaction and exchange, teachers plan and conduct their lessons with these questions in mind:

- ☐ What am I demonstrating?
- ☐ How is what I'm about to teach (and evaluate) going to contribute to children's learning?
- ☐ How am I building self-regulation and validation in the learner?
- ☐ Am I giving students sufficient opportunities to initiate learning and to practice what I have been teaching?
- ☐ Is the learning developing self-improving strategies?
- ☐ Am I promoting and supporting problem solving?

☐   Am I demonstrating respect for all learners?
☐   Are my teaching and materials helping students become more confident, proficient, and joyful learners?
☐   Am I invitational; that is, am I making it possible and likely that each learner will and can participate?

Work Toward Independence

Students who remain dependent on a teacher or program for all their feedback are limited in how much they can learn. When students have the strategies, confidence, and knowledge to continue learning on their own, not only does learning accelerate but also much of the responsibility for learning gradually (but actively) shifts from the teacher to student.

One example of that shift is an effective guided reading group (see Chapter 10 for a full discussion of guided reading). Previous demonstrations and shared demonstrations have focused on teaching students the necessary skills, strategies, and behavior of effective and efficient readers. When meeting with a guided reading group, the teacher is evaluating on the spot and teaching what is needed for students to read and problem solve successfully (see the examples on pages 175–182). The atmosphere is congenial, the teacher encouraging and affirming the students while providing the necessary supports to enable success.

It is not enough that we know how and what to teach; we teachers must, at the same time, provide the conditions—respect, joy, engagement, success, encouragement—that make continuous learning possible.

Promote Joy in Learning

At the same time we teachers monitor every aspect of each child's development, we gradually encourage that child to take over the learning responsibility. With continuous demonstrations, practice, and support, we make it possible for children to proudly assume the role of confident reader and learner. This is a very different from overrelying on a teacher-directed program, which promotes dependence for both teachers and students, or failing to provide opportunities for practice and independent problem solving.

Don Holdaway reminds us that effective language instruction—and, indeed, all learning—is social and dependent on relationships "with others, with context, with environment, with the world, and with self." Such learning is enjoyable as well as meaningful.

teaching tip

*Ask Reflective
Questions*

How are my teaching
demonstrations and
behaviors developing
readers, writers, and
thinkers across all
disciplines who:

☐ Monitor their own
learning?

☐ Are independent?

☐ Choose to engage
in literate acts?

☐ Evaluate their
own progress?

☐ Set goals?

☐ Are joyful learn-
ers?

☐ Are expansive
thinkers?

☐ Problem solve?

Put the Learning Model into Action

Like so many things we do in teaching, it's easy to put the pieces into place without adequate understanding. We do too much too soon. We fail to explain adequately. When that happens, I just tell kids something like this:

> You know what kids. We need to do this again in a different way. I didn't explain this in a way that was helpful enough. This time as I read I'm going to tell you *why* I make the decisions I make as I'm going along.

In a fourth-grade classroom in Huntsville, Ohio, I observed an excellent teacher, Jana McPherson, think aloud while reading a piece of nonfiction. Using a projected transparency, she demonstrated how she highlights important phrases to help her write a summary later. But she never told her students why highlighting aids understanding or how and why she selects particular words to highlight. Even though her demonstration was carefully done, her students were unable to take much from it. When she subsequently put them into small groups to collaborate on a similar exercise, they were unable to replicate what she had been teaching them to do.

In a follow-up lesson, Jana slowed down, reread, and explained every bit of her thinking—how highlighting helps her remember key points, why she highlights particular words and not others, how she takes the highlighted key phrases and puts them into her own words when she writes a summary sentence or two, why summarizing is important. And she added shared reading and writing—thus providing a scaffold and guiding their thinking—to her demonstration before expecting children to collaborate in a group. This lesson produced dramatically different results.

Thinking about the optimal learning model, Jana realized that she needed to give much more time and explicitness to demonstration and shared demonstration before she could "hand over" responsibility to students and expect them to participate effectively in guided practice in a small group:

> The significant gains in student understanding were amazing that second day and in the weeks that followed. I learned that it was so important to give students a gradual release of responsibility—to start out with a small chunk of text, and explain *why* I selected a word or *why* a specific idea made an impression. I realized how essential it was to work through many examples in this fashion before students could confidently be expected to attempt something similar on their own. It was an epiphany to realize that it wasn't about how *much* I did but rather how *well* I structured the learning situation.

We teachers work with much greater precision and effectiveness when we understand and apply the principles of learning. Not only that, both we and our students enjoy the teaching/learning process.

Integrate Basic Skills into Challenging, Relevant Curriculum

While many published programs and state frameworks separate basic skills from meaningful curriculum, there is no research to support such a dichotomy. Students do best when the skills they need are explicitly taught in meaningful contexts. This also holds true for students in economically impoverished areas. In fact, "individuals who are performing below their peers are *most* in need of opportunities to see how the discrete pieces of literacy learning cohere into a communicable whole" (see the lesson summary at end of this chapter on pages 55–62).

Breaking learning into bits and pieces can actually make things more difficult for students. One of the problems with teaching skills separately is that students don't understand how the skills they are learning in isolation apply to other contexts. Kids learn what we teach them, but "this advantage does not appear to transfer to everyday reading and writing tasks." For example, students can read or spell words correctly as an isolated task but often cannot read or write the same words in other contexts.

Focusing excessively on skills in isolation severely limits learning possibilities, and in my experience, contributes to the continuing achievement gap between black and white students. Isolated drilling in the basics hampers low-performing students because they fail to learn how to process new information effectively. On the other hand, when the basics are integrated into challenging, meaningful curriculum, these same students easily learn the basics because the work is interesting and relevant.

Suzy Headley, a first-grade teacher in Huntsville, Ohio, recently gave away all her phonics workbooks. She now has more time for real reading and teaching. She teaches phonics daily—explicitly and systematically—but now does so in the context of poetry, morning message, shared writing, journal writing, guided reading, and lots of "hands on" word work. Not only do all her students know and use phonics, they are also the best readers and writers she has ever had. She credits her students' success to her having integrated skills teaching into meaningful practice.

If kids can't apply what we teach them, our teaching is a big *So what?* I ask myself *So what?* all the time. *How is this activity or strategy helping students become more competent and independent as learners?* For example, if I've done a lesson and the students enjoyed it, but the lesson hasn't contributed to increased learning, it may have been a waste of time. Make sure your lessons are meaningful. Students who receive meaningful instruction are more likely to show an understanding of advanced skills by the end of the school year.

teaching tip

Check Phonemic Awareness

Instead of giving a test to see whether a student has phonemic awareness, examine a writing sample, such as a journal entry. If students are writing words with consonants and vowels, in correct letter combinations and sequence, then they have phonemic awareness.

Focus on Language Acquisition, Not Just Letters and Sounds

Language play, hearing lots of stories, and reading and writing stories and poems are not fads or add-ons but essentials if children are to become readers. If children do not have adequate and rich language to scaffold their reading and writing, their learning often stalls or regresses. Attention to print comes after an understanding of story and written language. That is why it is so critical for us teachers to be vigilant concerning what happens to our low-performing students. Sending kindergartners or first graders out of the room for a thirty-minute pull-out program to work on phonemic awareness or sounds in isolation when they are missing a read-aloud or shared reading or rich reading/writing experiences in the classroom makes no sense. In fact, the often cited "fourth-grade slump . . . is caused, at least in part, by the failure of schools to promote oral language development while children are still working on the mechanics of reading."

Be proactive so that your students who need to hear, speak, practice, and interact with the rich language of stories and literacy are not leaving your classroom for isolated skill and drill.

> To expect children to become literate before they have a base of language understanding is an exercise in futility. They may learn to sound out words but that is where the story ends.

In particular, teachers who read with young children and promote productive talk about stories are more likely to expand children's language development.

Ground Phonemic Awareness Work in Language Play

Kindergarten teachers have long observed that their first readers know their nursery rhymes. These predictable rhymes and structured verses help young children develop phonemic awareness as well as let them enjoy a tried and true literary form.

Most children easily develop phonemic awareness in literacy-rich environments—through activities that involve experimenting with and enjoying rhymes, poems, chants, and songs and manipulating sounds of words (substituting consonants, "clapping" syllables, using alliteration, repeating classmates' names), and by engaging in regular talk about words.

While invented spelling remains one of best ways to acquire phonemic awareness, it is, unfortunately, often neglected as an important teaching and assessment tool. Stretching out the sounds when writing is one of the easiest and most efficient ways to develop phonemic awareness.

Maximize Whole-Class Teaching

Whole-class reading is now routinely frowned upon, but it is not necessarily the problem. Typically, whole-class reading is based on round-robin reading and discussion. However, other approaches to whole-class reading—reading aloud, interactive reading, shared reading, shared reading aloud, and occasionally guided reading—can be productive (see especially the discussion of shared reading experiences on pages 139–149). When we use whole-class reading as a way to make our thinking and problem solving visible, demonstrate strategies, expose students to good challenging literature, guide discussion of that literature, and constantly evaluate how students are responding, we are doing important teaching. We always need to be clear about our purpose and the quality of the support (our grouping practices, for example) we provide our students.

Include Interactive Reading

In interactive reading, the teacher reads aloud and invites students to talk about the text during the reading, not just afterward. Such talk allows the teacher to help students make meaning as the story unfolds. The teacher may also make her own thinking visible to students while reading aloud, especially if it's a complex text with many new concepts. This explicit attention to oral language development and vocabulary are a crucial part of comprehension instruction.

Often, I do not want to interrupt a great story with questions or discussion, and I read it straight through to the end. The children's silence, appreciative looks, or spontaneous applause is response enough. Other times, we talk about the story—the theme, illustrations, characters, author's purpose—after we finish it. But in interactive reading we talk about the story in process. What I love about interactive reading is that I get to see children's meaning making—and how they support one another—in the midst of the story. Having a chance to talk about the story in process is especially great for second language learners and students whose language and vocabulary is very undeveloped.

When we give students the opportunity to talk with a partner or partners (through such contexts as interactive reading aloud and shared reading aloud), they think about the text more. When our instruction increases student engagement, student achievement increases. When students informally share their thinking with peers, rather than just the teacher, they listen and talk more. Their joint thinking and talking aids their reading understanding.

teaching tip

Rather than ask questions in a whole-class discussion—where typically just a few "stars" get to respond—have students talk to each other one or more times before the whole class shares at the end. Say something like this: "Turn to your partner (or small group) and talk to each other. Make sure you each get a chance to share your thinking. You'll have two or three minutes."

**TRY IT
APPLY IT**

During a read-aloud, stop several times at natural breaking points and have students "turn and talk" about:

Fiction

- What they think will happen next.
- Why the character is behaving in a certain way.
- How the story might end.

Nonfiction

- One interesting way the author (and/or illustrator) presents information.
- Something they learned.
- A question they have.

Poetry

- Images that come to mind.
- Words they especially like.
- Other language features they notice.

Pay attention to students' responses and notice if they are self-correcting, self-evaluating, confirming (at both the word and problem-solving level) and moving closer to independence. Ask yourself:

- Am I encouraging children to evaluate themselves realistically at every point?
- What do I need to teach next so students can become more independent as readers?

Connect Reading with Writing

The reading/writing connection is a powerful one. Young students often write before they read. In kindergarten classrooms, children's written texts often become their first reading texts (see Jessica's story on pages 18 and 19). In first- and second-grade classrooms, children's written texts are a jumping off point for reading and are often integrated into the curriculum as well. My integrated lessons are based on a principle stated by Linda McNeil:

> First, students learn the "basics" when they undertake purposeful instructional activities, when they have models of thinking to emulate, and when they can see how new skills can be applied at the next level.

teaching tip

Ask struggling older readers to write texts for younger students. When these older readers are aware of their audience, they take care to match their illustrations with text, choose their words and lay-out carefully, and delight in reading and giving their book to the intended younger reader(s).

How Much Written Response Is Appropriate?

Teachers always want to know what balance to maintain between reading and writing about what's been read. That's hard to say. A ballpark ratio is 80 percent reading to 20 percent writing. Certainly, having students deepen their thinking by writing about reading is worthwhile. On the other hand, having students spend large chunks of time searching for vocabulary words or metaphors or creating projects is questionable.

Of course, many students take high-stakes tests beginning in third grade, and these tests require written responses to demonstrate comprehension. It makes sense to familiarize your students with this practice. Don't overdo it. Use common sense, and be clear about your purposes for writing.

Create Your Own Texts for Shared, Guided, and Independent Reading

The texts students write themselves are highly motivating and engaging. This holds true for students of all ages. By generating written texts in shared writing, students create new texts to read: big books and little books, newspapers, labels, rules and procedures, brochures, booklets, and much more. The message we give students when we help them become authors of their own texts is this: "Your language, knowledge, experiences, interests, and culture matter." Writing our own classroom texts is a great way to bond with our students, value common experiences, and review content and curriculum.

Examples of shared writing texts that can become shared reading texts include a welcome booklet for students new to the school; an "All About Us" classroom book; a book about the heart (after a curriculum study of that body organ); a book highlighting each classmate's special talent ("What We're Really Good At," see page 57); a class book about pets ("Our Pets"); a fiction or nonfiction story. The illustrated "first editions" become part of the classroom library, and each student receives photocopies to read and enjoy at school and at home. These books can also become the basis of worksheets for practicing and evaluating specific skills (see the example on page 57).

Relevant texts that students write with our guidance are especially powerful for readers who struggle. Reading their own written text on a topic they are passionate about can be a springboard to becoming a reader. They willingly reread these texts and are almost always successful. I often write such texts in guided reading groups at the lowest levels because it can be difficult to find meaningful texts for these students. The most severely disabled reader I ever worked with learned to read as a fourth grader after we collaborated on texts about space, which he beautifully illustrated and proudly read to anyone who would listen. All our word work came from those texts. Shared writing texts are also a great way to differentiate instruction (see the example on page 58).

Put It into Action: An Integrated Reading–Writing Lesson

What follows on pages 55–61 is my summary letter to teachers after a weeklong focus on teaching reading and writing at the start of the school year. Notice how seamless the reading–writing connection is and how skills are integrated into all teaching.

Dear Teachers,

Most of the time spent planning for the week's instruction involved thinking rather than preparing activities that took a lot of my time. Here are some of my major beliefs and principles that guided my instruction with examples of related activities we did during the week.

Some Guiding Principles for Instruction and Learning

☐ Students become readers and writers by processing massive amounts of text. (Activities: shared writing, shared reading, guided reading, independent reading, providing interesting and well organized classroom libraries.)

☐ The more meaningful a task is, the easier it is for students to learn: the brain is a pattern maker and finder. (Activities: cut-up sentences related to relevant content, name word wall, shared writing a class story, reading student-generated texts.)

☐ You only have so much time: use it wisely. (Activities: integrating skills and strategies into authentic reading and writing.)

Some Guiding Questions for Instruction

☐ How is my instruction helping students become independent readers, writers, and thinkers? (Activities: constant modeling, small-group problem solving, guided practice, providing self-checking resources such as a cut-up-sentence on a projected transparency, providing accessible, appropriate books.)

☐ How am I accelerating learning for students? (Activities: teaching skills and strategies within meaningful contexts, making sure students read and write many texts, providing a useful and usable classroom library plus baskets of books on tables.)

☐ What messages about school and learning do the tasks I give students send to them? (Activities: connect skills—rather than isolate skills—to meaningful activities with clearly understood purposes.)

☐ How is differentiated instruction built into tasks? (Activities: word sorts, word work with white boards and/or tiles, writing a photo book, generating words, shared reading that allows for participation and extensions on various levels.)

☐ How do I know students are learning? (Activities: observe guided and independent reading; spot-check students working with cut-up sentences, magnetic letters, and tiles; observe independent writing—are students using the word wall, the name word wall, poems displayed on the wall, their peers, projected transparencies; record teaching dates of specific phonics skills on a phonics instructional record.)

Summary of Reading–Writing Activities

Here is a summary of activities that took place in Diana Brown's grade 1–2 class (also known as Team 30) during the last week of September in Adams Elementary School in Mesa, Arizona. Starting with a class-generated text created with Diana's and my guidance and direction, the students gradually moved toward independence as they were given many different opportunities to read the texts.

Text-Solving Activities

Shared Writing ▸ Shared Reading ▸ Partner Reading ▸ Independent Reading

☐ "What We're Really Good At" (illustrated book, an overhead transparency, individual copies for each student). Can be used for cloze activities.

Laura changes her brother's stinky diaper.

Breanna keeps her room really clean.

Two pages from our class shared writing book "What We're Really Good At" (see shared writing on page 60)

Mrs. Routman makes great jam.

Natalie puts her brother in the bath.

Laura changes her brother's slinky diaper.

Shawn is good _ _ rollerblading

Matthew makes his bed really good.

Breanna keeps h _ _ room really clean.

Chris is best at basketball.

Jazmine is really good _ _ drawing.

Viviana is good at math.

Cedric _ _ good at basketball.

A cloze activity: creating a worksheet from familiar text

☐ Team 30 text created from photos of class using disposable camera (a digital camera would work well too). The text is both open (a blank book for students to write their own text) and closed (individual copies of a class-generated book that contains the same text for all). Can be used for guided reading.

Our shared writing of our 8-page book—in process

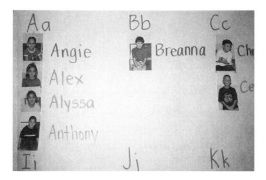

Writing our own 8-page text from classroom photographs we took

Students using the name word wall to write their own version of the 8-page photo-text

A close-up of our name word wall

Shared Reading ▸ **Independent Reading**

- ☐ "I Can Read Colors," a read-and-sing big book by Nellie Edge (individual copies to take home).
- ☐ "Little Red Hen," a read-and-sing story (overhead transparency, copy for each student). Read together as a class. Practice reading one section plus chorus.

Shared poetry reading with "Little Red Hen"

Guided Reading ▸ **Independent Reading**

- ☐ Read "Up, Down, and All Around" from the *National Geographic Reader*. Introduced the piece to "put the language in their ears"; each student read independently as Diana or I listened in; read aloud as a group; practiced with partners and individually. Whiteboard and marker were available for on-the-spot teaching.

Word-Solving Activities

☐ Used photo and name word wall (see page 58) as a reference for writing and learning basic rimes. Connected *an* to *Anthony, Angie,* and *Breanna* and to *can* in "I Can Read Colors." Connected *at* to *Natalie* (and *Mat-thew*).

☐ Added the rimes *an, at,* and *is,* highlighted in yellow, to the alphabetic word wall. ("If you know these words, you can figure out lots of other words.") Also added *his, her,* and *that* when they arose during shared writing.

☐ Presented daily mystery words (see pages 208–209). (If the context is familiar and meaningful, the consonants are sufficient to figure out the word.)

☐ Introduced tile work using one-inch-square shiny tiles that students wrote individual letters on and then manipulated. Diana and I determined the important words. (See *Conversations,* pp. 429–431 for specifics.)

☐ Wrote frequently used words quickly on individual whiteboard and walked around to check which students were able to write the words for themselves. Encouraged students to help each other and check each other.

☐ Helped students notice important words and word features. Used sliding mask to highlight *er* in many words (*her, brother, roller, diaper,* etc.) in "What We're Really Good At." Used highlighter tape to isolate *at, her,* and *good* in the same text. Used a small sliding mask in a guided reading group.

Using a sliding mask (chart-size version) to highlight features of print (see page 173 for directions on making your own sliding mask)

Shared writing into shared reading: highlighting "at" and "er" with colored transparent tape

☐ Students cut up a sentence (generated by the class) related to curriculum—"Our skin is like a rubber suit that keeps germs out"—into words. Diana and I cut up a transparency of the same sentence and projected the words as a model. Each day, we used the sentence for word sorts (see the following entry), pointing out features of text and stressing one-to-one matching when reading. At the end of week, the students pasted the words in the sentence in order on a blank piece of paper, illustrated it, and took it home to read to their family members.

☐ Introduced open word sorts (which the kids created) and closed word sorts (two-letter words, words that start with *s*, words that have *k* in them) using the cut-up-sentence. Asked kids, "What do you think the sort is?" "What do you notice?" "How are these words [*out, our*] alike, different?"

☐ Created worksheets from shared poetry readings:
  ☐ "Little Red Hen": circle frequently used words; circle pairs of rhyming words.
  ☐ "I Had a Nickle": circle sets of rhyming words.

☐ Conducted cloze activities using "What We're Really Good At" after it had been read and reread several times. (In a cloze activity, you delete words you would expect students to be able to predict and spell from the context. See the example shown on page 57.)

"Mrs. Routman, I can read!" A student who was downcast at the beginning of the week proudly seeks me out at the end of the week

Raise Your Expectations

Kids never let me down, no matter where I teach. If I expect them to achieve and I take the time to model carefully, provide lots of supported demonstrations and guided practice in which they can try out what I am teaching, and continually support their growing approximations, they always succeed. Of course, this assumes the tasks and materials are relevant to them and that they understand and value why they are learning what they're learning.

Do not let your students down. The data are stunning: we expect very little from poverty-stricken students in financially strapped schools. Children in these classrooms must have meaning-oriented instruction in order to succeed at high levels. The summarized lesson activities on pages 57–61 took place in such a school, and all the students—many of whom did not know all their letters and sounds—proudly and successfully read all the texts we created together. Yes, they were learning their basic skills but a whole lot more, too. Their principal, Devon Isherwood, says:

> Our first- and second-grade students excelled on both the Stanford 9 and the district criterion-referenced tests, doing better than any of the district's comparable schools. We teach reading, including phonics with real texts. Our students write for real reasons about things they care about.

In a recent residency in a school where 98 percent of the children received free breakfast and lunch, I found the students as eager and willing and smart as any I have ever worked with. Their stories were full of rich language; they delighted in the books I brought to read aloud; they loved reading the stories we wrote together. Only by teaching all of our students with a sense of urgency and joy can we hope to challenge them in appropriate and meaningful ways.

5. Organize an Outstanding Classroom Library

Until now, I never associated a successful independent reading program with a well-organized classroom library.

—Monica Carrera-Wilburn (multiage primary-grades teacher, English immersion, Mesa, Arizona)

My school residencies begin with a walk through the school building and into the classrooms to meet teachers and students. I am always impressed by the care teachers and administrators take to make their schools and classrooms inviting literacy environments. At the same time, I am startled by the absence of classroom libraries. When libraries do exist, it is rare to see them well equipped and organized according to teachers' and students' needs and interests. It is the same in just about every school I visit.

Whenever the weeklong focus is guided reading and comprehension—as it often is—we usually wind up working first on the classroom libraries. Even when books in the classroom are plentiful, teachers control how they are

63

organized, too few students know how to select books they can read, the collection is often hard for students to penetrate, and too little time has been set aside for reading. Classroom libraries are a literacy necessity; they are integral to successful teaching and learning and must become a top priority if our students are to become thriving, engaged readers.

It is difficult to maintain a strong independent reading program without an excellent classroom library. Sadly, while we have poured thousands of dollars into commercial programs, technology, and test preparation, it is rare for funds to be allocated for classroom libraries. When classrooms do have adequate libraries, most often, teachers have spent large sums of their own money. We need to lobby our administrators, superintendents, and school board members to allocate funds so that classroom libraries become a necessary literacy staple instead of an optional add-on.

Classroom Libraries and Books Improve Reading Achievement

The availability of reading materials greatly impacts children's literacy development. The most effective reading programs are generally supported by large classroom libraries. The better the libraries, the better the reading achievement as measured by standardized tests. Books contribute more strongly to reading achievement than any computer software does. Schools with lots of low-income families have far fewer books available for students, and classroom libraries can help level that playing field. Simply put, children read a great deal more when they have easy access to books, and well-designed, organized, ample classroom libraries provide the easiest access for students.

We need to use what we find out about students' reading interests to build our classroom library. If students are to choose to read and develop positive attitudes about reading, they must have access to engaging reading material. Knowing students' interests, whether it's a particular author, series, or genre, is critical for making the classroom library accessible to them and for encouraging the reading habit.

Additionally, we need to ensure that students have books and materials to read at home, both to borrow and to keep. Some ways to expand home reading materials include but are not limited to:

- ☐   Home-school literacy book packs.
- ☐   Reproducible books (The KEEP program of The Ohio State University; Nellie Edge; Newbridge).
- ☐   Book clubs (Scholastic, Lucky, Troll).
- ☐   Summer reading programs (PTO fund-raising, discarded library books).

teaching tip

Teacher Book Talks

Celebrate new books, and entice students with something interesting about the book:

- ☐ Setting.
- ☐ Writing style.
- ☐ Problem.
- ☐ Suspense.
- ☐ Characters.

☐ Library cards (helping all families obtain one, perhaps by inviting a library employee to the school on an open house night to sign families up).

☐ Suggested titles and resources for parents to purchase.

Expand Access for Struggling Readers

Access to interesting books is especially critical for struggling readers. One recent study found that when struggling high school readers were asked to suggest what books should be added to the classroom library and when teachers did brief "book talks" on new books, students read much more and developed positive attitudes about reading. I have found this to be equally true for younger and middle school readers.

Be Sure to Include and Value "Light Reading"

It really doesn't matter much what kids read as long as they read and enjoy what they're reading. By gently nudging them and introducing them to better literature—through reading aloud, co-reading, and putting books into their hands—their reading tastes will eventually grow to include more sophisticated materials.

I read primarily romance comic books—teenage dating and love stories—until I was well into my teens, and I'm a very good reader today. Mostly, I read secretly under the covers by flashlight so my mother wouldn't know. My mother, an avid reader, was so concerned with my lack of interest in reading books that she would check out classics from the library and read them aloud to me. Eventually, but not until I was about sixteen, I started to read literature in earnest. In fact, I believe it is because I did so much "light reading" through high school that I now seek out the "higher-brow" stuff.

"Light reading" is essential for turning our struggling readers into competent readers. Too often there are too few books available that struggling readers can actually read. Comic books, magazines, picture books—all with engaging text supported by lots of illustrations—appeal because they seem more manageable to students.

Series books also hold great appeal. The characters, setting, format, content, and writing style repeat somewhat in each book, making succeeding books easier to understand. Not only does such reading improve fluency, but also, as readers become increasingly familiar with the common elements in a series, they can more easily focus on meaning. Having strong background knowledge and familiarity with a particular series also makes it easier to predict and figure out new words successfully. Students' success and confidence with series books provides an incentive to do more reading and also brings them into the classroom community of readers who enjoy reading and talking about books.

Take a Critical Look at Your Classroom Library

It's difficult for students to spend lots of time reading if they can't easily find interesting materials. Since we know that the amount of reading students do positively impacts their achievement, it makes perfect sense for the classroom library to be the cornerstone of the literacy classroom. Remember, too, that your own enthusiasm for reading and talking about books will inspire and motivate your students to read.

ASK YOURSELF THESE QUESTIONS WHEN EVALUATING YOUR CLASSROOM LIBRARY AND THINKING ABOUT HOW TO MAKE IT CENTRAL AND VITAL:

☐ When you walk into your classroom, does the library or book nook jump out at you, or is it all but invisible?

☐ Does your library corner look beautiful and contain an inviting display of plentiful reading materials, or does it look bland and impoverished?

☐ Does the library include a variety of genres and literary forms— poetry, picture books, informational books, mysteries, fantasy, popular series—or does it house mostly fiction and textbooks?

☐ Are most of the books in the library written by well-known children's authors, or are they part of a program that has been created and leveled by a publisher?

☐ Do you have current books that accurately and aesthetically portray other cultures, or is your collection homogeneous and dated?

☐ Can children find books in which their language and culture appear, or are they unlikely to "see themselves" in the collection?

☐ Have students been involved in the selection and organization, or have you made all the decisions about design, how books are grouped, and what reading materials to include?

☐ Can struggling readers easily find books they can and want to read, or do they spend most of their independent reading time searching for books?

teaching tip

*Daily Book
Sign-Out*

☐ Put students in charge of the classroom book-lending process.

☐ Have volunteers or students attach an adhesive pocket on the inside back cover of each book. Place a card labeled with the book's title inside each pocket.

☐ Create a sign-out board with a name or photo pocket for each student.

☐ Are there comfortable areas in which students can sit and read, or can students only read at their desks or tables?

☐ Do you and your students rotate, change, and add to the collection based on changing needs, interests, and curriculum, or is your collection static?

☐ Does your library include children's favorite authors, books, and series, or is the collection limited to what you have on hand and your own preferences?

☐ Most of all, is the library a place children love to go to seek and find wonderful reading materials, or is it a rarely used appendage in your classroom?

Provide Lots of Choices and Books

An adequate classroom library will have at least two hundred books, but an excellent library will have more than a thousand. The more books in the collection, the less depleted it becomes as kids sign books out every day. Be sure to have several copies of the popular titles so that these books don't "disappear." Multiple copies also encourage reading with a partner, which is a great way to practice reading and enjoying texts. And include previous read-alouds and texts used in shared reading as well as class-authored and student-authored texts.

For new teachers and teachers new to a grade, having sufficient books and reading materials is a common problem. Money isn't the only issue; often teachers don't know what books to order when they do have the funds. See the following "Try It Apply It" for some ways to build your library collection.

**TRY IT
APPLY IT**

✐ Approach your Parent Teacher Organization. PTOs are often willing to raise money for books through fund drives and donations.

✐ Have students bring in favorite books from home "on loan." This is a great way to augment your collection. (Of course, book handling and respect for others' books will first need to be modeled and discussed.)

✐ Watch for sales at discount outlets and bookstores. (Our local Borders has a teacher appreciation weekend every spring where all books are discounted by 25 percent.)

- ✐ Find out what students are interested in, and borrow from school and public libraries. (Some public libraries are willing to rotate sets of fifty books or more to help classroom libraries get established.)

- ✎ Talk with your administrator. (If you are not ordering workbooks to go along with a basal anthology, see if that money can go toward trade books for the classroom instead. Or simply state your case and the research showing why classroom libraries are so critical for readers, and request a few hundred dollars to purchase books.)

- ✆ Take advantage of classroom book clubs such as Scholastic and Troll. Bonus points from orders can be used for free books.

- ✐ Seek donations from families. In your newsletter, suggest that parents donate a book in honor of a child's birthday or special accomplishment. Also, request that quality books in good condition that are no longer being used in the home be donated to the classroom library.

- ✎ Check out used-book outlets! Gently used titles can usually be found for less than two dollars.

- ✆ To keep your collection fresh, consider an occasional school or classroom "book swap." For each book in good condition, a student is given a coupon that can be exchanged for a different book. Teachers can trade some of their books, too. One teacher I know trades about 25 percent of his classroom library every year at a swap. (To ensure that all students can choose a book even if they have none to trade, some families donate extra books or the library donates some "carefully worn" discarded books.)

Find Out Students' Favorite Authors, Series, and Book Titles

teaching tip

Bookstore Fieldtrip

Take a class field trip to the local bookstore to note children's interests and choose new books.

A great way to begin organizing your library is to find out what your students like to read. Ask them, and chart their responses. (See charts on page 70.) Then, based on those responses, begin to create a library they will want to use. If students are unable to suggest any titles, find out the subjects they're interested in knowing more about and begin to read aloud appropriate authors, titles, and genres. Honoring students' choices is not just about considering their wishes; students read more when materials they are interested in are readily available.

Even middle school and high school students will choose to read if they can find stuff they like, and this usually includes more nonfiction and magazines as well as books with more illustrations. Other preferences include series books, scary stories, sports books, and even comic books. The top three choices for more than seventeen hundred sixth graders in twenty-three diverse schools were magazines, adventure books, and mysteries.

Young students love counting and concept books, predictable books with rhythm and rhyme, nursery rhymes, alphabet books, fairy tales, joke books, familiar stories by favorite authors (including themselves), and nonfiction animal books and other reference books. Kindergarten teacher Karen Sher, in Shaker Heights, Ohio, notes that her students also gravitate to picture dictionaries; they love to look at the pictures and read the captions under each one.

Students engage more when they are motivated to read, and a wide variety of captivating choices increases reading motivation. Engagement is not to be taken lightly: "reading comprehension test scores are more influenced by students' amount of engaged reading than any other single factor."

Pay Attention to Students' Interests and De-emphasize Leveled Books

It is disheartening to see classroom libraries in which most of the books are leveled. Some students identify themselves by that level: "I'm a level 8. John is a level 12." While levels can be a helpful guide for teaching students, we need to be careful to factor in the quality of the text and students' interests. When we show students how to select "just-right" books, even older struggling readers can appropriately choose books:

> No grade-level markings were put on the books, as is popular in some computerized book management programs. Students simply browsed through the books and determined if they liked the book and were able to read it. Teachers reported no problems with students finding books that they could understand and enjoy.

Students do not naturally gravitate to leveled or overly structured collections. When they can choose from a rich and varied assortment, a leveled book or a phonics reader is not usually a first choice.

TRY IT APPLY IT

- ✐ Make class lists of favorite books, authors, and series (see the following photos on page 70).
- ✐ Ask students to loan a few favorite books from home to the emerging classroom library. (Make sure each book has the student's name in it.)
- ✐ Borrow from school and public libraries to augment your collection. (Aim for a minimum of seven to ten books per student.)

Getting the library organized

Deciding how to organize the class-room library

Include Lots of Nonfiction

A big part of our job as teachers is to introduce books to readers. Many of these books need to be nonfiction, because nonfiction still tends to be scarce in classrooms. More nonfiction reading leads to more informational writing, which is related to higher reading achievement. Want proof? Nancy McDonough and Laurie Fox are second-grade teachers in Tenafly, New Jersey. For the past seven years, they have taught all their reading through nonfiction books connected to science and social studies. Not only do their students learn a vast amount about the world as they are learning to read, their test scores are exemplary. Almost all their students routinely test above grade level in reading on standardized tests.

In truth, students often prefer nonfiction. In surveying a class of first graders who could choose from over thirty categories of books organized in individual baskets, most students selected "nonfiction" and "animals" as top choices. A second-grade teacher was surprised to learn that her students wanted books about "sea life" added to the classroom library. And a multiage primary-grades teacher reported that her students requested more "how to" books, especially kids' crafts and projects.

I now regularly use nonfiction books in guided reading, even in first grade. (See the grade 1 guided reading lesson on pages 175–177, using a little book published by National Geographic.) It is all well and good for students to know

teaching tip

Book Share

Let students (usually one or two a day) request time in which to share a book they love with the whole class. The purpose is to get their friends excited about the book as well. Fifth-grade teacher Marnie Danielski, in Westminster, Colorado, reports that several students always want to read the shared books. They get a waiting list going so everyone has a chance to read the book.

their letters and sounds, but if they lack sufficient background knowledge, reading informational texts is very challenging. The earlier they become familiar with how nonfiction works, the easier it will be for them to read and understand informational storybooks.

Students also enjoy nonfiction magazines such as *Time for Kids, National Geographic for Kids, Sports Illustrated for Kids,* and *Kids Discover.* We need to make sure these are part of our classroom library and reading program.

Make Books and Book Talk "Hot" in Your Classroom

When I talk with students about how I choose books to read, I show them *The New York Times Book Review,* which I read weekly and rely on for some of my upcoming reading selections. I show them the "top-ten" lists for fiction, nonfiction, and children's books and tell them I read these lists every week. It's one way of seeing what others around the country are reading. I also check to see whether I'm reading, or have read, any of these titles. Usually one or two are familiar, and this gives me a feeling of being current as a reader.

Students love developing their own "top-ten" lists. In Mike Marinello's fifth-grade class, we talked about possible audiences and procedures for these lists (see the following photographs), and the excitement translated into authentic writing about ways to publicize the list (see below and see the photograph on page 72). One of the best things about the writing was the excellent quality. Because of the

Audiences for Top 10 list

Jotting down ideas for Top 10 list

Top Ten Book List

ownership the students felt and because their audiences were clear and important to them, students took the writing—including revising and editing for spelling, grammar, and word choice—very seriously. Best of all, all the excitement generated interest in reading and the students read more. Mike comments:

> Our "top-ten" discussion was one of the most important literacy events of the year. Of course, at first, my students all wanted their own favorites in the top ten. As the discussion progressed, however, they saw the importance of many people liking the book for it to be included. Later, I noticed my students were more persuasive in getting their peers to read their favorite books. A favorite title may not have made this week's top-ten list, but in time the books kids felt most passionate about would be recognized.

TRY IT
APPLY IT

Make Books and Book Talk "Hot"

- Give book talks on new and noteworthy books in your collection, and encourage students to do the same. These "commercials" help sell books to potential readers.
- Create best-seller lists of authors and titles, and share these with other classrooms and audiences. (See the list shown on page 71 for possible audiences.)
- Form a committee to nominate awards for "best books" or "favorite books." Vote on names for book awards and the winners. Establish selection criteria modeled on book awards such as the Newbery Medal

(for children's fiction), the Caldecott Medal (for children's book illustrations), the Orbis Pictus Award (for nonfiction), and the National Book Award (for adult fiction).

✐ Advertise books by designing posters, writing blurbs and reviews, and creating book jackets. (Note the following ad for a student's favorite series).

Replica Advertisement

Have you ever wanted to read a book series that is unique and exciting? If you have, then you should read the Replica series. It is about a 12 year old girl, who finds out she is a clone. A clone named Amy who is practically perfect. For example, she has amazingly quick reflexes, super sensitive hearing and incredible eyesight! She is so bright that she often finishes her school exams in one minute! She uses her special talents to read people's minds, travel through time, and enter a computer's virtual reality. Amy's adventures are both interesting and captivating. By reading one book, you'll be hooked and want to finish the whole series.

Brianna
Brianna Rae Neuenkirchen

After Brianna talked about and wrote the ad, she brought in books for peers to borrow. Many students began reading this series (which was previously unknown to them).

Make Classroom and School Libraries Attractive, Comfortable, and Accessible for Reading

Where do you read? My guess is that you don't do it sitting at a desk all day. I read in bed, on my living room sofa, on the floor, in a favorite chair, in doctors' offices, in school, in the car while I'm waiting for something or someone. I have books, magazines, and other reading material next to my kitchen table, piled high on the coffee table in the living room, on shelves throughout the house, in the bathroom, next to my bed, in my pocketbook.

My home library has sections for fiction, poetry, memoir, professional books, and children's literature (these last two are subdivided into many subcategories to help me locate books easily). I am constantly rearranging my shelves for easy access.

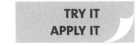

- ✐ Create an attractive reading corner with room for at least several students.
- ✐ Invite the students to help you create small reading corners for one or two students.
- ✐ Provide comfortable seating: bean-bag chairs, a special reading chair (maybe a rocker), a sofa.
- ✐ Evaluate the lighting in your room. Small lamps add a warm, cozy glow.
- ✐ Make the school office, principal's office, and meeting rooms reading places. Have baskets of books and various reading materials available.

Devon Isherwood, a principal in Mesa, Arizona, has always maintained a great collection of children's books in her office and allowed students to borrow them. Now her collection is also easily accessible: with her guidance, students have organized most of her books into bins, sorting by categories like books by the same author, poetry books, books about the environment, books about animals, fairy tales, ABC books, little books, easy books, chapter books. Now students can find books easily, and they make it a point to put them back in the right bin when they are finished with them.

A word about school libraries and media centers. While these spaces are ideally suited to be the heart of the school, too often dingy, outdated furniture, awkwardly arranged in rooms featuring dull colors, make them uninviting places.

Students reading during their lunch hour in principal Devon Isherwood's office (Mesa, AZ)

We need to see what we can do about repainting and reorganizing these rooms so they beckon readers. In Huntsville, Ohio, principal Diane Gillespie, along with her staff, spent part of a summer weeding out and giving away "ancient" books, repainting the room, and adding a reading loft (which Diane's husband built). While previously few students chose the library as a destination, now they can't wait to use it—it has become the most sought after space in school.

Involve Your Students in Library Design and Organization

When students help create the library, they use it more. Too often, we teachers do all the work. Not only does that take lots of teacher time that could be better spent elsewhere, but also students are less likely to find material they like, which, in turn, affects how much they read. I have watched some teachers work hard to create lovely looking libraries. But they organize these spaces for themselves, and the books are often not easily accessible to students—in terms of the types of reading materials that have been chosen and the way they are displayed and located. However, once teachers give up some control and let their students help make the decisions, pleasant surprises await. With demonstrations and guid-

Beginning to sort and organize books
for the classroom library

ance, even first graders can take full responsibility for categorizing, sorting, and organizing books and returning them to agreed-on places—and they love doing so. (Note a third-grade class's worksheet below for determining what categories and authors to include in their class library.) Not only that, students begin to take pride in "their" library. You'll be surprised and delighted at how neat and orderly students keep the library once they are involved in organizing it.

Given the physical limitations of the classroom and the expense of securing and housing sufficient quantities of good books, it can be a challenge to create a wonderful, accessible library space. However, it's a challenge we must undertake.

Circle the categories you think we should have:

Buddy Books	Mysteries
Magic Books	Realistic Fiction
Poetry	Animal Fiction
Natural Science	Interesting People
Applied Science	Tales & Legends
Animal Non-fiction	Chapter Books
History & Biography	Math Books
Picture Books	Favorite Authors
Magic School Bus	Duos
Funny Books	_____ Books
_____ Books	_____ Books

Who are our favorite authors?

Patricia Polacco	Barbara Cooney	Jane Yolen
Marc Brown	Roald Dahl	Eric Carle
Aliki	Dr. Seuss	Laura Ingalls Wilder
Lois Ehlert	Kevin Henkes	Chris Van Allsberg
Leo Lioni	Tomie dePaola	_____ .
Janet Stevens	Cynthia Rylant	_____
Helen Lester	Beverly Cleary	_____

Student worksheet for deciding what to include in their library (Jane Jones's grade 3 class)

When I am in classrooms with rich libraries created and maintained by the teacher and students, grand enthusiasm for reading and talk about books permeate every aspect of the curriculum.

**TRY IT
APPLY IT**

*Involve Your
Students
in Library
Design and
Organization*

- Invite students to submit design plans for a "new" library. Use graph paper, so students can draw to scale.
- Solicit parents for comfortable furniture they may no longer be using, such as a rocking chair and bean-bag chairs.
- Add a lamp or two to your library corner to make it cozy and inviting.
- If you don't have a carpeted area for reading on the floor, carpet squares are an inexpensive, portable alternative.
- Form a committee to evaluate present library design and make recommendations.
- Consider a special section for content-area books pertaining to current areas of study and thematic units. Include space for related objects such as nature collections (rocks, shells) or plants.
- Have students sort, label, and shelve books by genre, interest, difficulty, series, author, etc.
- Work out a manageable "sign out" system that students manage. (See the teaching tip on page 67.)

A section of a newly organized classroom library

Display Books So They Entice Readers

The next time you walk into a bookstore, notice how the best sellers are always displayed face out, with the full covers visible. The majority of books purchased at bookstores are displayed with their covers in full view. This is smart marketing that we need to apply to our classrooms. When you can see the cover of a book and can easily pick it up and peruse it, it's more likely you will choose to read the book. Yet, in our classrooms, we house most of our books so just the spines are visible, and our students barely notice them.

Recognizing the power of book display, fifth-grade teacher Mike Marinello, in Brookfield, Wisconsin, added a four-foot-high spinning display rack to his classroom. He put all the most popular titles in it, and by the end of the day he brought it in, it was almost empty. Mike notes, "It was unbelievable how that display was like a magnet to the kids."

Change your displays regularly. Feature different authors, content subjects, magazines—all based on students' and teacher interest and curriculum. And be sure to include a section for students' published writing—books, stories, nonfiction pieces, riddles, poetry, and more.

Students' interests may surprise you. One spring, first-grade teacher Suzy Headley and I gave each of her students a sheet listing all the categories of the dozens of book baskets she had placed in the classroom library. Each student was asked to circle their three top favorites, cross out any they didn't like, and add any they would like to see in the library. Joke books, not on the sheet, were the overwhelming number one favorite for most students. It was, by the way, rare for a student to delete an existing category. And, in a fifth-grade classroom, students surprised their teacher by choosing comic books as their second-favorite category.

Use Rain Gutters

Rain gutters are a fabulous, inexpensive way to display books so the covers are visible (see the photograph on page 79). Principal Mike Oliver uses rain gutters in his office and throughout his school to increase book display space. Rain gutters are easily installed under windows and chalkboards, and they enhance the look and atmosphere of the classroom. Ten running feet of rain gutter costs about three dollars. Teachers report rain gutter book displays influence students to read more and become more excited about reading, because the visible book covers attract their attention and "sell" the books.

Increasing space for book display with rain gutters

Use Book Baskets or Bins

Baskets to house books can be purchased inexpensively at discount stores, often for less than a dollar per basket when bought in bulk (see the photograph on page 80). Because students can easily see the covers and flip through books stacked one behind the other, access is increased. Spinning displays also provide easy access and let students see many titles at a glance.

Karen Sher has a personal book basket for each of her kindergartners. She interviews each child at the beginning of the year and asks what kinds of books she or he likes to read. She makes sure that her library includes books especially chosen to match each child's interests. Children love having their own baskets to house books they select to read.

Teach Students How to Care for Books

When teachers display their love and respect for books they own and bring these books in to share with students, students treat them carefully out of respect for the teacher. They don't want to let her down. We need to create that same sense of respect and caring for all the books in our libraries.

Books organized in baskets are easy to access

With your students, decide "book caring" policy and model expected behavior, which might include:

☐ Using bookmarks as placeholders.
☐ Handling books carefully to extend their life. (Don't leave books open at the spine; don't fold down pages; make sure your hands are clean.)
☐ Carrying books between school and home in a waterproof bag.
☐ Putting books back where you found them.

Start a Summer Reading Program

Research tells us that children who do not read regularly throughout the summer months lose approximately three months of reading growth, while those who do read during the summer continue to make gains. In order to stem this cumulative loss of years over a school career, we must make getting books into children's hands throughout the summer a whole-school priority.

When the staff of Huntsville Elementary School, in Huntsville, Ohio, heard about this research, they signed up to take turns coming in two days per week, on a volunteer basis, to keep the school library open all summer. To build excitement, they had an assembly the last week of school to explain the summer reading opportunities, which included "book bags" for children (free books donated by local businesses and Reading Is Fundamental).

Classroom Libraries Simplify Guided Reading

Finally, classroom libraries are essential to your guided reading program and working in small groups. Teachers are amazed that once they establish and value classroom libraries and connect them to a carefully monitored independent reading program, worries about management fade.

Typically, many teachers say, "I can only fit in one, or sometimes two, small guided reading groups each day. The groups take half an hour each, and what are the other students supposed to be doing anyway?"

In every school residency, before I demonstrate teaching reading in small groups, I first work with teachers to simplify their management. Mostly, that means making strong classroom libraries the number one priority along with making sure students knew how to select "just-right" books and are actually matched with books they can read (see pages 93–95 and 104). Once teachers establish excellent classroom libraries, fitting in small-group work and individual reading conferences becomes routine. Most significant, students spend most of their reading time *reading* as opposed to doing activities *about* reading (see pages 160–161). Often, this reading takes the form of partner reading (see pages 91–93.)

There Is No Substitute for Quality Books

You may need to be outspoken, proactive, and creative to get the money, space, and permission you need to put children's books in your classroom. In some California schools, teachers have been pressured to *remove* classroom libraries, the reason being that these books interfere with instruction. Ridiculous! In school after school where I have worked, I have seen excellent classroom libraries transform children as readers. Conversely, when there are no libraries, or poor ones, students often do not like to read and do not achieve their highest potential. Make sure you are doing all you can to provide children with interesting and outstanding reading materials and the time to read them.

Multiage primary-grades teacher Monica Carrera-Wilburn states:

> The impact of my evolving library has been tremendous. When I open the doors in the morning my students rush to the library to read. My goal is to transform my room from a classroom with a library in it to a library with a classroom in it! Can you imagine that!

We teachers need to become strong advocates for ensuring that our students read excellent books. Children's author Katherine Paterson reminds us that the future of literature depends on the reading diet we give our children:

> What are we feeding our children? Is there anything on the World Wide Web that can nourish a child intellectually and spiritually in the sense that the best of our books can?

6 Plan for and Monitor Independent Reading

If proficient readers typically read extensively on their own, as the research suggests, it would seem prudent, even scientific, to develop this habit in young readers.

—Thomas Newkirk

One August, I received a phone call from a colleague and friend who teaches fourth grade. "Confidentially, my students' proficiency test scores weren't as good as I expected. I have some questions about my reading program." She went on to tell that the students of the teacher down the hall had received similar test scores. "I can't figure that out," she wailed. "You know I do a much better job with guided reading. My students' test scores should have been higher."

My friend is one of the best teachers of reading I know. I've watched her conduct superb small-group guided reading lessons; she spends lots of additional time teaching comprehension strategies; she has occasional literature conversations; she assigns meaningful independent work.

"When do they read?" I asked. "When do they get to read books they can choose?"

"Well, the other stuff takes so much time, we only have ten or fifteen minutes a day for independent reading."

Aha. Here was the critical difference. The teacher down the hall started off each morning with an independent reading program, thirty to forty minutes in which the students read books of their own choosing and the teacher monitored how they were doing. I knew exactly what was going on in that classroom because I had demonstrated for and coached that teacher for a year. Even though she was a less skilled teacher of guided reading—and in fact was inconsistent about meeting with small groups—she had an excellent, carefully monitored, independent reading program in place, fully supported by an ample classroom library and daily reading conferences.

I suggested to my friend that she consider reallocating her reading time to include at least thirty minutes a day for independent reading. Just as important, I strongly suggested she think about putting a classroom library in place. Even though she had lots of books in her room, they were not organized so students could get at them easily.

Let me be very clear here. Just adding more time and space for independent reading is not enough. I'm advocating a carefully designed, structured reading program that includes demonstrating, teaching, guiding, monitoring, evaluating, and goal setting along with voluntary reading of books students choose.

Students Need to Do More Reading

My friend's story is not unique. Other teachers and principals have shared similar stories about doing lots of comprehension instruction and whole-class and small-group work with less-successful-than-expected results. I generally hear these stories after the test scores come in. Always, I suggest, "They need to be doing more reading." When an independent reading component is added, test scores go up.

Tragically, many intermediate-grade teachers are dropping independent reading as a regularly scheduled part of their instructional reading program. And even when time is allotted to independent reading, increasingly a computerized reading-incentive program (see pages 198–200) is in charge, not the classroom teacher. Additionally, many of our struggling readers lose their independent reading time, because this is often when they leave the classroom for supplemental reading instruction.

Any reading program that substantially increases the amount of reading students do will impact their reading achievement. Indeed, this is the main reason those computerized reading-incentive programs seem to work: students are required to read for long blocks of time. You can easily do the same thing without an expensive program. In fact, you can do better, because there is no teaching component in those incentive programs.

There is a caution here, however. Not all students automatically improve their reading just because we give them time to read. If students are reading mostly difficult books, if they don't understand what they read, if no one is monitoring their progress, not much changes. I have been in far too many classrooms where students are staring at books they cannot and do not read and where sustained silent/independent reading is largely a waste of time.

Struggling Readers Need Much More Time to Read

I recently spent a week teaching reading in a school in an economically deprived area. Low-performing readers spent the last hour of an extended day in a teacher-directed, regimented reading program while the rest of the students read independently. Since this was the only time of the day set aside for independent reading, struggling readers never got to practice reading and just read. What a sad irony. The kids who need to read the most are given the least amount of time in which to do so. Brian, who did not become a reader until he was a sophomore in high school, says it perfectly:

> My advice to anybody who wants to become a better reader is to read
> more, to read lower books and practice so you can move up to higher
> levels. If you want to know how to read better, just keep on reading.

If our struggling readers and learners with special needs are to become successful readers, they need more than good instruction. They need to do massive amounts of real reading and writing of authentic texts. Richard Allington found that struggling readers who are in classrooms with exemplary teachers read and write two to five times the amount of connected text that students in classrooms with typical teachers do. We teachers are the only ones who can make this increase in reading happen and put an end to the substandard instruction that many of our low-performing students receive. (See Appendix A for meaningful, proven ways to teach struggling readers and increase the amount of reading they do.)

What Do We Mean by an Independent Reading Program?

Although I use the terms *sustained silent reading* and *independent reading* interchangeably—and do so throughout this book—some educators see sustained silent reading and independent reading as two separate entities. Therefore, let me explain the differences as I see them. However, my definition of independent reading is the one I will be referring to whenever I use either term.

SUSTAINED SILENT READING	INDEPENDENT READING
Student chooses any book to read	Student chooses any book to read
	Teacher may guide selection
Daily time to read, 10–30 minutes	Daily time to read, 30 minutes or more
Optional classroom library	Excellent classroom library, essential
Book may be above reading level	Student reads mostly "just- right" books
No checking by teacher	Teacher monitors comprehension
No writing involved	Student keeps a reading record
No teaching involved	Teaching occurs during a conference
No reading goals set	Teacher and student set reading goals

Research Strongly Supports Independent Reading

A longstanding, highly respected body of research definitively shows that students who read more, read better, and have higher reading achievement. You need to familiarize yourself with this research, because the value of free-choice voluntary reading in classrooms has recently been called into question. In order to maintain this critical practice, you may well need to cite research linking independent reading with achievement (see Notes, pages A-22–A-23) and to share this information with administrators and parents. A sample letter to parents is included in Appendix C.

Connect Independent Reading with Teaching and Evaluating

Common sense tells us that if we want to get good at an activity, regardless of what that activity is, we have to practice it. Practice without feedback, however, is not as efficient as monitored practice. There is a delicate balance here. We need to set the learner up with just enough of a challenge so he can work out problems for himself and become self-monitoring, self-regulating, and independent. Too much challenge will lead to frustration; too little will eventually lead to boredom.

In my thirty-five years of teaching, I have always maintained an independent reading program, but it has never been just "take out your book and read." It has always meant making sure students are:

☐ Matched with a book (or other reading material) they can read and understand.
☐ Reading a text they enjoy.
☐ Practicing and trying out strategies we've been demonstrating and working on in class.
☐ Being monitored, assessed, and evaluated on the books they are reading.
☐ Being taught strategies and how to apply them to problem solve and read independently.
☐ Setting and working on goals to further improve their reading competency.

My years in the classroom have shown me that when a daily sustained silent reading program includes not only careful monitoring of students' progress but teaching what the student needs to know to be able to move forward, reading comprehension improves. This is not necessarily true when students are just given time to read. For example, with a computerized reading-incentive program, students do lots of reading and move through levels, but they may or may not be reading for understanding.

Notice Where Independent Reading Fits in the Optimal Learning Model

Revisiting the optimal learning model (see page 87; also see pages 43–50 and the chart on inside of the front cover), we see that independent reading is not just another activity to add to your reading program but is the crucial learning context in which the reader assumes responsibility for applying smart reading behavior in order to gain and maintain understanding. Independent reading provides the indispensable practice that literacy learners require to become

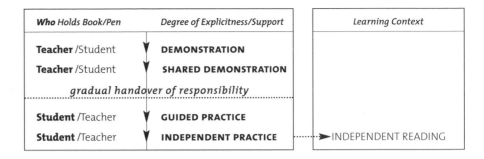

Who *Holds Book/Pen*	*Degree of Explicitness/Support*	*Learning Context*
Teacher /Student	▼ DEMONSTRATION	
Teacher /Student	▼ SHARED DEMONSTRATION	
gradual handover of responsibility		
Student /Teacher	▼ GUIDED PRACTICE	
Student /Teacher	▼ INDEPENDENT PRACTICE	┈┈▶ INDEPENDENT READING

The Optimal Learning Model's Progression of Responsibility

successful, self-regulating, self-monitoring readers. This independent practice includes response. That is, teacher feedback is necessary to ensure readers are applying what we've been teaching them, are reading for understanding, and are continuing to set new goals.

If you have an excellent, carefully monitored independent reading program in place, supported by a wonderful classroom library (see Chapter 5), guided reading is put into proper perspective. Also, by carefully monitoring individual students during independent reading (see pages 100–105), you learn what skills and strategies you need to teach next. Many of these skills and strategies apply to the majority of students and, as such, can be demonstrated through reading and thinking aloud and shared reading experiences.

An Independent Reading Program Is Essential

Ironically, when teachers are pressed for time, independent reading is usually the first thing to be cut. Yet a carefully monitored independent reading program is the single most important part of your reading instructional program. What's more, it's fun, it's easy to implement and manage, and kids love it. They get to choose books they're interested in, to talk about those books with their friends, and to have uninterrupted time in school—to read! There's nothing better. You get to read, too, if you choose to. I like to read one or two days a week and show students what I'm reading and thinking about. The other days I use for individual conferences. The exception is at the beginning of the school year, when I use each day to get to know students as readers—both through interviews (see pages 20–21) and reading conferences. (See pages 212–215 for some examples of how teachers changed their daily schedules to make time for—or increase the time spent on—independent reading.)

COMPONENTS OF AN INDEPENDENT READING PROGRAM

☐ A well-designed and well-stocked classroom library, one that has been set up with and by students, includes their interests and preferences (see Chapter 2), and provides comfortable seating areas.

☐ Sustained time each day in which to read.

☐ Teacher as reader (see Chapter 3).

☐ "Just-right" books.

☐ An array of genres.

☐ Time for sharing and book talks.

☐ One-to-one student-teacher conferences (to include teaching, assessing and evaluating on the spot, and goal setting).

☐ Well-maintained reading records (see pages 33–36).

☐ Procedures that have been developed in connection with the students, then modeled and understood, and that are followed by everyone.

Set Up Classroom Procedures

You will want to negotiate these with your students, but here are some simple guidelines you may ask them to consider:

☐ Be sure the book you are reading is one you like and understand.
☐ Have with you as many books as you might need for the entire period (including some student-authored work).
☐ Once you have selected your place to read, stay there.
☐ Read quietly.
☐ Maintain a reading record (essential for grade 2 and above, optional for kindergarten and grade 1). (Pages 33–36 discuss the criteria for reading records and present some examples.)

You will also want to discuss and agree on procedures and guidelines for handling books, deciding what to read next when you can't find a book, and transporting books between home and school. For your readers who struggle, you may need to preselect and set aside a group of appropriate books (but only until they have learned to select "just-right" books themselves) to ensure they are reading during this time and not wandering around the room searching for books.

teaching tip

Chatterbox

At the end of sustained silent/independent reading, have students take about five minutes to discuss their reading in pairs or as a small group. Walk around, listen in, observe behavior and responses, and make anecdotal notes.

Occasionally, you may want to have directed independent reading, when you ask students to read and do one of the following as a follow-up and evaluation of what you have been teaching. In other words, "When you are reading today:

☐ Try using the strategy (or strategies) we've been working on.

☐ Notice how your character is behaving and what makes him behave that way [for fiction].

☐ Visualize a setting the author describes.

☐ Make a connection to your life.

☐ Be on the lookout for a strong chapter lead—an enticing beginning.

☐ Reread when you lose meaning.

☐ Use what you already know to figure out what words mean

☐ Note how an illustration or visual helps your understanding."

For maximum engagement and application, instead of having students practice what you've been teaching using pieces in an anthology, have them read and practice with books they've chosen themselves. When they finish, students can share with a partner, in a small group, or as a whole class. You might ask them to read aloud a great lead or description or share a favorite passage.

Once you know your students as readers, you may occasionally want to walk around and spot-check each student while the class is reading independently. Also, you may want to devote some days to texts other than books—magazines, catalogues, instruction booklets, student-published stories, newspapers, comic books, raps, whatever.

Value Independent Reading in Kindergarten

In kindergarten, much of daily independent "reading" is really time spent looking at books. Students gain confidence as readers by browsing, interacting with, and enjoying reading materials they choose to "look" at. Often, these are familiar books, poems, charts, and texts that have previously been read during shared reading or read-aloud or created during shared writing. Many of these texts are predictable and have a rhythm and/or rhyme that supports developing readers' growing phonemic awareness, word competency, and fluency.

Independent reading in kindergarten should increase from about ten minutes at the start of the school year to about twenty minutes by midyear. Students can use this time to become familiar with the way books work, concepts of print, informational books, authors, fiction books, poetry, and more, and to develop positive attitudes about reading.

Beginning the day with free choice reading instead of worksheets

Many teachers walk around the room informally assessing students, both by "listening in" and by making notes as students are reading. Other times, teachers deliberately sit down next to students to observe them read, take anecdotal notes, guide students forward, give encouragement, set new goals, and celebrate successes. Some teachers are very deliberate about this assessment, seeing four or five students each day, dividing their class into Monday's children, Tuesday's children, and so on. Expert teachers observe what the child is already attempting to do as a reader and build on that rather than focus on deficits.

Once behavior, expectations, and procedures have been carefully modeled and practiced, a "book look" is also a great way for kindergartners to start each day when they enter the classroom. Kindergarten teacher Melanie Fry, in Huntsville, Ohio, who used to have her children begin each day with worksheets and structured tasks, has this to say:

> This school year I stopped doing worksheets to start the day, and I will
> never go back! I was wasting thirty-five minutes of class time each day.
> Now my children spend that time reading. Each day they prepare one
> or two books to take home and read to their parents instead of a
> handful of papers that will eventually end up in the trash can. What a
> wonderful change the reading has made! I have watched these children
> gain so much confidence in their abilities and the pride they have as
> readers is just amazing!

Depend on Partner Reading

Partner, or paired, reading is a terrific way for students to read independently and grow as readers. Partner reading helps students, especially developing readers, "become more self-sufficient and less reliant on the teacher for assistance." Kids love partner reading and readily do so with books of their choosing. What's more, research shows that taking turns reading increases reader involvement, attention, and collaboration.

I depend on partner reading as an easy way I can manage the classroom while I am working with guided reading groups and still accomplish important reading work. Partner reading first needs to be carefully modeled so students know "what it looks like" and "what it sounds like." Robin Woods's second graders in Westminster, Colorado, created the following partner reading guidelines during a shared writing.

PARTNER READING GUIDELINES

- [ ] The **reader** holds the book.
- [ ] **Sit close** enough so both partners can see the words.
- [ ] **Take turns** reading.
- [ ] Go back and **reread** if you don't understand.
- [ ] Turn and **talk**. (Tell your partner what happened. Both partners should talk.)
- [ ] **Problem solve** with your partner. (If one partner doesn't want to read so much, the other partner can read more.)
- [ ] If your **partner is stuck on a word:**
    - [ ] Give your partner time to think (wait time).
    - [ ] Go back and reread.
    - [ ] Read past the tricky word and come back to it.
    - [ ] Slide through it.
    - [ ] Put in what makes sense.
    - [ ] Sound it out with your partner.
    - [ ] Cover part of a word and ask, "What does it say?"
    - [ ] Look at the pictures.
    - [ ] Ask, "Would you like me to help you?"
    - [ ] Tell your partner what the word is.
- [ ] **ENJOY READING!**

Partner reading

<table>
<tr><td>Teacher
Talk</td></tr>
</table>

Modeling partner reading

☐ *I'm going to be working with reading groups [or individual reading conferences] and I can't be disturbed. You can read on your own or with a partner. Be sure you choose a book you can read and understand.* [I've already established guidelines for choosing "easy," "just-right," and "hard" books. See pages 93–95.]

☐ *Both of you need to be able to see the pages.*

☐ *What will you do if your partner doesn't know a word?*

☐ *Do the same thing I do in class: give your partner time to think.*

☐ *Stop after a couple of pages. Talk about what's happening.*

☐ *Partners read in quiet voices. Why is that important?*

☐ *Okay, Joey and his partner are going to show us what partner reading looks like and sounds like. Joey, read the first page. What will you do if you don't know a word?* [I let the class suggest strategies—see the list Robin Woods's second graders created, page 91.]

☐ *Kids, did you notice how they used quiet voices, how they helped each other and took turns? Okay, let's have another pair demonstrate for us and see how they do.* [If more modeling is necessary, I then demonstrate with a student.]

☐ *Find a place in the room where no one else is right next to you.*

Evaluate Partner Reading

When I teach students about partner reading—what it looks like and sounds like and what the expectations and procedures are—I offer demonstrations and guided practice and help students evaluate how well they are succeeding.

<table>
<tr><td>

Teacher
Talk

</td><td>

☐ *What went well in partner reading?*
☐ *You were acting just like a good teacher. You told your partner, "Try reading that again."*
☐ *Did you hear that? She gave him time to think, and they took turns.*
☐ *Good, you read a page, your partner read a page, and then you told your partner what happened.*
☐ *Were there any problems?*
☐ *What can you do if your partner is stuck on a word?*
☐ *You problem solved with your partner. When one of you didn't want to read so much, your partner did more reading, but you still took turns discussing. That's fine.*
☐ *Let's write down some of the things that are very important in partner reading.*

</td></tr>
</table>

Teach Students How to Select "Just-Right" Books

In classroom after classroom, I ask, "If you're going to become a better reader, do you think you should read mostly easy books, 'just-right' books, or hard books?" Almost always, quite a few students respond, "Hard books." I tell them, "Researchers [and I explain that a researcher is a kind of scientist] have found that if you read a steady diet of books that are too hard for you, your reading actually gets worse."

A "just-right" book seems custom-made for the child—that is, the student can confidently read and understand a text he finds interesting, with minimal assistance. These are books that make students stretch—but just a little bit—so that they have the opportunity to apply the strategies we've been demonstrating (and they've been learning), as well as become familiar with new vocabulary, genres, and writing styles.

While reading lots of easy books is important for building confidence and fluency as well as for focusing on meaning, once students are competent readers, reading only easy books is not enough for continued growth. Easy reading—"light reading" (see pages 65–66), pattern books, familiar books—is, however, critical for becoming a successful reader.

By the same token, reading "hard" books is fine once in a while—when the student is very interested in a particular topic, for instance—but a steady diet of challenging books is counterproductive. I share just two examples among many: a third-grade girl who "faked it" each day and told me, "I don't want anyone to know I can't read chapter books," and a boy who spent months "reading" detailed reference books during sustained silent reading. An informal reading conference indicated that while he was enjoying flipping through these books, he couldn't say anything specific about what he had learned. With guidance he set these books aside and selected a "just-right" book from the classroom library.

Making sure that students are comprehending and enjoying the texts they are reading is critical for students' reading success. A carefully monitored independent reading program as part of your reading workshop, total reading program, or literacy block is not an option. It is an absolute necessity. And having students spend most of their independent reading time with "just-right" books is a necessity, too, if students are to grow as readers. (See Appendix E, "Use the Goldilocks Strategy to Choose Books.")

Establish Selection Guidelines

When I ask students what a "just-right" book is, it is rare for them to talk about interest and understanding. Usually, they focus solely on getting the words right, and these days, lots of them also talk about the book being "on their level." Sadly, I am interacting with more and more students who use the level designation placed on the book as their only selection criterion. Without that designation, many are unable to select a suitable book. Once teachers become aware of that troubling deficiency, they deliberately take their students to the library and demonstrate how to select a "just-right" book and guide students in doing so.

To gauge what your students know and apply about book selection and, also, as part of the process of teaching students how to select appropriate texts for reading, begin to develop guidelines in shared writing. (See Appendix F for second graders' guidelines for easy, "just-right," and hard books. See the charts on pages 95 and 96 for first graders' and fourth and fifth graders' criteria for "just-right" books (developed during a shared writing). Notice the focus on enjoyment and understanding.) Work with your students and help them include selection criteria that go beyond level designations and reading the words. Other factors to consider include:

☐ Interest.   ☐ Supportive illustrations or visuals.
☐ Ability to understand the text.   ☐ Vocabulary.
☐ Adequate background knowledge   ☐ Book format and size.
☐ Writing style.   ☐ Favorite author or series.
☐ Genre.

TRY IT
APPLY IT

✐ Through a shared writing with your students, develop criteria for choosing a "just-right" book. Once you have excellent guidelines, glue a copy to the inside of students' reading records.

✎ Share criteria with caregivers and encourage them to use these criteria with their children when selecting books at the library or bookstore. (See letter to parents in Appendix D.)

✐ Save your present criteria to use as a guide when developing guidelines with next year's students.

A "JUST-RIGHT" BOOK FOR GRADE 1

- I like it
- I can read most of it.
- I understand it. (I can tell someone what it's about.)

"JUST-RIGHT" BOOKS FOR A GRADE 4–5 CLASS

It's interesting; you like it!
- The title is appealing.
- You know and like the author.

You are comfortable reading it!
- The print is the right size.
- You like the illustrations.
- Some places are smooth; some are choppy.

You can read it!
- You understand the plot and can predict.
- You can tell others what it is about.
- There are only a few words per page you don't know.

McPherson Just Right Book Criteria 3-18-02

* Something that you don't have too much trouble reading.
* It's your level.
* Words aren't to big or small
* YOU UNDERSTAND IT!
* It has personality, adventure and humor.
* You can visualize what the author wrote
* It keeps you in suspense
* You are interested in it
* You could read it over and over.

Criteria for just-right books by fourth graders

Demonstrate That Reading Words Accurately Is Not Enough

Lots of students, and parents too, believe that if they can read the words, the book is at their reading level. In fact, many students—especially older struggling readers—can read the words but are unable to say what the text is about. Fluency involves much more than smooth reading.

**TRY IT
APPLY IT**

- Bring in a text in which you can read the words but don't have the background and vocabulary to understand it—a physics text, a technical manual, a philosophy book, a methods textbook filled with impenetrable jargon, whatever is a very difficult text for you. Then, read aloud fluently and attempt to retell what you've read. Students will see that although you can read the words, you cannot make meaning.

- Read aloud a portion of a book that is "just right" for you. Demonstrate how you can talk about what you have just read, what the text is about, what you have learned, and what you think might come next. Confirm that reading "just-right" books means you are able to tell someone what the book is about and what you have learned.

- Congratulate the student who is able to say, "This book is too hard for me, because I don't understand what it is about." Help that child find a suitable book.

- Let students know that a book that may be too difficult now may be "just right" in a few months.

- If a student is interested in a book that is too difficult right now, send a note home requesting that a caregiver read the book aloud.

Don't Underestimate the Importance of Choice

Letting students choose what they read in a classroom and school that have excellent libraries is essential for a successful independent reading program and for turning students on to reading. And the choice needs to be real. One intermediate-grade teacher let her students choose what historical fiction book they would read for independent reading—but it had to be historical fiction, which left some students unmotivated. And a second-grade teacher who also taught summer school to low-performing second graders encountered this complaint: "In our classroom, we weren't allowed to pick our own books. We didn't have much time to read." The teacher took these students to the library to help them select books they were interested in, and they were amazed and grateful to be reading books they liked. Choice contributed greatly to their growth as readers.

A study of middle school students found that students preferred independent reading and teacher read-alouds above most other activities and, conversely, that assigned reading was rarely mentioned as a preference. Reading competence is closely tied to the amount of time children spend reading on their own, and students read more when they can choose their reading materials. Reading satisfaction, too, begins with personal choice.

7. Make Assessment Instruction's Working Partner

Assessments should bring about benefits for children, or data should not be collected at all.

—Lorrie A. Shepard

Lots of assessing goes on in schools these days. Students are taking so many tests there's scant time left for teaching. Unfortunately, little of that assessment gets used to improve teaching and learning, even when it's classroom-based assessment under our control. Partly, it's because we don't always know what to do with the assessment once we have it: often, we don't take the time to use the assessment to move children forward and determine next steps for teaching. This is a lost opportunity to support students' growing competence as readers.

Using assessment to inform instruction is not easy. Sometimes teachers are required to do assessments by district administrators or their principal, who want documentation that students are progressing. Many teachers report that they feel enormous pressure to move students through a series of competency levels. In that regard, many teachers routinely take and compile running records of a student's oral reading without using them to inform instruction. All these assessments take so much time that teachers are hard pressed to find the time to analyze and use the results.

Make Assessment Work for You and Your Students

As much as is possible, we teachers need to do our own ongoing assessments with our students using materials that students are already reading or are likely to read. Our own assessments are the ones that really drive instruction. Someone else's materials and notes rarely give the full documentation we obtain through first-hand observations of students we know well. (If our district requires a set assessment, we can at least make it user friendly.)

By making this kind of assessment part of our daily teaching, we will have the time to use our assessments to improve instruction and learning. We need to ask ourselves these questions:

☐ **Is this a valid and useful assessment:**
For this student at this time?
For our curriculum and standards?
To inform my teaching?
To share with the student?

☐ **How am I using this assessment:**
To note and celebrate the student's strengths?
To build on those strengths?
To note weaknesses?
To inform and determine my instruction?
To help the student become more competent?
To teach what the student needs to know next?

☐ **What goals am I setting:**
For myself as teacher?
For the student?
With the student?
(See the guide for determining student reading goals on pages 106–107.)

☐ **Who else do I need to inform:**
The principal?
Parents?
Support personnel?

Finally, we must make sure the assessment is worth the time it takes and that it is easy to administer. We have no time for cumbersome assessments that yield little useful information. In one school where I worked, teachers complained about being required to administer a monthly reading assessment to every student: the assessment yielded no useful information beyond a numerical reading level. Recognizing the principal's need and responsibility to know how every student was progressing so no one "slipped through the cracks," these teachers lobbied to replace these mandated assessments with ongoing informal reading conferences as described in this chapter. Being proactive by securing and administering appropriate and useful assessments is part of our job as responsible professionals.

Make Assessment and Evaluation a Daily Routine

Whenever I am with students, I am evaluating them and noticing what they need next to move ahead. Whether in the context of conferences, demonstrations, shared reading, shared writing, word work, or teaching on the spot, I adopt a mindset of evaluation. That is, I maintain an awareness that pushes me constantly to connect instruction and evaluation. Mostly, I do not teach and then assess. Assessment and evaluation are naturally interwoven throughout this book because that is how I teach. (They do, however, rate a separate chapter, in order to emphasize their importance.)

I assess (gather data) and evaluate (analyze that data) *as* I am teaching. Then I adjust my lesson to meet the needs and interests of my students. I abandon my original plan, I start again, I reteach, I allow more time for discussion, I constantly reflect. This is why all programs have to be modified. We can't just follow the directions of a manual and hope for the best. We don't know what our students will understand or not understand until we begin to work with them. As effective teachers, we are bonded to our students, know them well, and seamlessly integrate instruction with evaluation throughout the day. This is exactly what effective parents do to raise healthy, well-functioning children.

Regularly Evaluate Students Regarding the Texts They Are Reading

Sitting right next to a student, observing him read, probing her thinking, is the best way I know to evaluate all aspects of a child's reading and move the student forward. While there are many informal reading inventories available as well as all kinds of formal tests, the most accurate information is obtained by carefully observing the child by your side, in the act of reading. And when students are assessed in connection with a book they are interested in—rather than a decontextualized test passage—optimal and accurate assessment is more likely. Also, the students do not view the conference as a test but more as a "check-up," a conversation. Students love to talk about books, and they love the one-on-one attention.

Once a child is a good reader, usually by the middle of second grade, I do not require oral reading in the conference. I evaluate the student on a book in process. That way, the student is building on a chunk of connected text she has already read. A whole book provides a more accurate context for checking comprehension than a short, isolated passage. Once I have assessed that the student is reading with understanding, I ask her to read two or three pages silently while I read along, also silently. As I read, I jot down what I think might be difficult words, concepts, or ideas, and afterward I ask the student how she figured these out. (See the conference form on page 109.)

When I do ask a child to read orally, I take a running record for younger and developing readers and a modified running record for more competent readers. In a modified running record, I record what the child says on top, what the text says below, and I include the page number, so I can go back to it with the child at the end of the conference and do some probing, or teaching, if necessary. Here's an example:

p. 79   child: *monster*

text: *monstrous*

The page number also lets me easily relocate and reexamine miscues at a later date, perhaps during a parent conference or when writing a progress report. (To save the time required to go back and find the book, also jot down the type of error—meaning, syntax, visual.)

Conduct Informal Reading Conferences

Work out a manageable system that combines assessment with instruction and that is a regular part of your school day.

Having individual reading conferences with students as a regular part of your school day is a way to combine assessment with instruction that is easy and pleasurable to implement. Second-grade teacher Robin Woods, in Westminster, Colorado, says:

> I love the personal structure of a reading conference, since I get to talk
> with the children about what they have chosen to read. I get to discover
> how students select books, their reading interests, where they under-
> stand texts and how and why they don't. Reading conferences help me
> get at what they understand as a reader, how they connect new under-

standing to old. I couldn't see the evolution of their thinking by just taking running records. In reading conferences, I get to become a reading colleague with my children, and there is great power in that.

Confer with All Your Students

Once you make independent reading a priority, you can meet with all your students regularly. I recommend allotting twenty or thirty minutes for independent reading in grades 1 and 2 and thirty to forty minutes in grades 3 and above (see the suggested time frames on page 158). A conference with a student can take anywhere from five to twenty minutes, the average being about ten minutes. With practice, in thirty minutes, you can easily meet with two or three students.

While you will want and need to meet with your struggling readers weekly (and sometimes for a few days in a row), for most of your students once a month is sufficient. (For an outstanding reader, once every two months may be enough.) Remember that you are also monitoring students' reading records; observing their responses in shared, guided, and interactive reading and their interactions with partners following independent reading; and evaluating their occasional written responses.

Fifth-grade teacher Amy Kahn conducts her first informal reading conference

Adopt a Relaxed Stance with Your Students

After observing me confer with a few students, teachers comment on how easy and pleasurable the process is. A second-grade teacher beamed, "It's fun, it's easy, and they love to talk about books." A fifth-grade teacher noted that she went from being a "sergeant-general" to an interested, amiable observer and evaluator: "Instead of testing the student, it was more like a conversation." Because she changed her attitude, both she and the students found the time together rewarding and productive. Our disposition when we interact with students is crucial. This goes back to bonding: students achieve more when they trust us and feel comfortable with us.

Make Sure the Student Has His Book with Him at the Conference

I never assess a child without the particular book in hand. As the child is telling me what the book is about so far, I scan the back cover, flip through pages and chapter titles, and try to get the gist of the story. Teachers always ask me, "How can you tell whether the student understands if you haven't read the book?" I promise you, you can. When a student knows what's going on, his retelling is full of details, his language makes sense and has a flow, he has an obvious sense of what the book is about, and, usually, his pleasure is evident. When I have a doubt, I probe with questions like these:

Questions to probe for student understanding:

With fiction:

- ☐ *What's the problem in the story so far?*
- ☐ *What's the main character like?*
- ☐ *Tell me about the setting, where the story is taking place.*
- ☐ *What's your favorite part so far?*
- ☐ *What's happening in the story right now?*

With nonfiction:

- ☐ *What's the most interesting thing you've learned so far?*
- ☐ *What's your favorite part?*
- ☐ *What else are you hoping to learn?*
- ☐ *How is this book organized?*

If a student seems not to be understanding, I have him read a short passage aloud to see whether this will help me figure out the problem:

- ☐ Is the book too difficult—words, concepts, vocabulary?
- ☐ Does he lack sufficient background knowledge?
- ☐ Does he lack fluency?
- ☐ Does he fail to reread when something doesn't make sense?
- ☐ Is he aware that the text is not making sense to him?
- ☐ Does he know how to select a "just-right" book?
- ☐ Is he reading so slowly that he is not attending to meaning?

While all of this sounds complicated, with practice, it's not. Usually, in just a few minutes, I can tell whether the student has understood what he has read so far. Sometimes, just holding the student accountable with, "Where does it say that? Read that again and show me where it says that," is enough to coax him into reading more carefully. Once I am convinced that the student can read and understand the book in process, I continue with the conference.

If the student has not understood, we talk about what makes a "just-right" book, and I help him select one. It is our job as knowledgeable professionals to ensure that our students are reading when they are supposed to be reading; that means that they are effectively using phonics, word analysis, comprehension strategies, and whatever else they bring to the text to understand it. Otherwise, we are squandering precious time.

A FRAMEWORK FOR AN INFORMAL READING CONFERENCE

- ☐ *Bring me a book that you can read pretty well.* (Is the child able to select books she can read and understand?)

- ☐ *Why did you choose this book?* (Does the child take recommendations from peers? Is this a favorite author or series? Is she overrelying on designated book levels?)

- ☐ *What is the reading level of this book for you?* (Does the child know that understanding requires reading easy and "just-right" books? Is she overrelying on being able to read all the words?)

- ☐ *Tell me what the book is about so far.* (Can the child give an adequate retelling that shows she understands the gist and main ideas of the text? If not, check oral reading to be sure she can read the text. If oral reading is a problem, help her select an easier text. If not, probe to find out why she cannot say what the book is about.)

☐ ***Read this part of the book for me.*** (Have a younger student and developing reader read orally. However, once the child is a "reader," have her read silently, since most of the reading we do in the world is silent. Ask her to read two or three pages while you read along silently. Note the time she starts and finishes in order to approximate her reading rate per page. Jot down difficult vocabulary words so you can check to be sure she is figuring them out. Observe her as she reads silently. Does she subvocalize, reread, use illustrations and visuals, get the humor, seem to skip over hard vocabulary?)

☐ ***Tell me what you remember about what you just read.*** (If the child is reading fiction, does she understand character motivation and behavior? If she is reading nonfiction, is she also using charts, photos, and graphs to get information? Check whether difficult vocabulary is understood. Is the student going beyond literal events in her retelling?)

☐ ***Let's discuss your strengths and what you need to work on.*** (Always note first what the child has done successfully so she will continue to do it and be affirmed for her efforts.)

   ☐ STRENGTHS: (Focus on what the child does well—selecting a "just-right" book, retelling appropriately, figuring out vocabulary, inferring meaning, rereading when necessary.)

   ☐ GOALS: (State, and have student restate, one or two goals that have resulted from the conference. See the list on pages 106–107 for some important goals to set.)

☐ ***How long do you think it will take you to complete this book?*** (Has the student thought about it and set a realistic goal? For example, if there are eighty pages left to read, and she allots one hour a day for reading, thirty minutes at home and thirty minutes in school, at a rate of about one page a minute, she should easily be done with the book in two days or less.)

"CHILD-FRIENDLY" READING GOALS

☐ *Reread when meaning is unclear, when something doesn't make sense.* (Good readers monitor their reading to make sure they understand the text.)

☐ *Think about what you are reading and what's happening.* (Good readers use helpful strategies to understand text; they predict, check—and sometimes change—their predictions, question themselves, question the author, summarize as they are reading.)

☐ *Make sure you can decode and understand the words in the books you select.* (Good readers know that if they can't easily decode almost all the words, they won't understand what they are reading. Good readers recognize most words automatically, which allows them to focus on meaning.)

☐ *Think about why characters act and behave the way they do.* (Good readers understand that fiction, historical fiction, and biographies are largely about people—what motivates them, how they relate and change, how they attempt to solve problems.)

☐ *Make connections to your life and what you already know to help you understand the story.* (Good readers rely on prior knowledge and experiences to help interpret text. Good readers know they need sufficient background knowledge before reading nonfiction and some fiction.)

☐ *Read in your mind. Don't move your lips.* (Good readers read a lot and read quickly; they don't have time to subvocalize.)

☐ *Make a picture in your mind to help you understand.* (Good readers form mental and visual images in order to understand more as they read and remember more afterward.)

☐ *Try reading in another genre.* (Good readers balance their reading diets and know and understand how biography, poetry, nonfiction, and other genres work. This in turn increases their general knowledge and vocabulary.)

☐ *Read more, at least thirty minutes a day at home, plus thirty minutes in school.* (Good readers read a lot and in doing so increase their vocabulary, fluency, and prior knowledge.)

☐ *When you don't know what a word means, use surrounding words—or read the next sentence or two—to help you figure it out.* (Good readers have strong vocabularies and know how to determine concepts and word meanings from context.)

☐ *Use the pictures (graphs, charts, visual aids) to help get meaning.* (Good readers use and interpret visual sources of information when they read nonfiction.)

☐ Other goals might be related to **reading in a specific genre, becoming familiar with specific authors,** or **increasing vocabulary** (not knowing the meaning of an important word can make you misinterpret a whole section of text).

☐ **For younger students,** add goals related to **handling books, understanding the concepts of print,** and **using phonics strategies and the other cueing systems** you are teaching.

Teach Intentionally

Any time we spend with a child is an opportunity to teach. If we make an assessment and don't use it to move teaching and learning forward, the assessment is largely a waste of time. Use your informal reading evaluations to do needs-based teaching. Ask yourself, *What's most important to teach at this moment for this child to move him forward?*

Teachers who are not used to evaluating their own students initially find it difficult to know what reading goals to set. Keeping the above list, or one like it, right next to you during a conference may help. The goals listed above are the principal ones I usually set. Then, when I notice several students with a similar problem, I do teaching demonstrations with a small group—or the whole class if I think the majority of students will benefit.

For example, my reading conferences with intermediate-grade students reveal that most students do not read deeply. They can retell the events of the story and say what the character did, but they can rarely talk about why characters behave the way they do, what actions lead to other behavior (cause and effect), or infer character's intentions, motivations, and feelings. So, when I am reading aloud or conducting a shared read-aloud, I make sure that I think aloud and talk about and explain how and why characters behave and change. Then I say,

> Today when you are reading on your own, I want you to think about how and why your character is behaving in a certain way. Good readers predict how characters will act and then read to see if they are right or need to change their predictions.

After independent reading, I give students an opportunity to share their insights—with a partner, in a small group, or as a whole class (see the "Chatterbox" teaching tip on page 89.)

Students don't automatically apply what we demonstrate just because we teach it. We need to coax them to move on to application, both by directly telling them to do so and by making our own application process visible. Then, we need to give them time to practice, and we need to check to see if application is occurring—through sharing, conferring with students, and evaluating occasional written responses.

Try Some Informal Reading Conferences

Teachers are often surprised at how high my expectations are for students. I expect them to do their best work, to reread when necessary, to do lots of reading of books they like and understand, and to comprehend on a deep level. Check to be sure that even young students are going beyond a superficial understanding. Do they understand the vocabulary? Are they reading between the lines? Do they grasp the subtleties of an important character's behavior? Are they integrating new information with what they already know?

After I conferred with Morgan, a fifth grader, we went over her strengths and goals. See her *Informal Reading Conference* which is shown on page 109 exactly as I wrote it during our conference. (See Appendix H for the blank form.) Note that the page numbers in the left-hand margin refer to the pages involved. I write down only what I deem important. For example, it's not helpful to me at the time—or if I revisit the conference sheet—to list everything the student says in a retelling.

Use Standards and High-Stakes Testing to Improve Comprehension

If we teach well and deeply, use challenging material, make connections across the curriculum and to children's lives, teach explicitly, and make what is on the test visible to students, they—even ones in economically deprived schools—do well on high-stakes tests. Keeping the strategies in mind—and teaching and applying them—in the course of regular teaching has been instrumental in raising reading test scores in several schools in which I have worked.

For example, at a residency in a school in a poor part of Florida, we made the comprehension strategies tested on the high-stakes reading test, the F-CAT, apparent to all teachers, starting in kindergarten (see the list on page 110). We talked about these strategies, named them, posted them, shared them with parents, practiced them with students in natural classroom contexts—in other words, made them part of, not separate from, our daily teaching. Concentrating on the strategies that would be tested raised the level of teaching, particularly

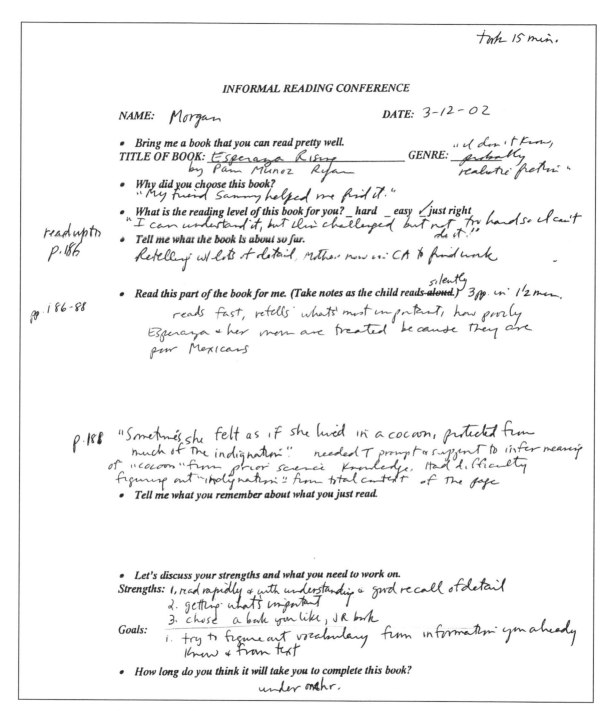

take 15 min.

INFORMAL READING CONFERENCE

NAME: Morgan   DATE: 3-12-02

- Bring me a book that you can read pretty well.

TITLE OF BOOK: Esperaza Rising   GENRE: "I don't know,
by Pam Munoz Ryan   probably
                                         realistic fiction."

- Why did you choose this book?
"My friend Sammy helped me find it."

- What is the reading level of this book for you? _ hard _ easy ✓ just right
"I can understand it, but this challenged but not too hard so I can't
                                                         do it."

read up to   • Tell me what the book is about so far.
p. 186   Retelling w/ lots of detail. Mother now in CA to find work

                                                       silently
              • Read this part of the book for me. (Take notes as the child reads aloud.) 3 pp. in 1½ min.

pp. 186-88   reads fast, retells what's most important, how poorly
              Esperanza & her mom are treated because they are
              poor Mexicans

p. 188 "Sometimes she felt as if she lived in a cocoon, protected from
        much of the indignation." needed T prompt & support to infer meaning
of "cocoon" from prior science knowledge. Had difficulty
figuring out "indignation" from total context of the page

- Tell me what you remember about what you just read.

- Let's discuss your strengths and what you need to work on.

Strengths: 1. read rapidly & with understanding & good recall of detail
           2. getting what's important
           3. chose a book you like, JR book

Goals: 1. try to figure out vocabulary from information you already
         know & from text

- How long do you think it will take you to complete this book?
                    under one hr.

Morgan's informal reading conference

with regard to struggling readers. Teachers who before had focused on factual recall began to raise their expectations for what they needed to teach and demonstrate. Students who had never been asked to think about an author's purpose or message or why characters behave as they do began to do so.

READING CONTENT ASSESSED BY THE FCAT (FLORIDA'S HIGH-STAKES READING TEST)

Students are able to use and understand:

☐ Strategies to determine meaning and increase vocabulary (including using prefixes, suffixes, root words, multiple meanings, antonyms, synonyms, and word relationships).
☐ Main idea or essential message (supporting details and facts; arrange events in chronological order).
☐ Author's purpose.
☐ Comparison and contrast.
☐ Appropriate reference materials; to read and organize information for a variety of purposes.
☐ Plot development and conflict resolution.
☐ Similarities and differences between characters, settings, and events.
☐ Cause-and-effect relationships ("What happened because of . . . ?").

Reading Essentials by Regie Routman (Heineman: Portsmouth, NH); © 2003

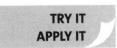

TRY IT APPLY IT

Use Standards and High-Stakes Testing to Improve Comprehension

✎ Review the strategies students need to apply on your state reading comprehension test. Make sure you and your colleagues are aware of them and understand them. Consider laminating the list and having it handy as a reference in every classroom.

✎ Integrate these comprehension strategies into your everyday teaching across the curriculum, starting in kindergarten. For example, during read-aloud, shared reading, or guided reading, talk about what the story is mostly about (the main idea), why the author may have written the story (the author's purpose), how this story or character differs from a related one (comparing and contrasting similarities and differences).

✏ Take a practice test yourself. What strategies are most useful for responding to the test questions? Teach those to your students.

Make Ongoing Accountability Central to Teaching Reading

We need to make sure we are documenting students' progress at the classroom and school level. Too often we move students ahead through a series of reading levels without data and analysis to back up our decisions. We must balance formal assessment (tests) with informal assessment (reading conferences, running records and modified running records, rubrics).

Have a School Policy in Place

Thommie Piercy is a highly knowledgeable, dedicated principal in Mt. Airy, Maryland; the teachers in her K–5 school of over eight hundred mostly middle-income students use various approaches to teaching reading. In 2001, this school outscored the other twenty elementary schools in the district on the rigorous, high-stakes Maryland School Performance Assessment Program. Why?

For one thing, to ensure that students in this school become excellent readers, Thommie and her assistant principal meet with each classroom teacher, several times throughout the school year, to review every student's progress. In these informal conversations, Thommie asks:

☐ Where are you now with teaching reading?

☐ Where do you expect each student to be by the end of the school year?

☐ Show me your data (running records, informal assessments, responses to comprehension questions, observations) on each student.

☐ Which students—and how many students—are below, at, or above grade level? How can we move all students forward?

☐ What can I do to provide additional support?

☐ What else (books, professional development, instructional support) do you need?

Thommie believes that explicit teaching, ongoing accountability through administrator/teacher partnerships and conversations, teacher collaboration at each grade level, a common school language for reading expectations, and more time spent reading have all contributed to her students' success.

teaching tip

Benchmark Books

Develop your own benchmark book assessments. In Shaker Heights, Ohio, where I worked for many years, we developed our own standardized assessments that we could administer as part of our daily teaching (see *Conversations*, pages 202b–204b). Students could select one of several excellent trade books to read and retell.

Work to Change Cumbersome District Policies

Everywhere I go, teachers complain about required procedures or assessments. Often, I find out that the policy is a district one, established with input from a committee of teachers. "Well, why don't you change it?" I ask. They always look surprised: "That's not possible!" Well, yes, it is. While state mandates and high-stakes testing may be a fact of life we have to live with, questionable practices and programs your district has implemented can often be changed.

When a group of third-, fourth-, and fifth-grade teachers I was working with voiced concern that there were too many indicators on checklists and report cards and that giving grades was arbitrary and difficult, we worked together to develop a simple rubric for reading (see page 113). Using the rubric simplified life for these teachers and their students—and for the students' parents. Everyone knew ahead of time what the expectations were for reading and what an A meant.

Students used the rubric as a self-evaluation tool each grading period. Teachers conferred with the few students who didn't evaluate themselves accurately. The rubric was then shared districtwide and used as a resource when new report cards were being written. In a similar instance, teachers were able to change the monthly assessment policy established by the principal by substituting a more meaningful and useful tool (see page 100). Instead of just complaining to administrators about what we don't like, we need to take a proactive, positive stance. Being a risk taker is easier to do as a group than as a single teacher. Think about saying something like the following:

> Here are the reasons we feel we can't go along with this policy or procedure. In its place, we intend to [do such and such], which will yield the same information and results you are seeking in a manner that is consistent with our beliefs, current research, and district expectations.

In particular, we need to be vigilant about new programs and materials that districts are thinking about adopting (see pages 195–198 for questions to ask *before* a program is adopted). While it takes time and effort to investigate, speak out, and advocate for specific changes, doing so will save us time and energy in the long run. When the practices we engage in improve instruction and learning and make school a more joyful place, everyone benefits.

Name:

Date:

Third, Fourth and Fifth Grade Reading Rubric

Indicators	Yes	No
1. Reads mostly "just right" books for daily independent reading.		
2. Reads a variety of genres.		
3. Keeps a reading record.		
4. Understands text using a variety of strategies.		
5. Is able to give a short summary.		
6. Contributes to discussion. Examples: starting conversations, piggybacking, questioning		
7. Comes to group prepared with:_____ .		
8. Sets reading goals and works towards them.		
9. Reads every day at school during independent reading time.		
10. Reads almost every day at home.		

Grading Scale

    9-10 = A

       8 = B

       7 = C

       6 = D

5 or less = Needs Improvement

Goals:

_____

_____

_____

Arapahoe Ridge Elementary, 2002

Reading rubric for use by students, teachers, and parents

Three

Teaching Essentials

ANY TIME WE SPEND WITH A CHILD IS AN OPPORTUNITY TO TEACH. USE YOUR INFORMAL READING EVALUATIONS TO DO NEEDS-BASED TEACHING. ASK YOURSELF, "WHAT'S MOST IMPORTANT TO TEACH AT THIS MOMENT FOR THIS CHILD TO MOVE HIM FORWARD?"

8. Teach Comprehension

Whatever approach is used, . . . it is important to emphasize to students that a targeted strategy is only part of a complex strategy system activated by skillful readers.

—Susan Kidd Villaume and Edna Greene Brabham

If we want kids to wind up with comprehension, we have to begin with comprehension. The current emphasis on word calling, automaticity, and fluency in the early grades is often at the expense of understanding. When we spend most of our energy focusing on words, students get the message that reading is about words rather than meaning. Additionally, we do lots of assessing of comprehension but not much teaching that makes it possible for students to comprehend on a deep level. Most students can give us the rudimentary facts but rarely an analysis of what they've read. We are turning out lots of superficial readers. They look and sound competent. They read smoothly and can retell what they've read with some detail, but they are unable to go further—to discuss why characters behave as they do, to give a concise

117

summary, to discuss the theme or big ideas, to talk about the author's purpose.

It's no surprise that the most recent NAEP results show a growing gap between our nation's highest- and lowest-achieving readers. We continue to focus on low-level skills (often using direct instruction programs) with our most impoverished readers. They learn to read the words, but by the time the focus shifts to comprehension, they have lost years of knowing what real reading is about.

In my continuing work in schools, it's rarely a lack of word work that prevents students from understanding. It's almost always not having the background, prior experiences, or knowledge of the way texts and authors work that stumps them—not knowing that good readers are aware of their understanding or lack of it and always do whatever is necessary to make sense of what they are reading. You can't start teaching comprehension in grade 3. You start teaching it the day kids enter preschool or kindergarten.

Start with the Texts Students Are Reading

We need to begin teaching comprehension by thinking about the texts students are reading as well as the texts we want them to be able to read and write. Teaching skills and strategies are important but only as they provide necessary supports for creating, understanding, and enjoying worthwhile texts. If we want readers to be critical thinkers, inquirers, and problem solvers, we need to introduce them to challenging, interesting texts. Then we need to show them not only how to process these texts but also how to reason strategically as they interpret, analyze, and appreciate what they read. This can be done even with developing readers (see the guided reading lesson "Making a Hat," conducted with first graders who are nonreaders on pages 175–177).

Demonstrate That Proficient Readers Use Many Strategies

A group of strategies have been identified as being key for achieving full understanding when we read. These strategies, which are having a major influence on how reading comprehension is being taught, include:

☐ **Make connections** (within this text, to another text, from known information to new information, to your life, to the world).

☐ **Monitor your reading for meaning** (apply "fix-up" strategies as necessary).

☐ **Determine what's most important** (distinguish main ideas from details).

☐ **Visualize** (see story in your mind's eye, create images).

☐ **Ask questions** (of yourself, of the author, of the text).

☐ **Make inferences** (predict, wonder, assess what's going on).

☐ **Synthesize** (apply new knowledge to what is known and generate new ideas).

Be Careful About How You Teach Comprehension

The good news is that comprehension has become a long overdue reading focus. The bad news is that comprehension strategies and exercises in isolation often dominate comprehension instruction. There are now many excellent books that help teachers think more strategically and concretely about how to teach comprehension, but many teachers have taken things too far. Strategies have wrongly become synonymous with comprehension, when, at best, they are a *tool for facilitating and extending comprehension.*

Students are spending massive amounts of time learning and practicing these strategies, often without knowing how to apply them and not understanding how they fit into the big picture of reading. Elaborate and expensive programs for teaching and practicing strategies are in vogue. Prepackaged curriculum, which often includes lots of coaching on taking tests, is thought to be the panacea. In many cases, what gets left out is enough time for the independent reading that enables students to use and practice these strategies.

In the typical classroom nowadays, reading instruction often focuses on practicing one comprehension strategy for weeks, whether it's asking questions, summarizing, or making connections to the text. Using sticky notes or bookmarks, students are expected to come up with lots of questions and connections as they read and then to write these down. Finally, either as a whole class or in small groups, students share their questions and connections in a teacher-led discussion.

So much emphasis on comprehension strategies can actually make reading harder. Students become so focused on identifying words they don't know, questions to ask, or connections to make that they forget to read for overall meaning. While it's fine to introduce and practice strategies one at a time, remember that when we read we use all these strategies at the same time and that our comprehension process is largely unconscious. Continue to ask yourself, *"How is this procedure helping my students become more proficient and independent as readers?"*

Balance Explicit Instruction with Lots of Time for Application

We need to be careful, too, about the amount of time we're devoting to strategy instruction; the act of reading still needs to predominate. Many students are held back by too much explicit instruction and too little guided practice. Keep in mind a 20-percent-to-80-percent rule:

> We learned that on average, dedicating about one fifth of each period
> to explicit strategy instruction was sufficient to provide students insight

into comprehension skills, which they then applied and extended in the remaining four fifths of the period.

Effective strategy instruction is about developing readers who actively and independently monitor and regulate their own comprehension. Key processes to teach include:

☐ Predicting.   ☐ Seeking clarification.
☐ Questioning.   ☐ Constructing summaries.
☐ Creating images.

Be sure to keep your teaching focus on strategic reading rather than on individual strategies. Ask yourself:

☐ Are students using and applying the strategies I am teaching?
☐ How do I know that? What's my evidence?
☐ Am I teaching for understanding of text?
☐ How am I assessing for understanding?

Teach and Apply Your Own Comprehension Processes

Just because we teach our students strategies doesn't mean they apply them. For many, it's akin to getting all the words right on the weekly spelling test but then failing to spell these words correctly in a notebook entry. They can "do" the strategy, but they don't apply it when they read. We have to make very clear why we are teaching a particular strategy. Then we must demonstrate how to use it by thinking aloud in front of the class. (See the example on page 49.) Only then can we expect our students to practice and apply the strategy. One fifth-grade teacher told me,

> My students can name and describe all the comprehension strategies good readers use. They can talk the talk, but they don't apply these strategies. I realize now that I have been telling them what good readers do and we've been practicing those strategies, but I've never shown them what I do as a reader.

Know What You Do as a Reader

While knowing research-based strategies is useful, don't forget to rely on what you do as a reader. Whenever I do a workshop to help teachers bring comprehension processes to a conscious level, we go through the following exercise using a current article about an educational issue:

- ☐ *Read one of the three articles you've been putting off reading* (choice so engagement will be higher, a little bit of a challenge so some reading work is needed).
- ☐ *Write down something you took away from the article*—a key point for you, a new understanding, a question, an affirmation (focus on meaning).
- ☐ *Take notice of the strategies you are using to understand the text* as *you read,* and jot these strategies down after you finish reading (thinking about your own thinking—metacognition).
- ☐ *With a partner or small group, talk about your findings.* Then, with the whole group, I ask, "*What did you each take away from the article?*" and we note the different personal meanings depending on interests, background knowledge, teaching situation. I always focus first on comprehension, just as I do with students, to emphasize that reading is always about making meaning.

Next, I make a list of strategies teachers consider most important for helping them understand as they read. The following is a typical list:

- ☐ Reread. (This is always the most frequently mentioned strategy.)
- ☐ Highlight (underline, circle, use highlighter pen, sticky note).
- ☐ Write (jot down comments or questions in margin).
- ☐ Survey (read ahead, skim, scan, read last paragraph first, read first lines of paragraphs, read first few opening paragraphs, predict).
- ☐ Connect (to past experiences, to prior knowledge) in order to understand ideas, figure out vocabulary.
- ☐ Monitor (adjust pace, pause and think, subvocalize, read aloud, talk to yourself).

The major research-based strategies don't dominate teachers' lists. No doubt we unconsciously employ these strategies, but if we don't often bring them up, perhaps we need to reevaluate how much time we spend teaching them to our students. We need to think deeply about our own reading processes, and trust what we do as a reader to guide our teaching.

Make Your Reading/ Thinking Process Visible

Students don't automatically comprehend just because they can read the words. Too often we assume they are getting meaning when they are not. Without our direct modeling and intervention, our students routinely skip words they can't read or don't understand, continue reading even when they don't know what's going on in the text, and rarely reread for clarification. Sometimes, they don't know they don't understand; more often, they fail to view reading as gaining understanding from text. In particular, our low-achieving students need to be taught comprehension strategies explicitly.

Our students are more likely to increase their reading comprehension when we show them how we understand a text and model a variety of strategies (such as asking questions, predicting, summarizing, and clarifying). We need to take care not just to model individual strategies in isolation and hope for a transfer of learning. Comprehending is a subtle, difficult-to-define process that changes according to the demands of the particular text.

> Being strategic is much more than knowing the individual strategies. When faced with a comprehension problem, good strategy users will coordinate strategies and shift strategies as it is appropriate to do so. They will constantly alter, adjust, modify, and test until they construct meaning and the problem is solved.

Teach Rereading as the Single Most Useful Strategy

No matter how many times I do the "Know What You Do as a Reader" exercise with teachers, rereading is always the number one comprehension strategy teachers cite. In fact, rereading is the strategy that is most useful to readers of all ages. When given opportunities to reread material, readers' comprehension always goes up. And research consistently shows that rereading is one of the most highly recommended strategies for struggling readers. Yet, we rarely teach rereading as a primary strategy.

**TRY IT
APPLY IT**

- Read aloud a short but challenging piece of nonfiction. Retell what you've read on the spot. In front of your students, rate yourself on your comprehension. Immediately reread the piece, retell it again, and rate your comprehension. Your students will witness your increase in understanding firsthand.
- During shared reading and shared writing as well as in guided reading, demonstrate how you reread to monitor and maintain comprehension. (This also works when reading aloud—when we discuss a text afterward, we sometimes need to go back and reread to recall information or clarify.)
- Model rereading when reading with a partner. Encourage partners to ask a peer to reread when meaning is lost.
- Demonstrate how you also reread charts, graphs, and captions to improve your comprehension of a text.

Use Writing to Help Recall Key Points

Writing can play a big part in aiding our comprehension, especially of nonfiction. One of the reasons I feel compelled to buy rather than borrow professional books is that I write in them. I underline, write comments in the margin, note key pages to return to. This writing aids my understanding and lets me reread, find, or verify information efficiently or summarize key points quickly.

I use lots of short nonfiction pieces with my students—photocopies of newspaper articles with white space for writing, excellent student news magazines (*National Geographic for Kids, Time for Kids, Scholastic News*), and children's magazines—any disposable text. Thinking out loud, I show students how I decide what to highlight or underline (what's most important or interesting or what I want to remember), how and why I write notes to myself, and so on.

Teach Students to Survey Text Before They Begin to Read

Even with nonreaders, I always start off a read-aloud, shared reading, or guided reading group by having students preview the book—notice the cover and title, go through the pages, examine the illustrations, predict what the story will be about. Surveying, or previewing, sets the scene for reading by giving a framework for what is about to unfold.

Surveying is invaluable with nonfiction. It teaches students how to be selective about their reading, how to hone in on exactly the information they're interested in. I routinely survey when I read the daily newspaper and news magazines. Using a short article, I show students how I examine the headings, captions, graphs, diagrams, and photos before I begin to read.

**TRY IT
APPLY IT**

✐ Give students copies of a current news article. Demonstrate how you preview and survey before you read and as you read. For example, I think aloud as I read the headline and opening paragraph(s). Depending on my interest in the topic and time available, I may skip whole chunks of the article and go directly to the conclusion.

✎ In pairs or in small groups, have students survey a news article. If necessary, first provide necessary background knowledge. Then, as a whole class, have students tell what they did.

✐ Make a class chart of strategies students use when they survey.

Make Connections

Making connections has become the comprehension strategy teachers love to teach. Students spend weeks looking for and noting connections as they read. While this is an excellent strategy, remember that when we make connections, we are doing lots of other things at the same time. If I asked you to read an article and *only* make connections as you read, you couldn't do it. You would also be integrating a whole range of other strategies. So while we want students to be aware of text-to-text, text-to-self, and text-to-world connections in order to enhance their understanding, most of those connections should be routinely demonstrated and practiced as part of the total reading experience. While it is important to teach a particular strategy explicitly to clarify and solidify it for the reader, use caution in how long you focus on any one strategy in isolation.

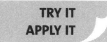

- Think about the way you make connections as you read, and teach what you do to your students. Adequate prior knowledge plays an important role here.
- Talk about how texts are related to one another in terms of characters, theme, plot, setting, author's purpose.
- When a student says, "I noticed that this book is similar to such-and-so," identify the strategy. Say, "You made a connection. That's what good readers do."
- As part of a shared read-aloud (see Chapter 9), ask students to make a connection to their life or to another text and talk about it with a partner.

Teach Self-Monitoring as Crucial to Understanding

Many studies have been done that show that readers are unaware of how they comprehend. Also, students do not automatically read for meaning: reading for meaning must be demonstrated, practiced, evaluated, and expected. (The students in the guided reading lessons on pages 178–179 could read the words but weren't understanding the story.)

Students cannot read for meaning until they can monitor the things they do to make sense of text and maintain comprehension—before, during, and after reading, yes, but especially *as* they read. Examine how important monitoring is to your own reading and teach it as a major strategy. I let my own monitoring processes guide what I teach my students. (See the list on page 125.)

Before students can monitor themselves and apply "fix-up" strategies, they need to know what understanding entails. That is, when they understand what they are reading, what are they doing, what's happening inside their head? And do they recognize when meaning breaks down, when they no longer understand what they are reading? Too many of our students don't have this awareness. We need to teach our students to ask themselves, as they read:

- ☐ *Does this make sense?*
- ☐ *Does this sound like language?*
- ☐ *Do I know what is happening in the text?*

When they answer no to any of these questions, they should stop reading and use one or more comprehension strategies to get back on track. We need to ask our students, "What will you do to be sure you understand?" and then be sure we have taught our students how and when to use and apply a whole range of strategies.

I KNOW I UNDERSTAND WHAT I AM READING WHEN I CAN

- ☐ Get the gist of the text even if I can't read or interpret every word and idea.
- ☐ Retell the text orally or in writing so that another person understands my re-creation.
- ☐ Connect or relate what I'm reading to what I already know, have read, or experienced.
- ☐ Reread a portion of text and clear up confusions.
- ☐ Use my knowledge of the subject or author to think and evaluate more deeply and critically—for example, to question, agree, or disagree with the text.
- ☐ Take clear notes that demonstrate my insights and learning.
- ☐ Use my notes to help me as I read or reread.
- ☐ Summarize or paraphrase what I've read.
- ☐ Use what I've read to think about other contexts and texts.
- ☐ Recognize gaps in my understanding and attempt to understand better by rereading, listing or highlighting key words or phrases, figuring out the meaning of unfamiliar words, writing notes to myself, asking pertinent questions, conversing with others.
- ☐ Consider multiple meanings.
- ☐ Recognize and use the characteristics of the genre to help me comprehend.
- ☐ Consider and understand comments of others.
- ☐ Make new meaning.

Talk to Yourself to Aid Understanding

When I come to a difficult or confusing passage or sentence, I not only reread it, I often reread it out loud to myself. I quietly subvocalize or speak aloud as I mouth the words. Saying the words aloud helps me focus on the meaning. Sometimes, I also talk to myself, in my head or out loud:

☐ *I wonder why he's doing that?*

☐ *Okay, I get that now.*

☐ *I've seen that word before.*

☐ *This doesn't make any sense.*

☐ *I better reread this part.*

Talking like this slows me down, which forces me to pay closer attention. I make this process visible to students when I think aloud in front of them as I read.

TRY IT APPLY IT

Teach Self-Monitoring

✎ Think about what you do as you read. Jot down your own list. Remember there is no one right list. Use what you do to guide your teaching.

✎ Be as explicit as you can about what's going on inside your head as you think aloud while reading in front of your students. Make your processes visible.

✎ Make a class chart: "What We Do When Meaning or Focus Is Lost."

✎ Have students share their strategies as they read with a partner.

✎ Conclude with a class discussion.

Interact with Peers to Increase Comprehension and Enjoyment

Talking with others about what we read increases our understanding. Collaborative talk is a powerful way to make meaning. Teachers who go through the "Know What You Do as a Reader" exercise (see pages 120–121) often mention how comforting it is to be able to talk over what they read and think with other adults. Not only do they feel supported, they gain new insights by hearing and considering other viewpoints.

TRY IT APPLY IT

- Provide more opportunities for students to talk with others about what they read through interactive reading, shared reading aloud (see Chapter 9), reciprocal teaching, literature conversations (see *Conversations*, pages 171–204), and partner reading.

- Take stock of how much talk about texts is teacher dominated. Make sure students are doing most of the talking.

- Model what productive talk looks and sounds like. With the whole class looking on, talk about some aspect of a text with a student partner. Then, with the bulk of the class still observing, have a few pairs of student volunteers try out what you have just modeled. Next, have the whole class work in pairs while you walk around, look on, guide, and coach.

- Add literature conversations (see *Conversations*, pages 171–204).

Use Texts That Are Easy Enough and Meaningful Enough to Support Comprehension

Students can't read for meaning if they are struggling over words or concepts. Too often we give students a text, even a leveled one, that does not support reading for understanding. Publishers' collections of leveled books may overrely on sentence complexity without paying enough attention to concepts, content, and sophisticated language. Too often texts are too difficult for the intended grade level or student, and most of the time students should spend reading is taken up helping them pronounce and define words they don't know. As a rule of thumb, if students are reading for understanding, they should know 95 percent or more of the words they encounter. (Some sources say 90 percent is sufficient, but I find that rate is too low for thoughtful comprehension.)

TRY IT APPLY IT

- Check your leveled book collection. Be sure these texts are mostly authentic literature written by authors to delight children.

- Examine how texts are leveled, especially at beginning levels where word recognition is critical.

- Seek out meaningful short texts—fables, short stories, short novels, newspaper articles, magazine articles, nonfiction pieces—to use to demonstrate, practice, and apply reading strategies.

- Through conferences with students (see Chapter 7), check to be sure that books and materials students are reading independently are easy enough to allow them to focus on meaning.

teaching tip

Build Fluency

Fourth-grade teacher Kari Oosterveen, in Vancouver, Washington, sets aside time several days a week for kids to partner-read short, easy, familiar material—picture books, poetry, even comic books. She asks them to read expressively and use special voices for the characters. They practice reading different print styles, and both listening skills and fluency improve.

Keep Fluency in Perspective

The National Reading Panel defines fluency as "the ability to read a text quickly, accurately, and with proper expression." I find this definition inadequate, because fluency without comprehension is not reading; it is calling words. Nevertheless, fluency, when it also involves understanding, is an important reading goal that can be taught in many contexts. In my experience, fluency is mostly a reliable predictor of reading comprehension in the early grades: by the intermediate grades, fluency no longer necessarily indicates comprehension. Many students can read all the words but are unable to talk about what they have read.

As teachers, we need to pay attention to our students' processing speed, especially that of our low achievers, but we need to use common sense in the amount of time we spend teaching fluency. Some teachers are required to report a reading rate for all students every week or month, not the wisest use of our time: fluency is easily assessed by listening to the child read aloud.

The best way to improve fluency is through repeated reading of familiar texts. Be sure that at least some of these are content-area texts, such as nonfiction trade books. Partner reading, shared reading, listening to tapes (when students can keep up), Readers Theatre, and reading series books are all great ways to help students gain fluency.

Teach Students How to Ask Significant Questions

Typically, we limit our students' comprehension by asking literal, right-there-in-the-text questions that require only shallow reading and understanding. Common examples are the comprehension questions posed by computerized reading-incentive programs and end-of-chapter questions in many content-area textbooks. Unless we ask and demonstrate how to ask questions that encourage in-depth reading, our students will remain superficial readers.

Mark Andrews is a conscientious middle-grades teacher in Mesa, Arizona. He often asks his students to make up comprehension questions after reading a chapter in a science or social studies textbook. However, observing students generating significant open-ended questions as part of a self-directed literature conversation made him question his practice. He found it "eye opening" that all 240 questions his students had generated on a science textbook chapter were literal ones. Mark reflects:

> I assumed my lesson was really stretching the students' higher comprehension skills. It wasn't until I analyzed their responses that I realized that I had not modeled appropriate strategies for students to engage themselves in true, high-level, open-ended questioning.

Use Caution and Common Sense When Teaching Strategies

Once again—but it's important enough to be restated—we must take care that teaching a particular strategy does not take precedence over reading and understanding text. Students can "know" lots of strategies and also document their use of particular strategies. But being able to complete a strategy exercise is not the same as knowing how and when to use and apply a strategy in the act of reading to gain understanding.

Also, it's impossible to read for understanding and only make connections or only summarize or only ask questions. When we read, we simultaneously and seamlessly employ a whole range of strategies, and we are constantly making refinements and adjustments according to the demands of the text and what we bring to it. Our comprehension process is invisible and difficult to document. So while it's useful to practice a strategy as students are learning it, make sure that most of your comprehension instruction uses strategies interactively. We teachers need to give explicit demonstrations not just on how to use a strategy in isolation but also on how to make the strategy a part of our unconscious reading process, so that students are able to combine any number of strategies to problem solve before, during, and after they read.

There is a huge difference between strategy instruction and strategic instruction. Just teaching strategies is not enough. Strategies must be "invoked" by the learner if they are to be used to increase understanding.

9. Emphasize Shared Reading

Shared reading is an important missing piece in many reading programs, especially in grade 2 and above. I find that when teachers shift their attention to give more time to shared reading, guided practice is more meaningful and efficient, and teachers don't have to work so hard in small reading groups. Also, and this is very important, teaching reading becomes much more enjoyable.

Make Shared Reading an Integral Part of Your Reading Program

In shared reading, a learner—or group of learners—sees the text, observes an expert (usually the teacher) reading it with fluency and expression, and is invited to read along. In the optimal learning model, shared reading is an ideal way to demonstrate and support what good readers do. The teacher not only makes reading visible and explicit for students but provides scaffolding so that students will be successful. Shared reading is also powerful because it helps students and teachers bond; students are partners in an enjoyable process and see themselves as ultimately capable. Furthermore, research indicates that shared reading typically improves reading achievement.

Here's how it works. Through teacher modeling and encouragement, students join with their peers to read a text collaboratively. In a relaxed setting, maximum support is provided, and there is no fear of failure. Perhaps best of all, shared reading is fun, and these days fun is sadly missing in too many classrooms. Students especially love reading a poem, chant, or piece of class- or student-authored writing together. At a lively pace and using expressive voices, teachers and students enjoy a terrific story or poem together. The learning is direct and explicit as well as incidental.

In kindergarten, grade 1, and early grade 2, shared reading focuses primarily on enjoying and rereading new, familiar, and favorite texts. As the teacher progresses word by word and line by line with a pointer or sliding piece of paper, students join in visually and/or orally. These repeated readings build confidence, fluency, and word familiarity as well as provide practice in phonemic awareness and phonics. Once students have read a text through a few times, shared reading texts are ideal for word work (see pages 60–61).

By mid–second grade and through the intermediate grades into middle and high school, shared reading—especially shared reading aloud—is a powerful context for demonstrating and practicing all aspects of the reading process. Following shared reading by guided silent reading and/or independent reading (supported by individual conferences) provides the necessary time for students to problem-solve, self-correct, self-evaluate, and practice all the other subtle aspects of successful independent reading.

Notice Where Shared Reading Fits in the Optimal Learning Model

Revisiting the optimal learning model (see page 132; also see the discussion on pages 43–49 and the chart on the inside front cover), we see that shared reading is not just a pleasant frill but a critical learning context for demonstrating and scaffolding learning. In fact, I do most of my teaching and demonstrating using shared reading. We need to examine our literacy schedule and make sure shared reading is a major part of our reading program. (See suggested time frames and teacher schedules on pages 157–158 and 213–215.)

Shared reading is an ideal context for guided participation (that is, while the teacher is demonstrating, students are encouraged to participate without any pressure or fear of failure). The enjoyable social interaction and exchange is critical to learning.

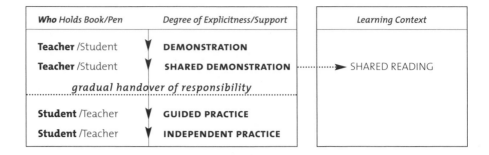

The Optimal Learning Model's Progression of Responsibility

Use Shared Reading to Demonstrate Reading of All Kinds of Texts

Shared reading is ideal for showing how any text works—nonfiction, picture books, short stories, newspapers, plays, poetry, chants, novels, textbooks, periodicals. In shared reading (usually with the whole class, but also in small groups or with a single student depending on my purpose), I model and guide students in all aspects of reading to comprehend—fluency, figuring out words, thinking, questioning, predicting, rereading. I rely on shared reading at every grade level as the medium for the bulk of my reading demonstrations.

While shared reading has traditionally been viewed as an activity for younger students and virtually ignored beyond grade 1, shared reading is a powerful teaching tool for students of all ages. Recently, however, even in kindergarten and grade 1, big books and enlarged texts have fallen out of favor as an emphasis on prepackaged programs and guided reading has dominated reading instruction.

Shared reading in the intermediate and middle grades should still include poetry and picture books (fiction and nonfiction) as well as longer texts, since students at all grade levels prefer short texts. Many unmotivated middle school readers need and prefer to read illustrated books and nonfiction materials in order to become engaged readers.

Additionally, shared reading is cost effective and works across the curriculum. When funds for materials are in short supply, all you need is one copy of a book. While I occasionally use class sets of books and photocopies of an article so every student holds a copy, I mostly use projected transparencies from one book, and it is often a library book.

Add Shared Reading Aloud

In shared reading aloud, the teacher combines reading aloud with interactive reading and shared reading. That is, using one copy of an engaging text, the teacher integrates and alternates reading aloud with interactive reading, shared reading, and partner or small-group discussion. (The Framework for Shared Reading Aloud for all Grades on pages 134–137 is a detailed breakdown of how it works.) Shared reading aloud works equally well with both younger and older readers, and with a picture book, basal anthology selection, or a chapter from a novel.

I use whole-class shared reading aloud to demonstrate and discuss:

☐ Fluency (phrasing, appropriate intonation).

☐ The author's craft (figures of speech, leads, endings).

☐ How to figure out vocabulary (phonics plus meaning).

☐ Character motivation and behavior (how characters change).

☐ Confirming (predictions, difficult vocabulary).

☐ How to read nonfiction.

☐ How texts work. ☐ Making connections.

☐ Summarizing. ☐ Inferring.

☐ Predicting. ☐ Learning new information.

☐ Asking questions. ☐ Enjoying reading.

teaching tip

Move the Book!

When reading and thinking aloud, move the book down or aside when you are speaking your own thoughts so students can easily distinguish between the text and your thinking.

In other words, shared reading aloud is a powerful context for demonstrating and practicing all aspects of the reading process in any genre. An added bonus is that it is quick and time efficient, with no need to worry about what the rest of the class is doing.

Also, for teachers who are frustrated when all students cannot read the stories in the basal text anthology, a shared read aloud is a great way for students to follow along and listen as the teacher reads and thinks aloud and invites participation. Do note that a shared read aloud is a purposeful teaching, discussing activity. (It is not just a shared reading of words.)

In addition, when used in connection with shared reading aloud, guided reading groups become more efficient—they boost and support what has already been demonstrated and practiced. Therefore, guided reading groups need only meet long enough to ensure that students are applying strategies. (Students above grade 2 certainly do not need to meet in guided reading groups every day.)

Additionally, shared reading aloud provides a context for students to talk with one another about a text. Such talk is not just enjoyable and enriching; discussion with peers improves reading comprehension and achievement.

A FRAMEWORK FOR SHARED READING ALOUD FOR ALL GRADES

Teacher

☐ Selects engaging, usually unfamiliar text, either nonfiction or fiction.

☐ Chooses several appropriate points at which to stop and discuss what has been read.

☐ Makes overhead transparencies (or reproduces copies for each student) of the pages of the book or text that are to be used as stopping points.

☐ Provides an appropriate introduction: discusses the cover, walks the students through the illustrations, makes predictions.

☐ Reads aloud in an expressive voice.

☐ Highlights features of text (a good way is to use a sliding mask to frame words—see the photo on page 59 and page 173).

☐ Poses questions for discussion (see pages 138–149 for examples).

☐ Guides and supports discussion.

☐ Demonstrates his or her thinking while reading (making connections, inferring meaning of text or vocabulary, confirming a prediction, summarizing to restate and recall important happenings before reading on).

☐ Observes students' responses and behavior and determines the appropriate next steps.

Students

☐ Read the text silently or orally along with the teacher.

☐ Learn the give and take of a small-group discussion (with one or two peers, usually for one or two minutes).

☐ Listen to and talk with one another, not just the teacher.

☐ Think about what's happening in the text or story.

☐ Respond orally as a class after talking in small groups, so everyone hears everyone else's thinking.

Text

☐ Is highly engaging, informative, entertaining.

☐ Is close to the reading level of the majority of students.

☐ Is clearly visible to all students.

☐ Contains elements that support fluent reading (clear, well-spaced text; illustrations; familiar vocabulary; easily understood concepts).

☐ Connects to students' interests, needs, culture, curriculum.

☐ May connect to other texts.

☐ Is worth students' time.

☐ Lends itself to high level thinking and comprehension.

Purposes

☐ Engages students through participation, not just listening.

☐ Gives all students a chance to be successful.

☐ Gets students thinking about what's happening in the story.

☐ Confirms or invalidates thinking.

☐ Demonstrates how reading works—the skills, strategies, and behavior of good readers.

☐ Makes reading an enjoyable experience.

Advantages

☐ Goes beyond listening to reading aloud or following a text visually.

☐ Encourages all the voices to be heard.

☐ Moves at a brisk pace that helps students stay engaged and focused.

☐ Provides lots of teaching and practice in a short period of time.

☐ Can be used effectively for teaching and learning across the curriculum (science, social studies).

☐ Is a good prelude to small-group literature conversations.

☐ Raises expectations for what's possible for students to do.

☐ Builds confidence and competence in struggling readers.

Procedures

☐ Introduce book; talk about cover, title, author; provide necessary background knowledge for understanding; encourage predictions.

☐ Discuss crucial vocabulary and concepts, at the start and throughout.

☐ Read aloud first several pages as students listen (and view illustrations).

☐ Make several text pages visible to all students, either through projected transparencies or individual copies, and have students follow along visually (use back-to-back pages of text of projected transparencies to increase continuity).

    ☐ Read the page aloud as students track the words with their eyes or read them chorally (student choice). To ensure all students are following along, track line by line or word by word.

    ☐ Use oral cloze: let students know you will occasionally pause in your reading and expect them to fill in the next word (sets expectation for students and lets teacher know if students are following along).

    ☐ Use occasional visual cloze to show that just seeing the beginning of a word in meaningful context is often enough to solve the word and maintain fluency.

☐ Occasionally ask students to read independently—or reread or read with a partner—a few sentences, a paragraph, or part of a page. Choose a section that most students can easily read and set a purpose:

    ☐ *Read to find out. . . .*

    ☐ *Find the sentence that tells what's most important on this page.*

    ☐ *Reread and find the words that describe [character's name].*

    Observe students' reading behavior, and teach supportive techniques as necessary.

☐ Have students discuss, with a partner or in a small group (not more than three):

    ☐ What they notice.

    ☐ What they wonder about.

    ☐ What they predict.

    ☐ Connections they make.

    ☐ What they are thinking at this point.

For fiction:

- ☐ Why a character behaves in a certain way.
- ☐ How they think problem will be solved.
- ☐ The author's intentions.
- ☐ How they think story will end.
- ☐ How a character or characters have changed.

For nonfiction:

- ☐ How the author conveys information.
- ☐ Something important they learned or are learning.
- ☐ Questions they have.

Evaluation Possibilities

- ☐ Observe students' attention and oral responses throughout the shared read-aloud and determine what, if any, demonstrations, explanations, rereading, and future teaching are called for.
- ☐ Have students do one of the following, depending on the purpose of your lesson:
    - ☐ Discuss why author wrote this text.
    - ☐ Turn to a partner and share a favorite part of story.
    - ☐ Draw or dramatize an important or favorite scene.
    - ☐ Alone or with partner, practice reading one page for fluency.
    - ☐ Read last page independently or with partner and then discuss as a class how the story ends.
    - ☐ Respond in writing to issues/questions already discussed (how characters change) or new issues (reaction to how the story ends). (Until written responses have been modeled and practiced, students can respond in writing with partner support.)

*Teacher
Talk*

*for a
Shared
Reading
Aloud
Lesson*

The language of thinking aloud

☐ *I'm thinking that....*
☐ *From the title and cover illustration, I'm going to predict that....*
☐ *You know that made me think about....*
☐ *And I'm now thinking....*
☐ *The illustrations help me to....*
☐ *I have a picture in my mind.*
☐ *I'm going to read that again. I'm a little confused.*
☐ *In this next part....*
☐ *What was going through my mind was....*
☐ *Let me rethink this.*
☐ *One of the good things that readers do is always think....*
☐ *I'm predicting that....*
☐ *Good readers are always thinking about their reading.*
☐ *I'm connecting this to when [such-and-so] happened to me.*
☐ *I think this character is....*
☐ *If I stop, that's means I'm waiting for somebody's attention.*

The language of partner work

☐ *Turn and talk.*
☐ *Read that with your partner.*
☐ *Find the line that tells you....*
☐ *Tell your partner what you're thinking.*
☐ *Face the person you're talking to.*
☐ *Give me a summary sentence.*
☐ *I should be able to call on anybody.*
☐ *Make sure each of you gets a chance to say what you think.*
☐ *Why do you suppose the author put that in?*
☐ *What are you thinking in your group?*
☐ *What do we know so far about . . . ?*
☐ *What is the most important idea on this page?*
☐ *What is this part about?*
☐ *Based on what we know so far, predict what will happen next.*
☐ *What makes you think that?*
☐ *What did you notice about . . . ?*
☐ *How did you figure that out?*
☐ *Talk with your partner about something new you learned.*
☐ *Why do you think the author wrote this book?*
☐ *Do you have any questions that were not answered?*

Observe Shared Reading Aloud in Action

Enjoy a Picture Book in a Shared Read-Aloud

LESSON FOCUS

☐ Reading and enjoying a story together.

☐ Learning how to think about and understand a story in process through small-group discussion.

☐ Understanding character motivation and how characters change.

☐ Practicing rereading to gain meaning.

☐ Verifying information from the text.

I conducted this lesson in a grade 4 class during a week of demonstration teaching. The book was *Keepers*, by Jeri Hanel Watts and Felicia Marshall. *Keepers* is the tender story of Kenyon and his grandmother, Little Dolly, who is about to turn ninety. Kenyon loves his grandmother's stories and wants to be the "Keeper" of them. His grandmother tells him that according to African legend, "The Keeper holds onto the past until she can pass it on to the next" Keeper, but that the Keeper needs to be a girl. When Kenyon spends all the money he's saved for a birthday gift for his grandmother on a baseball glove for himself, he is full of remorse and despair. Finally, he figures out what to give his grandmother, and she figures out that he will make a good Keeper after all.

I'd handpicked this book as a gift for the classroom library, because I thought these students would relate to and enjoy this story of a loving African American family. It's a great book to read aloud and discuss, and I often use it as a springboard for asking students to write down important family stories or traditions they themselves want to "keep."

While I generally prefer to have students—especially younger students—gathered close around me on the floor, it is easier to use projected transparencies when students are seated at their desks. So I asked the students to clear their desks so they wouldn't be distracted. (*Keepers* is unpaged, for my purposes here I have numbered the pages that have text on them.)

What I Do . . .	**What I Say . . .**

What I Do . . .

Pages 1–2

I hold up book, showing the cover.

In an expressive voice and stopping to show the illustrations for each page, I read the first two pages aloud.

I stop briefly to check that the meaning is clear.

What I Say . . .

Reading Aloud, Setting the Purpose, Getting Started

I have a wonderful book to share with you today. It's one of my favorites, and it's called Keepers.

I want you to be thinking about the story while I'm reading. Think about the title Keepers *and what it means. Think about the characters, Kenyon and his grandmother, what they're like as people and how they change.*

As Kenyon is listening to Little Dolly tell a "Keeper" story, she falls asleep (she's recently had a stroke), and he tries to sneak out the door to play baseball.

Do you know what a stroke is?

One student volunteers that a stroke is "like when you have a sort of attack and maybe can't move parts of your body."

Yes, that's right. And because of his grandmother's stroke, she has less energy.

Page 3 as a projected transparency

So students can more easily track the print, I expose the text line by line using a five-by-seven-inch index card as I read the entire page aloud.

I introduce rereading and talking with a peer to clarify meaning.

Shared Reading with Projected Transparency, Pausing to Check Comprehension and for Small-Group Discussion

Okay, now read this next page with me. You can read just with your eyes or out loud with me, but I want everyone looking at the screen.

As his grandmother gently chastises him to finish his homework before going out to play baseball, Kenyon's thoughts drift to "days like yesterday, days when Kenyon felt like a hitting machine that could not be denied. That had been a true wallop-bat day."

What does he meant by that, "wallop-bat day"? Talk about it with your neighbor. One of you read that paragraph aloud, and then talk about it.

A student shares with the whole class what he and his partner have figured out.

Yes, exactly. The author tells us what "wallop-bat day" means in the sentence before. Good readers can often figure out tricky parts by using what the author has already said.

Page 4 as a read-aloud

Reading Aloud

Kenyon goes off to play baseball, arrives late, and is teased by his teammates: "Did you have to help Granny into the sun?"

<table>
<tr><td>

Page 5 as a projected transparency

Students follow along, their eyes on the screen, as I read the entire page aloud and track the print.

I check to be sure meaning is understood, encouraging rereading as a comprehension strategy.

I help students get closer to the author's thinking and words.

I prompt the students to verify information.

</td><td>

Shared Reading with Projected Transparency

Kenyon, back at home, learns about the history and role of the Keeper and says, "Little Dolly, I'll be the Keeper. I love your stories." She replies, "You cain't be a Keeper if you a boy."

Turn to the person next to you and tell what this section is about. Who is the Keeper? What does it mean to be the keeper of stories in your family? Read the page again if you need to.

After a few minutes, relating again as a whole class, one student ventures, "To keep things in the family."

Where does it say that? Come up to the screen and find the line that tells us that.

Why can't Kenyon be the keeper? Find the line that tells that.

</td></tr>
<tr><td>

Pages 6–9 as a read-aloud

I encourage the students to predict and think ahead.

</td><td>

Reading Aloud, Continuing the Story, Predicting the Problem

Kenyon counts the money he has to buy Little Dolly a birthday gift and goes in and out of shops looking for the right gift for her. Then he spots a perfect new leather baseball glove on sale and buys it on impulse.

Okay, turn to your partner. What's the problem going to be? Several suggest, "He has no money for Little Dolly's gift."

</td></tr>
<tr><td>

Page 10 as a projected transparency

I state explicitly that I expect students to read along, with support. They follow along with their eyes on the screen as I read the whole page aloud.

I make clear that I expect students to predict this character's behavior.

</td><td>

Shared Reading with Projected Transparency, Making a Prediction

Read with me.

Kenyon happily tries out his new glove at the baseball field, and as he heads home he begins to realize what he has done.

Turn to the person next to you, and discuss how Kenyon can solve his problem.

After a few minutes of peer discussion, students respond, in whole-group share: "Maybe he can earn some money somehow." "He can't return the glove 'cause he's already used it." "His dad can give him money."

</td></tr>
</table>

Pages 11 and 12
as a read-aloud

I make sure students' have inferred the obvious conclusion from Kenyon's comment about using his grandmother's stories, in connection with the accompanying illustration showing Kenyon writing.

I ask them to confirm what they know.

Reading Aloud

Kenyon retreats to his room and explains to his dad that he's done something stupid that he's sorry about but that he can't change. His dad says that happens to everyone at times but you have to move on and try to do better the next time. Kenyon thinks, "Shoot, he didn't blame Little Dolly for not trusting him with her stories. . . . The stories. That was it. . . ."

Turn to the people in your group. What's he going to do?

Students discuss this for a minute or so.

Okay, let's see.

Page 13
as a read-aloud

Reading Aloud

Little Dolly enjoys all the festivities and gifts at her birthday party.

Page 14

Shared Reading with Projected Transparency

Read this part with me, silently or out loud.

The party is just about over, and Little Dolly finds Kenyon's gift of her handwritten, bound stories.

Final page, page 15
as a read-aloud

Reading Aloud, Understanding and Appreciating the Story

Little Dolly, overcome with emotion, decides that Kenyon can be the next Keeper and she will teach him what he needs to know. Kenyon smiles. The last line is, "It was definitely a wallop-bat day."

Talk in pairs. How has Little Dolly changed? What happened to Kenyon? How have they changed as people?

After a few minutes, students respond in whole-class share.

Students add to one another's thinking.

Who wants to add to that?

Students explain with examples of events and behavior from the story.

What made Little Dolly change her mind? What do you think about Kenyon?

Present an Informational Book Through a Shared Read-Aloud

LESSON FOCUS

- ☐ Reading and enjoying a text together.
- ☐ Learning how to think about and understand a story in process through small-group discussion.
- ☐ Learning how an informational story works.
- ☐ Learning about a historical period.
- ☐ Learning about an important achievement.
- ☐ Understanding character motivation.
- ☐ Verifying information from the text (predicting, confirming, rereading, summarizing).

---

teaching tip

To minimize the number of times you move from reading aloud to shared reading, use projected transparencies from two consecutive book pages. (See the example in this lesson, pages 7–8 and 15–16.)

Robin Wood's grade 2 class in Westminster, Colorado, had been reading, enjoying, and analyzing books by David Adler. Adler's biographies for this age level are some of the most well written, so his latest biography, *America's Champion Swimmer,* the story of Gertrude Ederle, who, in 1925, overcame great odds to swim the English Channel, was a great choice for demonstrating how to read informational storybooks. Not only was Miss Ederle the first woman to swim the more than twenty miles between France and England, she also broke the men's record by almost two hours. She became an international symbol of strength and courage to girls and women. (*America's Champion Swimmer* is unpaged; for my purposes here I have numbered the pages that have text on them.) The following lesson takes place in two sessions.

What I Do ...

I hold up cover. I am checking to see what students know. I encourage students to think about how and why an author writes as he does.

What I Say ...

Reading and Thinking Aloud, Getting Started, Setting the Purpose

What do you know about David Adler's biographies?

Kids respond that he "uses good repetition."

Well, I've brought you a wonderful book by him called America's Champion Swimmer. *I just love this book. Now this is a true story of an event that really happened. Yet there's conversation in this story. Conversation makes the story come to life. Be thinking about how that's possible. How could David Adler know what people said almost a hundred years ago when this story takes place?*

Page 1	

Reading and Thinking Aloud

When I'm reading, I'm going to be telling you what I'm thinking because good readers think as they read.

Page 1

In an expressive voice and holding the book so students can see the side-by-side illustrations, I read the first page aloud.

"In 1906, a woman's place was in the home but Gertrude Ederle's place was in the water." This page also tells about her family. I'm going to read the lead—that is, the opening—again, because I really like the way Adler begins. Wow! He grabs our attention immediately. I'm thinking I'm glad that I'm a woman today instead of then. I wouldn't have liked being told what I could do and not do, like women couldn't vote then.

Pages 2–3

I want students to "see" my thinking.

At the age of seven, Trudy falls into a pond and almost drowns so her father teaches her to swim. She quickly displays a natural ability for and love of swimming and begins to win races.

☐ *I'm surprised she took so quickly to the water after that disaster. I would have been terrified to get back in.*

☐ *She must have been very determined to learn so quickly and get good so fast.*

Page 4

I explain why the author uses conversation.

Trudy is the first woman to swim a seventeen-mile stretch from New York to New Jersey

Now here's some conversation in the story. Her sister Margaret yells, "Get going, lazybones!" Probably Adler made that up as something she might have said. Authors can do that to make the text more lively.

Pages 5–6

I read the next section of text aloud.

Trudy's accomplishments are noted in newspapers. She makes the U.S. Olympic team.
I predict she will help the team win a medal. I was right. She and her team won multiple medals and points.

Page 7, as a projected transparency

So students can more easily track the print, I expose the text line by line using a five-by-seven-inch index card as I continue to read the entire page aloud.

Shared Reading with Projected Transparency, Pausing to Check Comprehension and for Small-Group Discussion

Okay, now read this next page with me. You can read just with your eyes or out loud with me, but I want everyone looking at the screen.

Trudy is determined to try to swim the English Channel, but publicity of the day says she won't make it.

I introduce discussing with a peer and re-reading to summarize. A student shares with the whole class what he and his partner have figured out.

What's the most important thing that happens on this page? Talk about it with your partner. In one sentence, be ready to say what's the most important thing that happens on this page. Find the line that tells you that.

Yes, that's right, "She was going to swim the channel." With that sentence, the author tells us how determined Trudy is. Good readers think about what's most important in the story as they read. Okay, let's find that line and read it together.

Page 8, as a projected transparency

I allow one or two minutes.

The class takes one or two minutes and shares their predictions.

Trudy sets out from France for the swim, and her trainer, worried that she can't make it, pulls her from the water before she can finish.

Turn to your partner and predict what will happen next.

Okay, let's share our predictions.

Now let's read on and see if we're correct. Good readers are always predicting, checking, and sometimes changing their predictions as they read on.

Review, Partner Talk, Summarize

Students quickly review the story up to this point, retelling and summarizing. Retelling is easier than summarizing, because retelling includes all the details. Summarizing involves deleting less important information.

Turn to your partner. What's happened so far in this book? Tell each other. I should be able to call on anybody.

> I tell students, "Since each of you has had an opportunity to talk with your partner, I can call on anyone to give me a response." This sets the expectation for engaged participation. Occasionally, when a student seems unable to respond, I say, "Tell us which response that you've heard from a classmate that you agree with. You don't have to have your own idea."

Pages 9–10, as a read-aloud

Reading Aloud, Predicting, Thinking Aloud

Trudy attempts the English Channel swim again. Her father, her sister Margaret, her new trainer, and other swimmers are aboard an accompanying tugboat to cheer her on.

I make my thinking explicit.

□ *I'm thinking having a new trainer will help, plus all that support from family and friends. I think she'll make it this time.*

□ *The text and the illustration show another boat with reporters and photographers. I'm thinking that this is a "big news" story, especially if she makes it. It will be in all the papers.*

Pages 11–14, as a read-aloud.

Trudy is in good spirits and good form in the early part of the swim. As the sea becomes rough, her trainer orders her out of the water. She is scared but determined and refuses to give up.

□ *These illustrations really show how rough the water was. I can't imagine having that kind of courage.*

□ *I'm worried about her. Her body seems to be having difficulty. She's exhausted.*
□ *Listen to the last sentence on this page again: "She would either swim the Channel or drown." That says it all. It sounds to me like she's going to make it or die.*

Shared Reading with Projected Transparency, Pausing to Check Comprehension and for Small-Group Discussion

Read this page with me. Here's what I want you to think about as I read. What's the most important thing that happens on this page?

Trudy makes it to shore after more than fourteen hours and is greeted by hundreds of people.

Turn and talk. Face the person you're talking to.

Okay, let's come back together as a whole group. What's the most important thing that happens?

Several students eagerly respond: "She made it across without drowning." "She swam the Channel." "She didn't give up."

Those are all great summary sentences. Good readers think about what's most important as they read. Okay, with your partner find the sentence that tells how Trudy felt. Read that sentence.

Let's read this page together. As we read, think about what's the most important thing about what Trudy did. Reread the page with your partner if you need to.

Reading the Final Pages Aloud

Trudy receives a hero's welcome in New York City with a huge parade, praise from the Mayor, and congratulations from the President.

Turn and talk. What kind of a person is Trudy? What's a word you can use to describe her?

Students are eager to respond and come up with:

□ "athletic"   □ "courageous"   □ "smart"
□ "brave"   □ "excellent"   □ "marvelous"
□ "undefeatable"   □ "champion"

One student suggests "nice."

Is there something in the book to back that up?

She responds, "She was strong."

Yes, that's a much more precise word to describe Trudy. How many of you enjoyed this book? **All students' hands go up.** *I'll leave it here so you can read it again.*

Sidebar (left column):

Page 15, as a projected transparency

I want to find out whether students can choose the most important information from details and give a one-sentence summary. I do some oral cloze as they read through the page with me.

I wait two minutes.

I check whether students can locate information directly stated in text.

Page 16, as a projected transparency

We read the page together.

Pages 17–18

I give the class two minutes to focus on vocabulary and character traits.

I encourage her to reexamine her response and think harder.

Introduce a Literary Genre Through a Shared Read-Aloud

Shared read-alouds are a great alternative to reading aloud or interactive reading and a highly engaging way to involve students with long texts. Furthermore, the social nature and interaction of talking with peers as part of the lesson increases engagement and comprehension.

Typically, when shared reading is used with older students, students follow along in their own copy of the text as the teacher and/or students read orally. But oral reading and listening are not enough. We can make the most of our reading time with students by making it a richer instructional context: demonstrating a new literary form, connecting it to the curriculum, and inviting active participation. In particular, the opportunities for talk about the text are critical.

The shared read-aloud excerpted here took place in a grade 5 class and was spread out over two weeks. The book is the historical novel *The Witch of Blackbird Pond,* by Elizabeth George Speare. The book is a good choice in terms of the required curriculum (a study of colonial times in early America), a district requirement that students understand literary elements such as foreshadowing in fiction, and state standards that require students to be able to summarize, infer, paraphrase key ideas, and so on. Because the reading level is above sixth grade and many of the students would have had difficulty understanding this text independently, shared reading, including teacher read- and think-alouds and partner reading and discussion, make the book accessible to everyone.

In *The Witch of Blackbird Pond,* Kit Tyler, who has sailed from her home in the Caribbean islands, has to adjust to the cold, bleak life with her relatives in a Puritan Connecticut community. Because of her unorthodox behavior, she is accused of witchcraft.

Reading with a partner for a directed purpose

When I meet with students for this shared read-aloud, they have already "heard" and "read" the first thirty pages of the book in a whole-class shared reading, but they are unable to discuss the setting or what life was like in early colonial days, summarize what had happened, or predict upcoming events or problems. Before we continue the shared reading, we need to revisit the text so far.

What I Do . . .

I want to be sure students have sufficient background knowledge. Unless they understand the setting and the time period and know what the word *Puritan* means, the story can only be understood superficially.

I prompt the students to think about the author's craft.

I prompt students to infer.

I am checking comprehension, ability to determine the most important events, ability to infer attitudes.

I want to confirm students' understanding.

What I Say . . .

Building Background Knowledge

What do you know about the Puritans?

When no one responds, I tell them a little of what I know about life in Puritan days, essentially that it was harsh, simple, unyielding, religious, judgmental, and that people believed in witchcraft. We talk about what that might mean for Kit, who has come to America from a free and colorful island.

Introduce Literary Elements

Turn to page 13, middle of the page, and follow along with me. "Don't you know about the water trial? . . . Tis a sure test. . . . A true witch will always float. The innocent ones just sink like a stone." Kids, this is an example of what's called foreshadowing. *It's a technique authors use to prepare the reader for upcoming events, often troubling ones. For example, remember when Kit jumped overboard to fetch a dropped doll and the other passengers were suspicious because she could swim. Turn back to page 9. Careful readers know that foreshadowing can be used to predict what lies ahead in the story.*

Now, with your partner, reread page 20 and find the foreshadowing.

What are the clues that Kit's life will be difficult in her new home?

Talk about why the author put that in just here.

Review Key Understanding Through Rereading, Partner Talk, Guided Discussion

Go back to the first chapter. Something important happens that's surprising. Talk with your partner. Reread page 30 with your partner. Even if you can't read every word, you should be able to get the gist. What's going on here? What is the reaction when Kit arrives at her aunt's house?

Why were they so shocked? Turn to your partner and discuss.

I continue reviewing key events, stopping several times and saying, "Turn and talk" and asking questions:

☐ *Reread this page with your partner. What happened? Give a summary sentence.*

I want students to make a prediction based on the information they have so far. I want students to use foreshadowing and the events so far to predict what might happen next. I want students to delete the least important information and get to the most important ideas.	☐ *What's Kit's life going to be like with this family?* ☐ *What problems can you anticipate?* ☐ *Turn to your partner and summarize in one sentence what we've just read.*

Evaluate Shared Reading Aloud

After twenty or thirty minutes, ask:

☐ What did I teach?
☐ Where do I go tomorrow? What does my focus need to be?
☐ What did I learn about my students?
☐ How can I maximize my time with students?
☐ What are my students understanding or not understanding?
☐ What do I need to be demonstrating?

More Teaching Tips for Shared Reading

Tracking the Print

Sometimes I expose one line a time. Other times, I use oral cloze: moving word by word, I occasionally expose just the beginning of a word and wait for students to say the whole word based on the beginning letters and context of the sentence or paragraph. In that case, I use two index cards, one placed under the line I am reading, the other moving across the line, word by word. This ensures that all students are with me and have their eyes on the words as they are spoken. (This is very helpful to the reader who has difficulty staying focused.)

Easy Projector Screen

Tape a large white sheet of butcher paper on the wall behind you and put the overhead projector in the middle of the seated group. You won't have far to go to project a transparency, and students don't have to move.

Plan It!

I put most of my planning comments on sticky notes right in the shared or guided reading book. This serves as a reminder of key vocabulary to highlight, questions to ask, etc.

10. Examine Guided Reading

When I work in schools these days, much of the talk about teaching reading turns to guided reading. Kindergarten teachers question whether or not they need to have it. First- and second-grade teachers struggle with how to fit in all the groups. Third- through sixth-grade teachers wonder what guided reading is supposed to look like in the intermediate grades. Most also want to know, "How do I keep the kids productively busy when I'm with a small group?" and, "What about grouping?" And everyone asks, "Am I doing it the right way?" Only you as a knowledgeable teacher can make those decisions.

Clarify Guided Reading for Yourself

Guided reading is most often defined as meeting with a small group of students and guiding and supporting them through a manageable text. Students are grouped with others at a similar reading level and supported to use effective reading strategies. Often, there are "before, during, and after" activities and discussion in which students talk about, think about, and read through the text.

I view guided reading more broadly and see it as any learning context in which the teacher guides one or more students through some aspect of the reading process: choosing books, making sense of text, decoding and defining words, reading fluently, monitoring one's comprehension, determining the author's purpose, and so on. In guided reading, the teacher builds on students' strengths and supports and demonstrates whatever is necessary to move the child toward independence. Therefore, an informal reading conference as described on pages 108–109 becomes a guided reading lesson once the teacher uses that assessment to evaluate the child's progress, teach the child what he most needs to know, set goals with the child, and move him forward in the reading process.

Small-group guided reading remains the heart and mainstay of guided reading but must not be seen as an end in itself. The teacher provides a text with just enough challenge so the learner is able to do most of the reading and problem solving on her own by integrating strategies over which she is gaining increasing control. Most of these strategies have previously been demonstrated by way of teacher explanation and modeling and shared experiences.

Understand Where Guided Reading Fits in the Optimal Learning Model

Looking at the optimal learning model (see below), as described on pages 43–49 and shown on the inside cover, we see that guided reading is an excellent opportu-

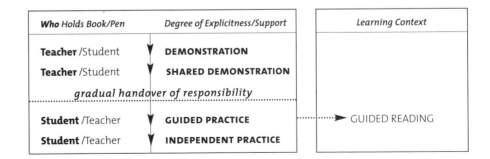

The Optimal Learning Model's Progression of Responsibility

nity for guided practice: that is, *the student is practicing what has already been demonstrated* by the teacher via:

☐   Thinking aloud.
☐   Explicit instruction and explanation.
☐   Guided participation.

These demonstrations have taken place in such contexts as:

☐   Reading aloud.
☐   Interactive reading.
☐   Shared reading.
☐   Shared reading aloud (see Chapter 9).
☐   Shared writing (to include interactive writing)
☐   Reading conferences.

What is significant about guided reading is the guided practice as described on page 46, not the guided reading group. The student could also receive guided practice through other means: partner reading, reciprocal teaching, reading one-on-one with a teacher or tutor, shared reading.

We need to think about our own guided reading program and how we use it to support students in becoming more accomplished readers. We need to keep the learning model in mind and decide whether or not a small guided reading group is the optimal way to teach, guide, and evaluate these particular students at this particular time. Students need ample demonstrations and support before we "hand over" most of the learning responsibility to them. When students have not had enough demonstrations and guided demonstrations, we wind up spending too much time on word work, concepts, and strategies in guided reading—work that could easily have been taught in guided demonstrations.

For guided reading, as for all optimal learning contexts, the social aspects of learning are also paramount: that is, in a congenial environment of acceptance and trust, students are encouraged to share their thinking, try out what they've been learning, and, with teacher support, approximate, regulate, and expand their reading competency.

Be Cautious About How You Group Children

In the schools in which I work, I am noticing a troubling trend—the return of homogeneous grouping. I have encountered many classrooms, especially in the intermediate grades, in which students are ability grouped for all guided reading. Once students are already reading, grouping students so narrowly is unnecessary. More important, except for nonreaders, students want and need to be in mixed-ability groups.

When guided reading is strictly interpreted (as it often is) to mean meeting with students with similar reading processes, we do a disservice to students. As in the past, students who need challenging material will often be relegated to skills work. I make an exception here for developing readers with similar needs, those students in kindergarten, grade 1, and grade 2 who are learning to read and focusing on reading strategies as they make sense of text. Of course, it makes sense to group these students, and this is where leveled texts are very helpful.

Personally, I am no longer comfortable ability grouping beyond second grade. I worry about the message such grouping sends to students—a message that they are somehow less capable. If you group by ability, make sure you keep it short (ten or fifteen minutes) and provide daily opportunities for more-varied groups—whole-class shared reading, heterogeneous small groups, partner reading, independent reading.

Create Opportunities for Flexible Grouping

teaching tip

Limit your group size to no more than six students. While you can "work" with larger numbers, it's difficult to customize instruction, give opportunities for all students to talk, and assess individually.

Take an honest look at your grouping practices. (Also see Chapter 12 for time management suggestions.) Make sure that your groups really are flexible—that is, that groups are based on students' needs and interests and your purposes and that students are not "stuck" in a particular group all year. All students need to experience guided reading in many contexts.

Some possibilities for flexible groupings include but are not limited to:

- ☐ Participating in literature study and literature conversations, often called literature circles. (Initially, it may be a teacher-chosen book; later, students may sign up to read a text from among several choices.)
- ☐ Rereading and discussing a story, or part of a story, that has been read aloud.
- ☐ Reading with a partner.
- ☐ Reading a small chunk or passage from a book begun during whole-class interactive reading.
- ☐ Engaging in reciprocal teaching.
- ☐ Rereading part of a familiar text as Readers Theatre (on the spot, not from a formally prepared script).

Choose Books for Guided Reading Carefully

Many classrooms and schools have leveled texts, primarily to ensure that students are matched with appropriate texts for guided reading. Be sure that the texts you use are of the highest quality. *Your guided reading lesson will only be as good as the text you use.* A mediocre book will not adequately support your students as they problem solve and read for meaning and can, in fact, make reading for meaning difficult.

Publishers have hurriedly mass-produced thousands of leveled "little books" to meet market demands, and schools have purchased whole collections without knowing what they're getting. A good number of these "little books" are fine for independent practice, but many of the stories and illustrations are not suitable for guided reading. Even when they are suitable for word work, too often the language and story structure are not substantial enough to promote reading for understanding.

Examine Your Book Collection for Quality

Because the quality of books varies widely, be sure you carefully examine the ones you use for guided reading. In some schools where I've worked recently, teachers were beginning to realize that their struggles for better guided reading lessons were related to the lack of meaningful stories and texts in their leveled book collection. A group of these teachers spent several afternoons reviewing all the guided reading books to decide which should remain in the collection and which should be moved into classroom library baskets/bins for independent practice. They determined which levels needed more meaningful titles so that additional materials could be ordered for the next school year. Their main goal was to ensure that all leveled books used specifically for guided reading were excellent literature written by authors whose aim is to delight and inform children.

For older students, put more emphasis on interest than on levels. Once a student is a competent reader, you don't have to worry so much about exact levels. In fact, it is not the best use of your time to level every book in your room.

Make sure texts you choose for guided reading, including literature discussion, are manageable—that is, the text is not so long that it is overwhelming for students or so complex that it requires substantial background explanation. If I am using a chapter book in the intermediate grades, I like relatively short books that pack a wallop. Two favorites are *Because of Winn-Dixie* by Kate DiCamillo and *Every Living Thing* (connected short stories) by Cynthia Rylant. While I tend to stay away from very long books (more than 250 pages) because they take so long, I always put the quality of the book first. Three other excellent titles are *Holes* by Louis Sachar, *Bud, Not Buddy* by Christopher Paul Curtis, and *Esperanza Rising* by Pam Munoz Ryan.

Also be sure that most of the titles in your collection are recent and in good condition. Too many of us tend to stick with the same titles year after year. While we of course want our students to read some "classics," most books for guided reading, shared reading, literature discussion, and independent reading should

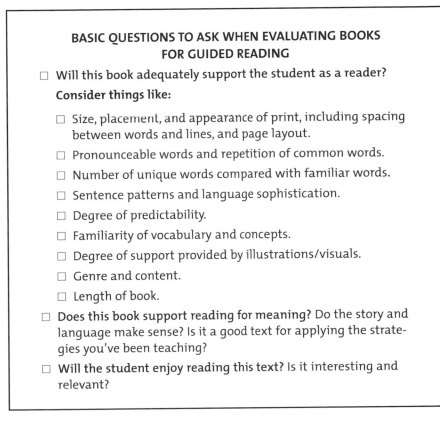

be current and relevant. There is no shortcut here. Teachers need to get together and make decisions on what new titles to add to grade level and school reading collections, consulting excellent resources in making their choices.

Qualities of an Excellent Text for Guided Reading

A text is appropriate for guided reading if it engages students and supports their ability to:

- ☐ Figure out and understand the words.
- ☐ Make and confirm predictions.
- ☐ Follow the story line or organizational structure.
- ☐ Use the book's layout and organization to help make sense of text.
- ☐ Use the illustrations or photos to support understanding.
- ☐ Read most of the text with minimal teacher support.

☐ Learn new information.
☐ Make connections to life or to other books.
☐ Make inferences (read between the lines).
☐ Retell the story.
☐ Reread for practice and pleasure.
☐ Find other stories of similar theme, style, or author.
☐ Demonstrate success (apply strategies and read for meaning).

An excellent text makes it easier for students to focus on meaning. Texts with contrived language, poor layout, insufficient visual supports, and complex concepts that are not well explained are more difficult to read and understand.

**TRY IT
APPLY IT**

*Qualities of
an Excellent
Text for
Guided
Reading*

✐ Form a committee (at your grade level or across several grade levels) to select the best of your leveled book collection for guided reading. Organize the remaining books in independent-reading baskets.

✎ Using benchmark books, set your own leveling criteria (see pages 154–155). (Levels assigned by book companies are not always accurate and are often determined by a formula.)

✐ Be sure that many of your books are nonfiction. For the early grades, check out the latest "little books" from National Geographic and Newbridge.

✐ Become familiar with publishers' materials.

✐ Give books not suitable for guided reading to students to take home for vacation or summer reading (these are periods when students typically lose ground).

✐ Invite your students to help you establish criteria and evaluate a book once you have used it for guided reading to determine whether it is "good enough."

Establish a Workable Schedule

While small-group guided reading should be an integral part of a reading program, you don't need to meet with every group every day. On the other hand, meeting with a group once a week—especially in the early grades—is not enough. Use common sense, and conserve your energy.

In grade 1, it's important to see your readers as often as possible at first to put them on the road to independence. If you are well organized, meeting with four reading groups during an hour-long literacy block is very doable. In grades 1 and 2, you will want to see your low performing readers every day, or at least four days a week.

Once students are independent readers at their grade level, you will not need to see them every day in a guided reading group: two or three days a week is sufficient, especially if you have a strong shared reading program and a well-monitored independent reading program. In grades 3–6, for example, you might have guided reading two days a week and use the other days for shared reading or independent reading with one-to-one conferences. (Sample schedules are provided on pages 158 and 213–215).

Broaden Your Groups and Shorten the Time You Meet with Them

teaching tip

Use Time Wisely

Evaluate how you spend your group time. Typically, most of our teaching time focuses on accuracy, not comprehension. Both are important.

Some teachers attempt to match every student to an exact, finite level and wind up with six or seven groups. Handling more than four or five groups can be exhausting and unmanageable. Just as important, teachers become so focused on "getting through" all the groups that they fail to enjoy teaching reading—and to pass on that enjoyment to students. An excellent text can bridge the gap, allowing you to combine students at adjacent levels.

In the intermediate grades, I rarely meet with more than two guided reading groups a day. These groups are likely to include such focuses as learning how to read and discuss a chapter book, how nonfiction works, how to figure out unknown vocabulary, how to determine character motivation, how to appreciate an author's craft.

Examine Your Instructional Reading Schedule

Take a careful look at your schedule and make sure guided reading is not dominating your instructional reading time. Remember that what you teach in guided reading can also be taught in other contexts (see the optimal learning model on page 151 and the inside cover), like reading aloud and shared and interactive reading. Skip guided reading one day to allow more time for independent reading and informal reading conferences. Use more shared reading in all grades as a medium for thinking aloud and demonstrating comprehension strategies that students can then practice applying in both guided and independent reading.

If you think about your reading instruction going across the entire curriculum, you will be able to fit it all in. Some days, for example, your reading may be totally devoted to social studies or science texts.

POSSIBLE DAILY SCHEDULES FOR YOUR READING PROGRAM

Grade	Reading Activity		Time Frame
1–2	Reading aloud ⎫ may be		20–30 minutes
	Shared reading ⎭ combined		30–40 minutes
	Guided reading		50–60 minutes (10–15 minutes per group)
	Independent reading		20–30 minutes
3–6	Reading aloud ⎫ may be		20–30 minutes
	Shared reading ⎭ combined		15–20 minutes
	Guided reading, reciprocal teaching, literature circles		20–30 minutes (2 or 3 times a week, 10–15 minutes per group)
	Independent reading		30–40 minutes

Make Time for Independent Reading Your First Priority

Be flexible with your reading instruction, especially in grades 3–6. The same schedule every day can become routine and boring for both you and the students. Be consistent about reading aloud, maintain a daily (monitored) independent reading program, and implement shared reading and guided reading flexibly as contexts for demonstrations, strategies, and practice. See the sample schedules on pages 213–215.

One fourth-grade teacher I know rearranged a one-hour reading block that had been equally divided between shared reading and guided reading. She and other teachers in her school had been using shared reading to "get through" the basal, which was too hard for many of the students. But there was no teaching going on during that time, just reading aloud while the students followed along. She changed her schedule to:

> shared reading—10 minutes
> guided reading—20 minutes, several times a week
> independent reading—30 minutes

For the first time, independent reading became a major part of her reading program. Also, by not having guided reading every day, on some days she increased the time for independent and shared reading. In addition, she continued to read aloud for thirty minutes each day, sometimes as shared reading aloud.

Be Flexible About Guided Reading in Kindergarten

Some kindergarten teachers, especially if they are fortunate enough to have aides or volunteers, are able to manage guided reading groups. Others choose not to have guided reading groups at all and teach all their reading through whole-group contexts, individualized conferences (both planned and "on the run"), and occasional small groups. Many kinds of arrangements can work successfully in kindergarten—and in other grades too—as long as the teacher is knowledgeable and purposeful in teaching reading.

My concern is that guided reading is now required in some kindergartens. That necessitates inordinate amounts of time in which the children are working independently. Also, increased pressure on teachers to have children reading in kindergarten has often meant limiting or usurping such crucial activities as playing, building with blocks, painting, acting out stories, and even reading nonfiction and fiction aloud.

In my experience, kindergarten teachers as a group are the most philosophically grounded in knowing what's appropriate best practice for children. I believe kindergarten teachers need to take the lead and become vocal and proactive to reclaim kindergarten as a critical childhood learning experience that embraces all aspects of child development—social, emotional, and physical as well as academic.

Karen Sher is an outstanding kindergarten teacher in Shaker Heights, Ohio, whose students do as well at becoming readers and writers as any kindergartners I know. Like all conscientious teachers, Karen struggles to meet the needs of kids who require lots of individual attention. She has many students who enter her classroom with little experience of being read to and very limited sound and letter knowledge. She does not have guided reading groups. She does have:

- ☐ Book baskets (with carefully selected books) for every child.
- ☐ Intensive letter and sound work for students who need it, focusing on:
    - ☐ Accuracy.
    - ☐ Awareness.
    - ☐ Automatic recognition.
- ☐ Daily read-alouds—at least five or six—of new, familiar, and favorite texts in varied genres.
- ☐ Daily morning message.
- ☐ Direct, explicit instruction as well as instruction at the point of need.
- ☐ Daily writing opportunities—shared writing, journals, charts, labels, sentences, notes, messages, letters.
- ☐ Daily reading opportunities—shared reading, "book looks," partner reading, poems on big charts, songs, big books, free choice.
- ☐ Ongoing assessment.

☐   Reading and writing integrated into the curriculum—science, social studies, health, math.

☐   A carefully thought out reading/writing program that constantly changes to meet the needs and interests of her students.

Keeping your focus on learner-centered reading instead of on group-centered reading enables you to make the best teaching decisions for your students. Once again, you teach students, not programs. Decide first what it is you want and need to teach and then what the best contexts are for teaching to ensure students are learning and enjoying learning to read. Guided reading may or may not be a priority.

Make Management Easy and Meaningful

When I work in classrooms, teachers always ask not only "What does a guided reading lesson looks like?" but also—and especially—"What are the other students doing?" So that I can support a teacher's efforts, I always first observe what the teacher has in place—both how she conducts the guided reading group and how she manages her classroom.

In classroom after classroom I see teachers working way too hard devising worksheets, projects, centers, and procedures. Many teachers tell me classroom management takes up most of their preparation time. Some boast of spending more than fifty hours putting their "centers" together. Others say they cannot "do" guided reading with more than one group a day. Something is amiss here, especially when most of the activities teachers devise are "time fillers," exercises in isolation, tasks unrelated to helping students become better readers.

Have Students Spend Most of Reading Time Reading

The first thing I do to help teachers simplify their management in all grades is to make reading the primary activity for students not in a group. Sometimes the reading is assigned, a follow-up to guided reading (see the examples on page 179 and 181). Often it is free, voluntary reading, alone or with a partner (see pages 91–93). Mostly this involves having assorted baskets of interesting, readable books on tables or otherwise easily accessible in the classroom. (A classroom library is also essential; see Chapter 5.) Usually there is one basket for each group of three, four, or five students sitting together, but sometimes one basket may be hand-selected for a struggling reader. Keep in mind that students—especially low-performing readers—need to process massive amounts of easy, and "just-right" comprehensible texts in order to read well.

Reading during guided reading

Having students spend most of reading time reading is a shift for many teachers. Several teachers have admitted this is difficult because it means trusting children. While it's easy, though time-consuming, to check a worksheet or written assignment, there is no way to check every page a child reads. This is as it should be. Keeping the optimal learning model in mind, students need lots of time to practice reading. If we make sure students are matched with a text they can read—which includes being able to apply the strategies we've been teaching them—we can trust that learning and understanding will occur.

Monitor Comprehension

You can and should, however, check to be sure that comprehension is developing on the level you expect. Before students leave a guided reading group, whatever the grade, assign an additional reading or rereading, either alone or with a partner (or for older students, a directed or open written response). A quick check like this lets you know what students got out of the reading, what the difficulties were, and how they attempted to problem-solve to maintain meaning (see the examples on pages 178–181). Use that information to decide how and what next to demonstrate, discuss, and practice in continuing to support students as readers.

teaching tip

Check Self-monitoring

Asking kids to cross words out (see pages 179 and 180) rather than erasing them lets you see their thinking. When you see a crossed-out response that has been replaced by a new response, you can ask, "How did you figure that out?"

Connect "Seat Work" to Your Curriculum

In the primary grades, I often give students a simple project related to what we are already doing in the classroom. Often it is completing and extending a text we have created in shared writing and used for shared reading by now making that text into a little book for each student (see page 58). The book always goes home as a reading text at the end of the week. Children insist on reading these books to and with their families, which encourages constructive parent involvement.

In grades 3–6, more writing is appropriate for extending comprehension and literary appreciation, but even here, be careful that response to literature does not dominate. Some appropriate responses include but are not limited to:

☐   Making entries in a reading response log (see page 36).

☐   Raising questions for an upcoming group discussion.

☐   Writing book reviews for classroom and school use.

☐   Advertising or promoting a favorite book to peers.

☐   Performing the piece as Readers Theatre.

Limit Written Responses and Projects

Make sure that written responses to guided reading don't take up a lot of time. Too often, students spend hours writing about their reading. While written response is important and can deepen a reader's understanding, students need to spend most of their time reading.

> **My usual assignment to students not involved in a guided reading group is:**
>
> ☐ Reading connected to the guided reading (always to be done first).
>
> ☐ Independent reading (a second independent reading time).
>
> ☐ A related project (often stemming from a shared reading).

Students do need to be comfortable writing about what they've read: written responses like this are required on many high-stakes reading tests. However, they first need to be fluent readers who will not be overwhelmed by lengthy passages.

Make Sure Your Literacy Centers Are Worth the Time They Take

Centers have become another orthodoxy: teachers feel they have to have them for management and learning. In some places, "literacy centers" are actually mandated. If "centers"—structured activities for small groups of students while the teacher is meeting with a guided reading group—are worthwhile, have a meaningful purpose, and are contributing to reading achievement and enjoyment, great. If not, rethink how you and your students have been spending your time.

Make Sure Your Management Techniques Are "Manageable"

It is critical that your ten or fifteen minutes with a guided reading group not be interrupted. Sometimes the structure set up to accomplish this takes so much explaining and monitoring that too much time and energy gets spent on it. Make whatever you do easy to plan, execute, and understand—for students, teachers, administrators, and parents. Most important, make it an activity that will enhance and increase student's reading achievement and enjoyment. (Chapter 12 includes some timesaving suggestions.) Above all, your expectations for students need to be clear, easy to accomplish, and worthwhile.

Because so many teachers find classroom management—"What's the rest of the class doing?"—an obstacle to meeting with guided reading groups (especially several groups each day), I have outlined some detailed but easy management plans in Chapter 12 and here.

Model Exactly What You Expect Students to Do

To ensure that my time working with students is productive, I carefully structure and demonstrate what is expected of those students not in the guided reading group. I require the rest of the class to work quietly while I am with a group, but each teacher has his or her own level of acceptable noise and movement.

Modeling exactly what we expect students to do must start the first day they enter our classroom. When we have established a classroom where we have bonded with our students and treat them respectfully, they return that respect. They understand how important it is that the teacher is free and undisturbed to teach.

Expect Students to Manage Their Own Behavior

My single best piece of advice is to ignore distracting behavior. *Do not intervene unless it's an emergency.* (I have yet to have had a true emergency.) You are letting

---

teaching tip

Quiet Please!

Rather than call out the names of the students you want to come to reading group, walk over to each student and lightly tap her or him on the shoulder. This simple gesture helps keep the tone of the room peaceful and quiet.

students know that the teaching you are about to do is critically important and that they are now in charge. Initially, teachers find this "handover" very risky, but it works. If students know we will take over as soon as there is a problem, there is little motivation for them to monitor their own behavior. As soon as we have to get up—or even look up—to give a reminder or reprimand, we have lost precious teaching time and instructional focus.

Every time you are with a child—or group of children—is an opportunity to teach. You are only with your guided reading group for ten or fifteen minutes, and you don't have a minute to waste. If a student elsewhere in the classroom is off task, it is only for a little while on one day. Use a guided evaluation at the end of every guided reading session to address problems and set up expectations for improved behavior (see page 165–166 for an example). Once students assume full responsibility for routines, procedures, and management, these daily evaluations will no longer be necessary.

teaching tip

Grouping

Limit group size so you can effectively support, teach, and evaluate. As a rule of thumb, try for a maximum of four low-performing readers or six average readers.

Here are the guidelines I set for my students:
- ☐ I cannot be interrupted for any reason.
- ☐ Students remain in their seats, or at their group table, and work quietly.
- ☐ Students have all necessary materials with them. (I keep dozens of sharpened pencils on hand.)
- ☐ Students' main job is to read, alone or with a partner.
- ☐ Students may also be expected to work on one literacy project connected to curriculum.
- ☐ The facilitator or monitor (who changes every week) reminds students to stay on task and speak quietly, and assists as needed.

Model What It Looks Like and Sounds Like

The behavior I model includes:

- ☐ Whispering.
- ☐ Choosing a book to read.
- ☐ Reading a book.
- ☐ Reading on in a guided reading group book (read on, reread, predict ahead, read with a partner).
- ☐ Reading with a partner.
- ☐ Working on a project.
- ☐ Responding to reading.

teaching tip

Keep guided reading books in school. Do not send books home or assign them for homework. That way, every student has the book available for reading group, and you know what students are able to do on their own. (Once the book has been completed in group, then it can go home and be shared.)

- ☐ Asking a peer for help.
- ☐ Politely reminding a peer to follow established guidelines (most often the monitor's job).

Using the optimal learning model (page 151 and inside cover), I first model and explain an expected behavior, such as whispering or reading with a partner (demonstration). Next, I have two students model the behavior or activity as the rest of the class looks on (guided practice). If the students have difficulty, I model again, this time with a student (shared demonstration). We talk about what the behavior or activity looks like and sounds like, and then I have a whole group of students try it, while I give support, more modeling, and explicit teaching as needed. If necessary, I will demonstrate again and provide more modeling and practice before expecting students to work independently.

Model What Students Do If a Problem Arises

The facilitator and group members are responsible for helping one other. Some expected behavior includes:

- ☐ Finger to mouth (reminder to work quietly).
- ☐ Gently tap student (reminder to focus on work).
- ☐ Quiet reminder to whisper.
- ☐ Help student find a book to read.

Teacher Talk	*I'm going to be doing the most important job there is, teaching you to read. I cannot be interrupted for any reason except an emergency. An emergency would be if someone is very sick or hurt; I don't expect any emergencies. When I am with a group, I need to focus all my time and energy with the group so I can do my best work with them. I expect you to manage your own behavior exactly as we talked about, modeled, and practiced. I will count on you to do it. I know you can do this. When it is your turn to have a reading group, you will not want our group interrupted. Our group time is a special and enjoyable teaching/learning time.*

Evaluate How Well Students Not in a Guided Reading Group Have Managed Themselves

Initially, this daily evaluation after all guided reading groups have met will take about ten minutes but is well worth the time. After a few weeks, it will be mostly procedural and take just a minute or two. I go from group to group and ask:

- ☐ *What did your group do well today?* (Focus: note strengths)
- ☐ *Were there any problems?* (Focus: acknowledge difficulties, support appropriate behavior)
- ☐ *What could you have done to solve the problem?* (Focus: make problem solving students' responsibility)

First I call on the facilitator. He calls on others. Students know it is the entire group's responsibility to evaluate their behavior and set goals for improvement. As students are orally self-evaluating their behavior—and we always begin with what they did well—I scaffold their language:

- ☐ *What could you have said?*
- ☐ *Try saying. . . . Let me hear you say it.*
- ☐ *Let's not use anyone's name because we're working as a group. Say instead, "One member had difficulty. . . ," or "Our group. . . ."*
- ☐ *Next time, let's try. . . .*

After the facilitator responds—and then calls on other group members to add anything important he has missed—I give feedback. I only add what students have left out. I use the language I want students to use:

- ☐ *I noticed. . . .*
- ☐ *One thing that was really great was. . . .*
- ☐ *One problem we had was. . . .*
- ☐ *We need to. . . .*

With continued modeling, coaching, encouragement, and feedback, students work appropriately and "cover" everything in the group evaluation. After a while, intervening comments from me aren't necessary.

At first, however, a few students are unaware of their off-task behavior. (Still I have not intervened or even looked up during my guided reading group.) For example, perhaps Monica talks in a loud voice. Even with a gentle reminder from the monitor, she's unaware of how loud her voice is. This becomes clear when we do our evaluation. So privately, a little bit later, I take Monica aside and we practice what a quiet voice sounds like.

Once in a great while, I encounter a student who cannot work independently. I move this student right next to me. I say something nonpunitive like, "I've noticed it's hard for you to work on your own when I am with a group. I'm going to move your desk right next to me so you can concentrate more easily." I may occasionally need to touch the student gently on the shoulder as a nonverbal reminder to refocus or get back to work, but I do not make eye contact with or directly attend to him or her. My 100 percent focus is with the students I am teaching.

My guidelines for behavior assume that students are sitting in clusters, because this is always my preferred seating arrangement for promoting collaborative thinking and group work. However, if your students are seated in rows, you can still ask self-evaluation questions of individual students.

Plan Your Guided Reading Lessons with a Focus on Meaning

If the first question we ask students after reading is, "What words did you have difficulty with?" we are giving them the message that reading is about getting the words right. I always ask first—even with nonreaders—"Tell me about what you just read" so students always know we read for understanding. (The lesson on pages 180–181 is an example of how this can work.)

Within a meaningful context, guided reading in grades 1 and 2 focuses on automatically recognizing common words, comprehending what is read, reading fluently, integrating a range of strategies, correcting, monitoring, working with words, and knowing when you understand and don't understand. In grades 3–6, guided reading also takes the form of studying and talking about literature, learning to read nonfiction, internalizing more sophisticated comprehension strategies, introducing reciprocal teaching, and learning to read texts across the curriculum.

The guidelines for and details of a guided reading lesson have been spelled out by many. If you are unfamiliar with these procedures you will want to bone up on them either on your own or as part of a professional study group made up of other teachers at your school.

HERE ARE QUESTIONS AND CONSIDERATIONS FOR THOUGHTFULLY STRUCTURING YOUR OWN GUIDED READING LESSONS WITH YOUR STUDENTS:

☐ Why are you meeting with this group today? Make sure you and the students know why they are reading this text.

☐ Is your purpose related to moving students forward in their reading? How will you know that your lesson has been helpful to students?

☐ Is guided reading the best context for teaching or supporting these students? In other words, might they be better served—or served just as well—through some other means—whole-class shared reading, for example?

☐ Have you given the students an opportunity to demonstrate their growing independence as readers?

☐ How are you ensuring each student is reading for understanding?

teaching tip

In the intermediate grades, use guided reading to practice what students are almost ready to do on their own (and what you have already been teaching through demonstrations and shared demonstrations), such as, reading nonfiction, creating summaries, understanding character motivation, discussing literature on a deeper level.

teaching tip

When meeting with a guided reading group, once students have met or demonstrated whatever goal was established, send those students to their seats to continue reading. Then, spend more time with the students who need it.

Some Important Purposes for Guided Reading

When we set a purpose for guided reading, we need to make sure it's worthwhile. "Getting to a higher-level book" doesn't cut it. Underlying all purposes for reading is the question, *How is what I am doing today going to help students become more independent readers?*

When I meet with students for guided reading, as a whole class and as individuals as well as in small groups, I want students to:

☐ Experience success and pleasure.

☐ Actively engage in reading.

☐ Think deeply about what they are reading.

☐ Easily decode words and know how to help themselves when they run into trouble.

☐ Monitor their comprehension—know when meaning breaks down, be able to use "fix-up" strategies (reread, predict, confirm) for word analysis and understanding, know how and when to seek help, know when comprehension is occurring or not occurring.

☐ Always read for understanding—be able to tell (orally or—briefly—in writing) what they have read.

☐ Learn how fiction works—understand story structure.

☐ Learn how nonfiction works and is organized—how we read nonfiction differently than fiction, how we read to gain new information.

☐ Converse intelligently about a book—literature study, character motivation, how characters change—as a prelude to self-directed literature conversations.

☐ Apply strategies we've been working on in other contexts, such as shared reading and reading conferences.

☐ State what they did as they read to make meaning, clear up confusions, figure out words.

☐ Determine what's most important in what they read.

☐ Think about what they already know to help them read and understand text.

Teacher Talk

for a Guided Reading Lesson

What it sounds like to focus on words

- ☐ *Sound it out.*
- ☐ *Look for a chunk you already know. Use your finger to cover part of the word.*
- ☐ *Start that word again. Say the beginning sound and read the rest of the sentence.*
- ☐ *I will start the word for you to help you figure it out.*
- ☐ *Read the word without the vowel. See what would make sense there.*
- ☐ *Here's a word you already know that's like this one....*
- ☐ *Try reading that again.*
- ☐ *Look at the picture to help you.*
- ☐ *Make sure that sounds right.*
- ☐ *Does that make sense?*
- ☐ *I liked the way you tried to help yourself.*
- ☐ *I noticed you tried ... when you had trouble. That's what good readers do.*
- ☐ *You worked out the hard part. I saw you checking....*
- ☐ *Try reading that sentence again.*
- ☐ *The word is....*

What it sounds like to focus on meaning

- ☐ *What kind of information would you expect to find in this book? Think about what you already know about the topic [or author or series].*
- ☐ *Let's start reading to see how the author presents....*
- ☐ *Let's think about how chapter books (or nonfiction) work as we read through....*
- ☐ *What do we learn about the main character?*
- ☐ *Let's look through the table of contents.*
- ☐ *What's something you learned?*
- ☐ *Where does it say that in the text?*
- ☐ *Read to find out ...*
- ☐ *What do you think will happen next?*
- ☐ *Was your prediction confirmed?*
- ☐ *Did anything surprise you?*
- ☐ *Why do you think ...?*

**A FRAMEWORK FOR THINKING
ABOUT A GUIDED READING LESSON**

This is a flexible guide showing some possibilities for applying what you have already been demonstrating and practicing with students. The student is in control of his or her reading and is reading for understanding. Don't get bogged down filling out complex forms or plans or trying to do everything in one lesson. Think about your students' needs, not a set of required procedures.

☐ **Choose an appropriate book or text that offers many supports and just a few challenges.** Make sure each student has a copy.

    ☐ **Supportive features**—familiar language, inviting layout, accessible storyline, many common words, interesting.

    ☐ **Challenges**—a few opportunities for readers to problem solve.

☐ **Briefly introduce the book with students.**

    ☐ **Predict**, using cover, back cover, title, illustrations.

    ☐ **Provide background** and **key vocabulary** necessary for understanding text.

    ☐ **Sample the text.** Point out and read words and sentences, call attention to visuals. Students may preview the text.

    ☐ **Use oral cloze.** Read first few pages aloud to help students get into the story quickly. As you read aloud, stop and have students fill in the next word (this is also a good way to monitor that students are following along.)

☐ **Have students read the book or text mostly silently.** It is not necessary to "listen in" to each student's reading (asking each to read aloud quietly while in group) if you are conducting individual reading conferences (see Chapter 7) and know your students as readers.

    ☐ Use **occasional oral reading** to judge appropriateness of text for readers, for fluency, for pleasure.

    ☐ **Observe readers** and provide necessary assistance.

☐ **Monitor comprehension.** This is critical and is often a missing step.

    ☐ Carefully **observe students** as they read. Are they rereading, checking words against the pictures, using other reading strategies?

- ☐ **Have students read silently** for a specific purpose and briefly respond in writing so you can check everyone's comprehension. (Once one student has given an oral response, we have no way of knowing if the others "got it.")
  - ☐ Use small spiral notebooks.
  - ☐ Use reading response logs.
  - ☐ Use sticky notes.
- ☐ **Take running records** or modified running records, analyze them, review them with students, and set new goals.
- ☐ **Talk about the text** and raise questions.

☐ **Support and teach as necessary.**
  - ☐ **Notice** and **anticipate** what students need to move forward on their own.
    - ☐ Word work.
    - ☐ Strategy work.
    - ☐ Monitoring methods.
    - ☐ Ways to use visuals.

☐ **Read on.** Once students demonstrate they can read and understand the text, encourage and assign further reading and discussion. (Do this in group and after group as you meet with other guided reading groups.)
  - ☐ **Read with a partner** (see the guidelines on pages 134–137).
  - ☐ **Reread a portion of the text** read in group (for fluency).
  - ☐ **Continue reading the group text.** As you read, think about:
    - ☐ Why the character behaved in a certain way.
    - ☐ What will happen next.
    - ☐ What's the most important thing that's happened.
    - ☐ The most important thing author is trying to say.
    - ☐ Share something new you learned.

Check comprehension of text read at start of next guided reading group.

☐ **Occasionally, extend and respond.**
  - ☐ Dramatization (puppetry, acting out).
  - ☐ Readers Theatre.
  - ☐ Reading response log.
  - ☐ Illustrations for key scenes.

ESSENTIAL MATERIALS FOR GUIDED READING

☐ **A copy of an appropriate text** for each child.

☐ **Whiteboards** (approximately nine inches by twelve inches), **dry erasers**, and **markers**, for word work (some teachers prefer magnetic letters; some like **chart paper** for making teaching points) and for writing directions for a reading assignment that extends guided reading group work.

Writing/Reading component on a whiteboard

☐ **Small notebooks, bookmarks**, or **sticky notes** (for students and teacher) to capture and monitor thinking, comprehension, planning, and responses to reading.

☐ **Sliding mask** to assist in word work. (I have three sizes—5" by 2" for books, 6½" by 2½" for enlarged texts, and 8" by 4" for handwritten charts.) Sliding masks are great for gradually exposing a word or for oral cloze. See following template.

1¼"

← slot

1⅝"

¼"   2"

outline window
in black marker

5"
(actual size)
6"

slide

1"

**Assembled Sliding
Mask
(shown reduced)**

More Teaching Tips for Guided Reading

Share Center Stage

Instead of sitting at the center of a kidney-shaped reading table, sit off to the side (but so you can still see the rest of the class). Not assuming the center-stage position encourages more student talk and gives the message that students are doing most of the reading work.

Timesaver

As students follow along, quickly read through the beginning of a guided reading book—or a section that isn't that meaningful—to get to a substantial section and maximize group teaching time. Try this reading aloud using some oral cloze.

Evaluate and Reteach

When most students aren't "getting it," read those pages aloud with the group and discuss them together. If just one or two are unable to demonstrate comprehension, zero in on why:

☐ *Read this part aloud. Think about what's happening.* (Is there a problem at the word level that impedes comprehension?)

☐ *Reread this page.* (Has the student just read too quickly? Is the student not thinking as he is reading?)

☐ *Reread just this part again. Find the line that says….* (Can the students understand when directed to a specific line or section?)

Hold It!

Don't jump right in when a child makes an error. Students need opportunities to problem-solve in order to learn to monitor and correct themselves.

Save This Assignment!

I have three or four whiteboards, one for each guided reading group. At the end of group time, I write the reading assignment on the whiteboard (see the photo on page 172) and leave it posted. Not only does that serve as a visible reminder (and is helpful if a student has been absent), referring to the whiteboard assignment when the group meets next gets us quickly focused.

Excerpts from Guided Reading Groups

For the following four lessons, I utilize "A Framework for Thinking About Guided Reading" for planning and working with students. In each of these lessons, I am building on an established group already in process (after observing a previous lesson by the classroom teacher).

GRADE 1, READERS WHO STRUGGLE

group: Four nonreaders at midyear.

context: This was a group that knew a few letters and sounds. Most of their previous work had focused on highly structured texts.

focus: Realize texts have to make sense, learn common words, use illustrations to support reading, learn to read nonfiction, increase vocabulary and concepts, enjoy reading, meet success as readers.

text: *Making a Hat* by Kate McGough

What I Do . . .

Each child receives a copy of the book.

I want students to learn to preview and predict before they read. I give them wait time to think.

What I Say . . .

What do you think this book is going to be about?
   No response.
Look through the pages . . . what do you think?
   After about two minutes spent looking through the book, a student predicts "A girl is having a party."

| I check to be sure students have one-to-one matching of spoken to written words. | *Why do you think that?*
  "She looks happy."
What do you think the title says? How many words to you see here? Point to each word and count them with me. Good. Do you see a word you know?
  I see "at." |

Why do you think that?
  "She looks happy."
What do you think the title says? How many words to you see here? Point to each word and count them with me. Good. Do you see a word you know?
  I see "at."

I check to be sure students have one-to-one matching of spoken to written words.

Yes. Now look at the whole word and look at the picture. What is the girl doing? What is she making?
  "She's making a party hat."

I draw students' attention to the print.

Everyone, point to the word hat. *Turn the page. This is the title page. Read it with me as you run your finger under each word:* Making a Hat.
What does she use to make the hat? Look on page 4.
  "Scissors."

I continue in a similar fashion through page 7, and ask students to find particular words and confirm their response.

Point to scissors. *Good. What does it start with?*
  "It starts with an *s*."
Try reading that page on your own. Point to each word as you read.
Look at the next page. What does she use?

Page 5.

Find the word stapler.

Page 7.

Find the word tape. *What letter would you expect to see at the beginning of* tape? *Find it. Point to it.*
Try to read the first page yourself. [Page 3 in the text.] *Use the picture to help you.*
  Students attempt to read and confirm using the picture. The word *can* is familiar from a previously written three-page, shared writing book: "We can read. We can write. We can draw."

I encourage problem solving, observe what students do, and teach what's needed.

Now, read the whole book to yourself. You can do it. Try to figure out the last page on your own.

The last page deliberately has not been discussed to see what students can do independently. Students subvocalize as they read through the book.

Let's read the book together now.

Each student reads a page as others follow along.

Let's look at the last page. Who can read it?

"I can make my hat."

There's one word you need to figure out. "I can w _ _ _ my hat!" Point to the w. What sound does that make?

/w/

I want students to use phonics and meaning and to confirm for accuracy as they read.

Yes, it starts just like William's name. When you read, it has to look right and sound right and it has to make sense. Good readers check carefully when they read. Let's read the last page together. "I can wear my hat!" Everyone, point to wear.

How many of you can read this book?

All hands go up.

I want students to feel successful as readers.

Good. Go back to your seat and practice reading it three or four times until you can read it perfectly. Tomorrow we'll read it again and possibly do some word work too.

All follow directions and independently reread the book at their seats.

GRADE 1, HIGH-ACHIEVING READERS

group: Five "top" readers in late fall.

context: This was a group of fluent readers. Most of their previous work had been at the word level. They were quickly "moving" through texts but were not able to say what the story was about.

focus: Comprehension, monitoring, slowing down.

text: "The Garden," *Frog and Toad Together* by Arnold Lobel (1971, NY: HarperCollins, pp. 18–29).

What I Do . . .

Each student receives a copy of the book as well as a small spiral notebook (to monitor comprehension).

I want students to be able to use a table of contents.

I write "What does Toad want?" on a whiteboard for them to keep it in mind as they read. This is a literal, "right there" question; on page 18 of the text It says, "'I wish I had a garden,' said Toad."

What I Say . . .

Look through the book. What kind of a book do you think this is?
   Students flip through pages. One says, "It's about a frog and a toad."
What else do you think? Any other ideas?
   No response.
Does it look like other books you've been reading?
   "It's longer."

Let's look at the contents page. How many stories are there?
   "Fifty-two."
That's the page number where the last story begins. Look again and count the number of titles.
   "There are four."
We're going to read "The Garden." What page do you have to turn to?
   "Page eighteen."
"How did you know that?
   "I looked at the page number after the title."

When people plant a garden, what happens?
   "Flowers grow."
Read the first two pages to yourself and be able to say what Toad wants.
When you find the answer, write it down. If you can't figure it out, read it again.
   One student finds it right away; another has to read the text three times; a third needs prompting to find the answer.

Okay, Jason, read aloud the sentence that tells us that. How do we know what Toad wants? It's right there in the story, isn't it?

The answer is not in the book. Students have to connect to world knowledge that seeds don't immediately grow.

Read the next two pages silently. Why don't the seeds grow? Read it to yourself and think as you read.
Write down your answer in just a few words. Also write down any words that are hard for you
Several students are unsure and are prompted to reread and think.
Think about what you know about what happens when you plant a seed.
Eventually, all the students "get it." We discuss how good readers think about what they already know as they read.

I write the word on the whiteboard. I am supplying vocabulary essential for decoding and reading for meaning.

Go back to your seats and finish the story. You will need to know this word—frightened—to finish the story.

I write the sentence on the whiteboard and students copy it. I am guaranteeing their success as there are five things Toad does to make the seeds grow: shouts at them, reads a story, sings songs, reads poems, plays music. When the seeds don't grow, Toad decides they are very *frightened*.

Here's your assignment: "Find two things Toad does to make the seeds grow."

If you find a word you don't know or can't figure out, write it down, along with the page number it's on. If you figure the word out with your strategies, cross it out by drawing one line through it. If you have no words written down, then you can be our expert and help other students when we meet tomorrow.

Go back to your seat and finish reading the story. Bring your notebook with you. If you need more time to copy the question, I'm putting the whiteboard here.

This lets students know I will be checking self-monitoring.

In the next day's follow-up lesson, I examine all the spiral notebooks for comprehension and assist with any problems. If and when a student does not understand, I try to figure out why and to teach what is necessary: Does the student need to reread, slow down, connect to what he knows, have help figuring out words, read an easier text? Meanwhile, for the students who "got it," I ask them to do one or more of the following, which extends the text for them and gives me time to zero in on one or two students:

☐ *Find a part you like and practice reading it so you can read it aloud to the group.*
☐ *Write down the other three things Toad did.*
☐ *What made the seeds finally grow?*

Then as a group, we read favorite sections aloud and discuss the story.

GRADE 2, AVERAGE READERS

group: Seven average and "low average" readers in the spring.

context: This was a group already in process. I observed the teacher and group one day and did demonstration teaching the next day.

focus: Overall comprehension—that is, are the students understanding what the story is about?

text: *Young Wolf's First Hunt* by Janice Shefelman, illustrated by Tom Shefelman. This is the story of how Young Wolf wins his father's (Eagle Feather) trust to hunt buffalo on his own. (The students had already read and discussed the first two chapters. We began with a review.)

What I Do . . .

What I Say . . .

DAY 1

I check students' understanding of the story so far before we read on.

The reason we are meeting together is so you can be the best readers you can be. Let's talk about what the story is about so far. What's happened?

In the first two chapters of this easy chapter book with illustrations on each page, it is buffalo hunt time in the village. Young Wolf feels he is ready to run buffalo, but his father says he is too young. Without his father's knowledge, Young Wolf trains his mare to run.

Students demonstrate partial understanding of what has happened so far.

The notebook jottings allow me to see who is comprehending and who is not. In this case, a few got it and others did not. In the story, Young Wolf's father now allows his son to go on the hunt because he "acted like a man" by getting along with a boy who had previously taunted him. The ones who understood become our experts. The others reread to find information and cross out their first response.

Grade 2 guided reading with *Young Wolf's First Hunt*

I ask students to reread so I can observe where comprehension may have broken down.

Reread pages eighteen and nineteen. Why did Young Wolf's father change his mind? Read carefully and write down your answer in as few words as possible. If you don't know, reread.

Students reread those pages silently and jot down their answers in small spiral notebooks. (See shaded box above.)

We read pages 20–23 as a whole group using an oral cloze procedure.

I check comprehension assignment from Day 1 (Young Wolf felt scared), and teach/scaffold as necessary.

Your assignment is to read pages twenty-four and twenty-five. "How does Young Wolf feel?" Write that question down. Copy it.

DAY 2

Read pages 27-28 silently. Discuss the advice Young Wolf's father gave him.

> Some students have to reread to find the "right there" information, that he should ride very close to the buffalo. Some students get confused because the mother gave advice too, but the father's advice came afterward. I send those students who understand back to their seats to complete the next assignment (below). I work with the four children who still seem to have some confusion. We read and talk about the text line by line. After their confusion is cleared up, they copy the assignment, continue reading, and work at their seats.

Read chapter 4. What problem does Young Wolf have and how does he solve it?

The question is on a whiteboard (which allows students to take the time they need to copy it and also allows me to immediately call up the next group). When students go back to their seats, they do their reading assignment first, next read independently, and third, if they have time, work on a literacy project.

The second jotting shows a student's response, the result of my teaching and his rereading the material in guided reading group the next day, Day 3.

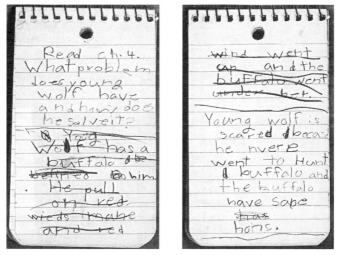

Writing the assignment on the white board

Notebook jottings demonstrating comprehension (or lack of it).

GRADE 4, HIGH AVERAGE READERS

group: Eight readers at midyear.

context: The group was in process. The focus had been silent reading with the teacher "listening in" and talking with each student, as well as whole-class, teacher-led discussion.

focus: Learning how authors craft literature, checking for understanding of key ideas and themes, learning how self-directed literature conversations (literature circles) work before students attempt them on their own.

text: *Because of Winn-Dixie* by Kate DiCamillo.

What I Do . . .

Students are assigned to read this easy-to-read 182-page text in chunks, either alone or with a partner. For Chapters 3 and 4, our discussion question is, *What do we know about Opal's life?* Our discussion lasts about ten minutes.

I begin on the literal level where all can succeed.

I give wait time to encourage students to take charge but jump start the discussion when necessary.

What I Say . . .

Kids, today, our group is going to be a little different. First of all, I'm not going to sit at the head of the table, because I'm not going to be in charge of the discussion. You are. Over the next couple of weeks, we're going to be talking about books during reading time, and you will be leading your own discussion groups. Today, and this week, we're going to learn what that looks like and sounds like.

Here are some of the procedures we'll follow: You don't have to raise your hand to talk. Just politely jump in when you have something to add. You could say, "I'd like to add on to that," or "I agree because . . . ," or "I disagree because. . . ." Back up your thinking with what's in the book. Okay, let's get started. I'll begin.

Well, I can tell Opal is a kind person. On page twenty, it says how she took lots of time to clean up Winn-Dixie by bathing and brushing him.

"Yes, I agree, and she also brushed him real carefully."

Yes, that's right. Look on page twenty-nine. It says his fur was all stuck together, and she worked hard to get it untangled.

Silence for ten seconds.

I think that Opal finally has a friend. On page twenty-one—everyone turn to page twenty-one—it says "I don't even have any friends" because she had to move. But now, she has Winn-Dixie.

"And her mother left her when she was three. It says that on the same page."

"And they're both like orphans."

Tell us more about that.

"Opal doesn't have a mom, and Winn-Dixie didn't have a mom either."

"Opal has her dad, the preacher."

I can tell Opal really misses her mom because she asks her dad to tell her ten things about her mom. . . .

Four

Advocacy Is Also Essential

... WE MUST KNOW WHAT RESEARCH TO PAY ATTENTION TO AND WHAT RESEARCH TO IGNORE. AND THEN WE MUST BE BRAVE ENOUGH TO ASK THE HARD QUESTIONS AND TAKE A STRONG STAND ON BEHALF OF WHAT'S REALLY BEST FOR OUR STUDENTS.

11. Build on Best Practice, Know the Research, and Use Programs as a Resource

None of the exemplary teachers were tied to commercial materials. Exemplary teachers taught children, and typical teachers taught programs.

—Richard Allington

It was the end of the day at a state reading conference. I was sitting and talking with eight teachers from a local public school. They were a disheartened lot, lamenting that they were mandated to use a direct instruction program with their fourth graders. Several of them were talking about leaving teaching. It was midyear, and they didn't think they could last the whole year reading the rigid scripts that focused on rote learning. Most of them were experienced teachers.

"Are you tenured?" I asked them. They were. "Why are you going along with this?" They just looked at me. "If I were in your school, I'd say no to this program. In fact, I'd be leading the charge," I told them spiritedly.

One finally spoke up. "We're just too defeated and exhausted. We don't even know that we would have any power to change things."

Whenever I talk with teachers, in whatever part of the country, there is a sense of resignation and helplessness. Teachers go along with programs and practices they know are not working well for many of their students because their energy is spent meeting the rising demands of curriculum, standards, and high-stakes testing. Time for collaboration and reflection—necessary for all good teaching and advocacy—is missing. Yet it is our professional obligation to assume the role of advocate for our students and make the time to ensure that they receive excellent instruction. No one else will do it.

Billions of dollars are being spent on "approved" reading programs to "close the achievement gap." Rather than investing in the professional development of the nation's present and future teachers, our new education law embraces "scientifically based" programs. When there is professional development, much of it is directly linked to prescribed instructional materials rather than focused on how to teach reading. Never before in our history has so much federal money been set aside for prescribed programs. Teachers have been bombarded with so much data about miracle reading programs that some have begun to doubt that they can improve test scores and instruction without a $50,000 program.

We had better know what these programs are, what research is behind them, and how we can intervene on behalf of our students. In too many schools, but especially in our schools that serve economically disadvantaged students, the "right" program has become the panacea. Without our direct intervention and leadership, we remain at the mercy of politicians and policy-makers, and we will continue to give our students far less than they deserve and can handle.

Build on Best Practices in Teaching Reading

Effective teachers are constantly re-evaluating and rethinking their practices in the light of the students in front of them, curriculum requirements, new information and research, and the daily demands of teaching. Only you, as a knowledgeable teacher, can decide what your reading program should encompass and how it should be organized. There is no best program or perfect model of teaching reading.

In spite of the fact that there are and probably always will be disagreements on how to teach reading, there are some common agreements and key research to guide your teaching practice regardless of the approach you favor. Use these as guidelines for your thinking, planning, and teaching.

All of the following statements have been discussed and elaborated on throughout this book:

BEST PRACTICES IN TEACHING READING

☐ Students need caring teachers.

☐ Readers need to have a large bank of words that they can read automatically.

☐ Phonics instruction is most effective when largely completed by the end of first grade.

☐ Phonemic awareness is necessary for students to become readers and is acquired by most children through rhyming and word play in rich, literacy contexts.

☐ All good readers miscue (make errors), correct themselves (when necessary for meaning), and problem solve as they read.

☐ Students need to be matched with books they can read.

☐ Struggling readers need to spend more time reading, not doing activities about reading.

☐ Avid readers can talk about favorite books and authors.

☐ Effective readers integrate many strategies to comprehend text.

☐ Access to books and libraries positively impacts reading achievement.

☐ More nonfiction texts need to be housed and read in classrooms.

☐ Interest plays an important role in engaging readers.

☐ Readers who enjoy reading and are motivated to read do read more.

☐ Students learn more when basic skills are integrated and connected to relevant and challenging curriculum.

Be Knowledgeable About Relevant Research

Research is driving reading instruction both nationally and locally. In fact, "research-based" practice is one of the hottest topics in education. Therefore, we must know what research to pay attention to and what research to ignore. And then we must be brave enough to ask the hard questions and take a strong stand on behalf of what's really best for our students.

Reasonable and sensible practice may be lost without our strong voice and action. Too often, parents, politicians, and some educators as well form their views by relying solely on "research" reported—not necessarily accurately and fairly—in the news media. If we as professionals continue to remain silent and passive, people outside education will continue to determine our reading practices.

It is extremely difficult for us as teachers to know when studies are seriously flawed or misrepresented, when publishers have put their own interests first, or when an analysis of research is misguided. However, when respected scholars and educators question research that is being used to influence and, indeed, mandate teaching practices, we need to pay close attention and question that research ourselves.

We also need to value all kinds of research—observational research in our own classroom as well as evidence-based research. The strong message we teachers are being given is this: unless it's scientifically based, it's not a proven practice. That flies in the face of everything we know about excellent practice in the complex world of the classroom.

SOME KEY FINDINGS ON TEACHING PHONICS

- ☐ There is no one best way to teach phonics.
- ☐ Effective teachers use a combination of approaches.
- ☐ Phonics instruction is most effective if it is mostly completed by the end of first grade.
- ☐ Intensive phonics instruction is not effective for older, struggling readers.
- ☐ Students need both systematic, explicit phonics, and phonics taught in the learning context, at the point of need.
- ☐ Children learn a lot about phonics through invented spelling in their writing.
- ☐ Excellent phonics instruction is necessary but not sufficient for becoming a reader.
- ☐ An early phonics emphasis does not necessarily translate to increased comprehension.
- ☐ Phonics and reading need to go hand in hand: "Phonics instruction should aim to teach only the most important and regular letter-to-sound relationships. . . . Once the basic relationships have been taught, the best way to get children to refine and extend their knowledge of letter-sound correspondences is through repeated opportunities to read."

Be Informed About the Influential National Reading Panel Report

One piece of research you must become familiar with is the National Reading Panel report, which has been widely embraced by the U.S. Congress, politicians, policymakers, and many educators. Federal reading policies, practices, and funding have been determined from this one report, which is now driving reading instruction in the United States—especially in the early grades. While the report deals with fluency, comprehension, teacher education, and technology, it is the phonemic awareness and phonics sections that have received the most emphasis and publicity.

When you use the NRP report to guide reading instruction, keep the following facts and concerns in mind to maintain perspective. Also, take a look at the "Minority View," written by panel member and elementary educator Joanne Yatvin, which appears at the end of the full report. And remember that some claims in the news media for the study's findings are not supported by a close, careful look at the full report.

Facts	Concerns
The panel members were predominantly scientists; there were no elementary teachers on the panel.	Out of fourteen panel members, only two were school based, an elementary principal and a middle school reading teacher. The remainder included a physicist and university chancellor, a neuroscientist, a pediatrician, several educational psychologists, an accountant, and other professionals without practical knowledge of the daily, complex world of teaching students in real classrooms.
The panel relied on "scientific" research; few studies relied on classroom teachers.	The research used a medical model—short-term control studies—rather than descriptive studies over time. Typically, the phonics studies were based on intensive small group or individual tutoring conducted by graduate students outside classrooms. The studies generally taught one small skill intensely and then tested children on that fragment.

The report focuses on phonemic awareness and phonics and short-changes comprehension and motivation.	The report favors a subskills approach to reading and ignores other approaches.
The studies were done with low-performing and disabled readers.	The studies' results were generalized to apply to normal and high-achieving readers as well.
The report ignores second-language learners.	EAL—English as an additional language—students are an increasing part of our student population.
The report questions the value of independent, voluntary reading.	It misinterprets previous "nonscientific" studies.

Additionally, I have a major problem with what the panel did not consider (see below), most of which involves the complicated, messy, daily work of teaching reading in real classrooms with real kids, which cannot be easily and simply quantified. For example, while it's easy to assess a child's phonics knowledge, it's difficult to assess how that knowledge contributes to reading comprehension. It would be easy to come to the erroneous conclusion that a practice not examined by the panel is not supported by research.

SOME IMPORTANT TOPICS NOT ADDRESSED BY THE NATIONAL READING PANEL

The impact of:
☐ Home culture and language on learning to read.
☐ Social contexts on learning to read, including talking about books.
☐ Skills instruction embedded in rich, authentic literacy contexts.
☐ Writing (including invented spelling) on learning to read (the integration of reading and writing).
☐ Access to books and well-stocked libraries with engaging reading materials.
☐ Ongoing assessment, informal and formal, to move students forward.
☐ Relying on professional teachers rather than commercial programs.

Know and Apply the Research on Effective Teaching

Students in classrooms with effective teachers are better readers regardless of the approach, program, or materials the teachers use. (Of course, the lowest achievers make the most gains. This is common sense.) Researcher Richard Allington cites six common, interactive practices of these effective teachers:

☐ Their students spend about 50 percent of the day reading and writing; in less effective classrooms, students may spend only 10 percent of the day reading and lots of time on "stuff."

☐ Their students spend enormous amounts of time reading easy texts that they can successfully read with fluency, accuracy, and comprehension.

☐ Well-crafted, explicit demonstrations and explanations during all aspects of reading instruction—whole class, small group, individual—are standard practice.

☐ They promote purposeful, open-ended talk (teacher to student and student to student) that is "more conversational than interrogational."

☐ The tasks they assign are meaningful and challenging, involve some student choice, and often integrate several content areas (reading, writing, and social studies, for example).

☐ They evaluate student work more on improvement and effort than on achievement. They prepare rubrics students can use to evaluate their own work. They spend little time preparing their students to take standardized tests.

My own observations of effective teachers, which are also supported by research, are included in Appendix B.

Use Programs Only as a Resource

On the one hand, teachers are often expected to create their entire curriculum; on the other hand, many teachers are expected to follow—explicitly—a scripted program. Both extremes exist, and neither one works very well.

In general, my experience has been that the more dependent teachers are on a program, the less knowledgeable they are. As our knowledge increases, the more we can rely on our experiences, modify the program to suit our beliefs, needs, and contexts, and trust our own judgment. Without exception, every excellent teacher of reading knows her students' needs and interests, the latest research, and a range of approaches and exemplary practices. Expertly, she demonstrates, applies, and tailors that knowledge for every student. At best, any program, no matter how good it is, is a resource and tool. It can never take the place of the knowledgeable teacher. As far as I know, no student has ever written to a teacher thanking him for using a particular commercial program. Our students know that it is teachers that make the caring difference.

Teachers ask me if I'm against programs. Absolutely not. There are some terrific published programs that provide much-needed frameworks, excellent guidelines, easy management, model lessons, and relevant student work. For a novice teacher, programs are a lifesaver. What I'm against is having a published program become the entire reading curriculum, year after year. Any reliance on a scripted or rigid program should be temporary. Here's what I believe and what I tell teachers.

> Use this program as a resource and beginning framework. Learn from it. See what works for you in teaching students to read. But if in a few years you're still using this program exactly as is, something is wrong. You as the teacher need to become knowledgeable enough to pick and choose from this program, to adapt and change it. That's what good teachers do to meet the needs of their students.

There is just no way one program can appropriately challenge and meet the needs of all your students. *Kids are different and have different needs.*

Here are some of the common problems with programs:

- [ ] All the students receive the same instruction at the same pace.
- [ ] The text turns out to be too hard for many of the students.
- [ ] The manual offers little guidance on teaching explicit strategies.
- [ ] There are too many low-level and disconnected supplemental activities.
- [ ] Not all the students need all the lessons.
- [ ] Most of the questions posed to students are factual ones.
- [ ] There is often not enough intervention for students who need extra support.
- [ ] The program makes up the bulk of reading instruction.

Since published reading programs—and the "scientific" research that supports them—are driving reading instruction, we need to be well informed. We simply cannot speak out, use our influence, and make the hard decisions about how to teach reading otherwise. Even if we teach older students, we need to know what's going on in the preceding grades so we can understand the reading behavior of these students when they become ours.

Take a Close Look at Your Commercial Basal Reader

Be sure you know what you are getting and what you are giving up.

ADVANTAGES	DISADVANTAGES
Provides a framework	Often requires following a set sequence
Allows for easy management	Can overfocus on whole-class grouping
Provides all materials	Usually expensive
Gives a complete lesson plan	May not provide the flexibility a teacher needs
	not tuned in to individual student needs
	little student choice
	too many activities
Manual provides detailed plans	Plans often not well designed
Purpose for reading provided	Purpose may not relate to student needs
Uses excerpts from literature	Illustrations may be altered; excerpts may be edited
Anthology looks like a textbook	Student may not ever see a whole book
Provides frequent assessment	May be too much assessment; not always authentic assessment that informs teaching
Often views reading as a precise process of "getting the words"	Not enough focus on reader getting meaning from text
Includes detailed skills activities	Often has too much focus on "skills" in isolation

Become Knowledgeable About Direct Instruction

Direct instruction refers to a sequenced skills-based commercial program, often directed toward low-performing readers. The focus may be on sounds and letters, words, sentences, and/or "stories." The teacher follows a script (from which he cannot deviate) and reads the statements and questions provided. In other words, he cannot interject his own questions, change the pace, or skip anything. Students cannot volunteer answers, work ahead, or ask their own questions.

The use of direct instruction is increasing, and, in many cases is being mandated. In order to make informed decisions about direct instruction programs, we must know what these programs entail and how research is used— or misused—to support them.

EXAMINE THE VALUE OF DIRECT INSTRUCTION PROGRAMS

These are some questions we need to ask when examining a direct instruction program:

☐ Is the lesson teaching a student to read?

☐ What kind of thinking and problem solving are involved for the student?

☐ What is the role of the teacher?

☐ Can we expect students to read beyond the word level?

☐ What kinds of attitudes about reading are being communicated?

Look Carefully at the Research

Most of the research on the success of direct instruction, which includes commercial phonics programs, is controversial. One problem is that the majority of direct instruction research has been done by the program developers themselves. Additionally, the promise of higher test scores has not materialized in a number of schools. Be sure you look at the test scores over a period of years. Scores in grades 1 and 2, when most of the teaching and testing emphasis is on decoding, are typically high. However, after several years of direct instruction, the reading test scores can decline sharply, particularly once students hit the greater reading demands in the intermediate grades. Futhermore, direct instruction research is sometimes selectively reported, as the following story illustrates.

A teacher in Anchorage recently told me that his school had voted to become a direct instruction school. Two years later, when test scores had not risen sufficiently and could not be used to make the program look favorable, the school was blamed and dropped from the program. The teachers were devastated. I asked why they had signed on in the first place. He said, "We were told it was 'research-based.' That swayed me. I wasn't informed enough to know what questions to ask. I just went along with it after I heard the word *research*." Had the teacher and his colleagues first asked whether they could see the research, discuss it, and then help decide whether the program would work for students at their school, the program might never have been adopted—sparing everyone wasted time, effort, and dollars.

Too often, direct instruction programs proliferate in schools in poor areas that have few resources and a large teacher turnover each year. Sadly, our students who need the best instruction often receive the least challenging and least relevant. Of course, there are exceptions—committed, professional teachers in schools without adequate resources who necessarily rely on direct instruction programs because there is little else. However, the more common scenario is that direct instruction programs are adopted districtwide with little or no feedback or commitment from teachers.

Perhaps the biggest problem with direct instruction is that teachers and students have no voice and no choice. The program assumes the role of instructor, to exact and rigid specifications. Eminent educator Linda Darling-Hammond reminds us, "The evidence suggests that highly prescriptive curricular mandates do not improve student learning, especially if they effectively control teaching." Keep in mind, also, that often a program, even a bad one, gets credit for students' success when the teacher should. Good teachers don't let their kids fail regardless of the program.

Ask Questions Before Any Program Adoption

A red flag should go up whenever you hear "research-based." Watch out for language and exaggerated claims like "innovative research-based program," "accelerates learning," "failure free." Make sure the claims and evidence are credible and valid. Respected researcher Richard Allington cautions us to be on the lookout for research that is unsupported by the claims being made for it:

> In other words, virtually every proponent of any method, material, or program can find some sort of evidence that what they have to offer works somewhere, some of the time. By selectively reviewing the evidence, by creating magazines to publish your own supportive data (because no peer-reviewed journal would accept it as unbiased), and by controlling the design of the evaluation and the implementation of your favorite method, material, or program, almost anyone can create the impression that "research shows" positive effects for their product or pedagogy.

There are some big questions about research to ask *before* you change your practices or support a new program.

Is the research relevant for my students?
Find out whom the test population includes. Have low-performing students been excluded? Is the student retention rate high, artificially raising scores because students are older? For example, the phonics studies in the National Reading Panel

report are based on studies of children in kindergarten or grade 1 at risk for developing reading problems, low-achieving readers, and older disabled readers. However, the results were generalized to include normally achieving and high-achieving readers. Generalizing research across populations not examined is not permissible.

Always ask, "What assessments were used, and what were they designed to measure?" And, "Are these results relevant for my instructional program and students?" As a knowledgeable professional, resist subscribing to a program for all your students based on results that apply only to a small group. We need to remain skeptical until we are solidly convinced that the research claims are, in fact, valid and applicable to our students and teaching contexts.

Who are the researchers?

Do the researchers or those interpreting the research fairly represent the audience for which the research is intended? Keep in mind that teachers and teacher research are routinely by-passed and ignored. For example, the National Reading Panel included no teachers from the elementary grades (and only one teacher of reading—from middle school—and one principal). Most of the panel members were scientists and educational psychologists, who chose to consider only empirical research based on a medical model and control groups. No doubt their backgrounds led them to emphasize phonemic awareness, phonics, and fluency as these are easy to quantify.

Had the panel had a fair representation of teachers, the research considered would also have included descriptive, classroom-based data relative to topics teachers deem important (those listed on the chart on page 190, for example). That would have greatly altered the results and recommendations for teaching practice and changed the message disseminated by the media.

Do the researchers or interpreters of research fairly and broadly represent the evidence available? Are the questions being posed significant ones?

Has all the research on a subject been considered? If qualitative research or case studies using rich descriptions of complex behavior and interaction exist, have they been included in an effort to examine all facets of a question? If only quantitative studies using a medical model are considered, then important information has been excluded.

The NRP reportedly considered only scientifically based (quantitative) research, as I've already mentioned. The same problem exists with the influential 1998 report *Preventing Reading Difficulties in Young Children*. That report, for example, examines research cited in several hundred journal articles, less than 5 percent of them published in journals teachers rely on, such as *The Reading*

Teacher and *Educational Leadership.* The journals and other resources cited are primarily medical, scientific, and special education—*Journal of Educational Psychology* and *Journal of Memory and Language,* for example. Also of note, of the nineteen PRD panel members, only one was a classroom teacher. (Current talk heard coming from the Department of Education stresses local control and the value of teachers, but these teachers are often excluded from policy-making projects like PRD and NRP.)

How current is the data researchers are relying on?

Some direct instruction programs rely on outdated research to make current claims for success.

What views do the researchers hold? Can they be objective?

While we want to believe researchers and interpreters of research are free from bias, all of us, if we're not vigilant, can be guilty of only seeing what you're looking for. That is why independent evaluations are so critical—peer reviews by respected researchers with no possible personal or financial gain, published in reputable journals such as *Reading Research Quarterly* and *Educational Researcher,* not the program developer's in-house newsletter.

Whether the researchers stand to profit from the program's success is a critical question. Sometimes the researchers or those paying for the study are the very people who created the program or who analyze the results or write the conclusions. If that is the case, objectivity is not possible.

Research can be twisted to support particular views. As an example of such bias, note how two prominent educators are quoted in an article in *The New York Times* entitled "Voucher Study Indicates No Steady Gains in Learning." Jeanne Allen, director of the Center for Education Reform, a group that supports vouchers, says, "The report appeared to confirm some positive effects in certain instances." Jack Jennings, director of the Washington-based Center on Education Policy, a group that opposes vouchers, says, "No substantial body of research shows a significant benefit for student achievement." We often explain findings based on the worldviews we already hold. Keep this bias in mind when reading research findings such as those reported by developers of commercial programs or members of the National Reading Panel.

Is the evidence compelling? Does it fit with what we already know?

In order to be considered truly "scientific," the evidence from a study must be so convincing that someone with an open mind would be persuaded to reconsider his views. This is perhaps most important to us as teachers. We need not abandon our common sense, lose our confidence, and change our practices based on the latest study when that research contradicts what we solidly know from our teaching experiences.

For example, because of the findings of the NRP report, many kindergarten teachers who have successfully integrated phonemic awareness into their rich literacy program now believe they must treat phonemic awareness as a discrete skill. There is no compelling evidence that systematic training in phonemic awareness or any other narrow skills makes students better readers and increases their comprehension in the long run. In the short run, students get better on the discrete skills we teach them but do not necessarily transfer these skills to reading.

What are the long-term results?

It is not unusual, especially when discrete skills are being measured in isolation, to have impressive short-term reading gains that do not hold up over time. Be sure to ask questions like, "What are the effects of early intervention on later, fifth-grade, reading achievement?"

A Word About Computerized Reading-Incentive Programs

Computerized reading-incentive programs are school library and classroom collections of popular children's books that have been leveled by difficulty. The book level appears on the back of the book as a number in a colored circle. After students complete a book on their level, they take a factual test included on the accompanying computer program. Passing the test earns a designated number of points (determined by book length and level of difficulty) that can be exchanged for prizes. Program developers tout the fact that students are motivated to read more and better books, but few peer-reviewed journal articles support these claims.

Evaluate Computerized Reading-Incentive Programs for Yourself

Teachers and schools using computerized reading-incentive programs need to take a hard look at what's going on. Too often, these programs have a stronghold where teachers are not knowledgeable about how to teach reading. If you are using such a program, make sure that your students can select a "just-right" book (without a level designation) and that they are truly reading for meaning.

Mike Oliver is a principal in Mesa, Arizona, who took a strong stand after such a careful evaluation. Having tried the program for several years in his school, he was concerned that the disadvantages he was seeing far outweighed any benefits. He declined to participate any longer. He requested that the eight thousand dollars that would have been spent for the testing software be allotted for books for classroom libraries in his school.

Recently, third-grade teacher Angela Beland, in Tampa, Florida (with whom I had worked in a school residency), wrote to me about her changing views. She witnessed that her students were unable to select a book without a level designation and were unable to understand key elements of a story even though they had passed the electronic test. Those two eye-opening events led her to rely less on the program and more on her own teaching and evaluation.

A word to the wise. If you are using a computerized reading-incentive program, make sure that it is not your total reading program, that your students are choosing and reading books they really like, and that you, not the program, are the instructional decision maker.

ASK THE HARD QUESTIONS RELATED TO COMPUTERIZED READING-INCENTIVE PROGRAMS

- ☐ *Can each of my students successfully select a "just-right" book if there is no designated level for the book?* If not, what am I doing to ensure students can choose appropriate books to read independently? How am I ensuring that students are looking beyond levels to appealing titles, authors, genres, and topics when making their book selections?
- ☐ *Are students motivated to read primarily because of the points they amass?* If yes, reconsider the role of extrinsic motivation, which undermines voluntary reading for pleasure in the long run.
- ☐ *Do students like to read?* Are they choosing books they are interested in? Do students talk about enjoying reading? If not, how is the program influencing their attitudes?
- ☐ *Am I putting struggling readers at a disadvantage?* Many of the lower level books are poorly written and, therefore, hard to read. Also, struggling readers, who particularly need individualized and small-group instruction, are left on their own to read.
- ☐ *Am I teaching and demonstrating high-level comprehension?* If you are relying on the electronic test to assess comprehension, recognize that literal questions overwhelmingly predominate.
- ☐ *Can students talk about a book beyond the surface details?* For example, can they discuss the major themes, setting, conflicts, and resolutions?
- ☐ *What messages about reading are we sending to parents and students?* Are we just pushing for higher levels or are we stressing understanding and enjoyment?

Take Professional Responsibility for What You Believe

We are teaching in difficult times. Increasingly, restrictive programs and materials are becoming part of our classrooms without our input or approval. The voices wanting to "fix" education are loud and insistent, but they are not teachers' voices. We must become brave and knowledgeable enough to articulate our concerns in a respectful public manner.

And we must go even further. For the sake of our students and for the healthy future of education, we must become visible, active agents for change. When programs are of questionable value, we must not allow ourselves or our students to become involved with them. We must stand up and say to our administrators and board members, "These are the reasons I cannot use this program with my students. Instead, I will be teaching such-and-so." We cannot just complain; we must offer a positive alternative. This is not easy, but it is essential. Current federal funding guidelines do not encourage customizing instruction to fit the needs of students and teachers.

We educators will succeed with our students—including the low-performing ones—when we stop looking for the perfect program and begin relying on our own informed professional judgment.

12. You Only Have So Much Time

I have been reevaluating everything I do to see if the activity has a true purpose or if it's just busy work and a time filler.

—Donna Kline (special education teacher, primary grades, Huntsville, Ohio)

How do we do it all and not work sunrise to sunset every day of the week? Teachers are burning out and retiring as quickly as they can in our district.

—A group of K–5 teachers in Colorado

I called a friend to say hello. "You sound exhausted," I said to her after she picked up the phone. "Well, you know what teaching is like. I have so many challenges this year, I can't seem to keep everything going."

Teachers are working too hard. We are always tired, and there is never enough time to do it all. We have the same twenty-four hours a day we've always had, but more keeps getting added—curriculum, standards, mandates, new students, programs, in-service, materials, testing requirements—and that doesn't include the demands of our own personal lives.

The elusive balanced life remains a mirage. Your time is valuable. Spend it in the most meaningful, productive ways possible.

Live an Interesting Life

When I work in schools, one of the first things I tell teachers is that one of my goals is to make their teaching lives easier and more productive, that everything I do with students does not require time-consuming work before or after school. You can't come to work each day enthusiastic about teaching if all you did the night before was grade papers. You want to be able to have dinner with a friend, go to a movie, read a book, cook for fun, reflect about what's just happened. We are not only role models for learning; we are role models for living.

I have previously told the story of a teacher who was going to decline an invitation to an evening out because she had papers to grade. "Leslie, go the ballet. Be an interesting person," I advised her. So many teachers have told me how much they love that story. I think it's because we all want to "have a life" but feel overburdened with demanding responsibilities and tasks. We need to stop feeling guilty if we leave school at a reasonable hour so we have time for our families. Staying till six or seven each evening doesn't necessarily make us more effective teachers.

Our students will not become better readers because we create fabulous projects and centers, give them lots of paperwork, and grade lots of papers. They will become better readers if they receive excellent instruction and have lots of time to read and talk about books. There are many things we can do during the school day to make our teaching lives easier and more efficient. Use the following information and suggestions to rethink how you spend your time.

Spend Most of Your Time *Thinking*

I spend a lot of time planning for teaching and learning, but it is mostly thinking. This thinking goes on all the time—early morning before school, on my way to school, while I'm eating, in between doing other things. It's exactly how I work as a writer. The thinking about composing goes on all day long, not just when I am in front of my computer screen.

I cannot work with students effectively until I have met them and their teacher. Together we determine needs, interests, purposes, and goals. Then, every lesson plan is customized for that particular group of students, those learning goals and expected outcomes.

I KEEP THE FOLLOWING QUESTIONS IN MIND ALL THE TIME:

☐ *What do I want them to know and understand?* Expectations, content, curriculum, big ideas, skills, strategies, standards.

☐ *How can I help them know and understand it?* Provide necessary background knowledge, demonstrations, guided practice, appropriate resources, differentiated instruction, supportive language, reteaching.

☐ *How will I know when they know and understand it? How will students know that they understand and let me know that they do?* Observations, conversations, conferences, performance assessments, tests, evaluations, self-evaluations, reflections.

☐ *What are my new expectations for students?* Goals (theirs and mine), action plans, lessons, demonstrations, resources.

And with that it's back to question number one.

Trust Your Own Experiences to Help You Plan Well

While teacher's guides and program manuals can help us plan, they are at best resources. Part of our job is knowing which resources, materials, and suggestions to use and which to ignore. When the "teacher's notes" are twice as long as the story and take an hour to read, we need to exercise our common sense and good judgment. Do not overrely on teacher's editions, and be sure to include and trust your own knowledge, judgment, and experiences.

Don't forget, either, to be responsive to what your children are doing and attempting to do. Kindergarten teacher Karen Sher says,

I have learned to use my own classroom experiences as a guideline to help me understand what's going on with my students. Now that I do that, I'm having a lot of fun with them. For example, I try to take what they do on their own to see how they're making sense of print. Then I look to see what I can do as a teacher—using the pathways they've chosen—to clarify and extend their thinking.

Keep Work Meaningful

Students will happily engage in work that is connected to their lives and in projects in which they can see value. As much as possible, ensure that the work students do is literacy centered—that is, that students are reading and writing worthwhile texts that provide opportunities to expand their skills, knowledge, and thinking.

The literacy tasks we ask students to do impacts their motivation for learning and their views of literacy. Authentic reading and writing in which students have some challenge, choice, control, and opportunity to collaborate motivate students most.

**TRY IT
APPLY IT**

*Keep Work
Meaningful*

- ✐ Create your own texts for reading and writing "on the spot" (see pages 57–61). These can include narratives, retellings, factual accounts, instruction booklets, guides, reviews, poems, photo documentaries, and much more. For younger students, include charts, big books, little books, books for guided reading, books for the classroom library, take home books. Older students might publish newspapers, parent information pieces, brochures, handbooks, stories or poems on their or the school's web site, issue-oriented letters and requests to the school board, the city council, the principal, nonfiction books for younger students.
- ✐ Make your own meaningful worksheets from shared reading and shared writing. (See the example on page 57.) Make sure that when you use worksheets they are tailored to your students' needs and not just a time filler.
- ✐ Rethink and review the "must-dos" you assign students (see page 209). Are these tasks engaging and motivating for students, or are they merely time fillers?

Keep Work Simple

Make sure the work you plan for students to do independently is something they can do without your on-the-spot guidance. "Seat work" needs to be easy to manage and prepare. Some suggestions include:

- ☐ Simple book projects.
- ☐ Reading with a partner.
- ☐ Reading an assignment that has been posted on the whiteboard (see pages 172 and 181).
- ☐ Finishing the story started in guided reading.
- ☐ Independent reading.
- ☐ A whole-class project stemming from a read-aloud, shared writing (see pages 56–57), shared reading, or other common experience. For example, an intermediate grade class adopted an acre of rainforest and boycotted Nike for its foreign labor practices.

☐ Word work that builds on what you've already taught and practiced.
☐ Responses to reading.

Make Every Minute Count

If students need to process a great deal of text to become great readers, then they must spend most of reading time reading connected texts. To ensure that our struggling readers make the necessary gains, we also need to offer explicit instruction in many contexts (for example, morning message, meaningful word work, shared reading and shared writing experiences, guided reading).

We're spending way too much time creating "seat work" and activities that fill time without increasing students' knowledge and skills. Recently a teacher told me she had just attended a workshop and had spent thirty hours over the weekend creating activities and literacy centers for her classroom. Not a particularly good use of her time, or her students'.

Continually ask yourself when planning work for students, *How is this activity helping my students become more independent as readers, writers, and thinkers?* If it's not, set it aside.

Use All Time Spent with Your Students to Teach and Assess

teaching tip

Check yourself. How long is it taking you to state your expectations and give directions for independent work? If you can't do this in just a few minutes, the requirements are probably too complicated for students to work without your guidance. Lots of time spent giving directions is time lost from reading instruction and practice.

In optimal teaching and learning, teaching and assessment go hand in hand. There are many planned and unplanned moments for explicit teaching throughout the day. Every moment spent with a child is an opportunity to teach:

☐ Assess, evaluate, and teach during independent reading.
☐ Take a running record during guided reading, analyze it on the spot, and make one or two teaching points.
☐ Informally check a new student's reading the day she enters the classroom: ask her to select a book she thinks she can read from the classroom library, or ask her to choose from a group of books you've preselected.
☐ During shared reading and writing, notice individual strengths and weaknesses and explicitly teach to move a student forward and build confidence.

Make Ongoing Evaluation Part of Every Literacy Activity

The most effective teachers constantly evaluate students' learning and needs *as* they are teaching. When I work in classrooms, I integrate teaching and evaluating all day long. One easy way to do that is through individual reading conferences. Rethink assessments that are time consuming and are not being used to improve instruction.

**TRY IT
APPLY IT**

*Make
Ongoing
Evaluation
Part of Every
Literacy
Activity*

- During shared reading, have a student lead the class in rereading a text. Stand back and observe how students are following along and redirect those who need help.

- Take a few minutes to observe partner reading. Notice which pairs are working well collaboratively and which need additional demonstrations.

- Use most of independent reading time to confer with students one-on-one.

- Before school and during "book looks," walk around and observe readers. Encourage and teach "on the spot."

- When students "turn and talk" during shared and interactive reading, notice which students are engaged and participating. Encourage those who are not, move distracted students closer to you, reassign matches that don't seem to be working.

- During shared writing, call on students who do not volunteer and guide and support their responses.

- Structure small-group reading so that you can easily evaluate who is reading for understanding (use small spiral notebooks to check comprehension; introduce reciprocal teaching).

- Think about making standardized reading assessment part of daily teaching rather than separate from it. You might also develop your own assessment (see pages 112–113).

Keep a Lively Pace

Recent brain research indicates that we have kids' attention for less than ten minutes before they need a "cognitive rest." This means we must allow lots of time for students to process new information, to interact in conversations and collaborative responses. When the work is interesting and we move along at a fast pace, we keep kids engaged. (Pages 57–61 show examples from fast-paced, engaging lessons.) I find that when the lesson is relevant, interesting, and moves along at a good clip, I rarely have to stop and discipline a student. Teaching that keeps kids engaged saves us time and energy.

teaching tip

Don't "stuff" your lessons trying to do everything—it's a sure way to lose kids' attention and interest. Focus on one or two important teaching points, and do them well.

Time Yourself

I am always looking at my watch. Morning message? I want to be done in five minutes. Modeling journal writing? Ten minutes. What are the key teaching points I want to make? Make them and move on. When we try to "do everything" in one lesson that goes on and on, we lose students' attention. Not only that, we tire them out so that they don't have the will or energy to continue when we're ready to have them work on their own. A first-grade teacher who observed me lead students in shared writing commented:

> You stopped after fifteen minutes, at a high point of excitement in the story. I would have run the lesson into the ground and kept going till they were exhausted. These students left engaged and wanting more.

Create Structures That Maximize Participation and Learning

Students learn more when they are able to talk to one another and be actively involved. Learning structures that promote maximum participation include simultaneous student-led groups, literature conversations (small student-led book groups), discussion groups in science and social studies, joint reading of newsmagazines, partner reading, and shared reading. After demonstrating with the whole class, have students work in groups, monitoring their own behavior and thinking, while you guide one group.

Combine Activities

Combine reading aloud with shared reading and teach comprehension strategies at the same time. Teach reading in social studies and science, not just in reading and literature classes. Evaluate your readers while they are reading independently. (Chapters 6 and 7 discuss some specifics.)

Fight for More Time for Students Who Struggle

Mostly, we send our struggling kids out of the room for skill and drill and "corrective" programs, and they miss the valuable instruction they need most. Don't pull students out during reading aloud or shared reading—if you must do it, do it during social studies or science instead. Remember the importance of language development for low-performing students (see page 51). And don't expect support personnel to assume the full responsibility for remedial reading—classroom teachers are responsible as well, and students need at least a double dose of excellent practice.

Use Transitional Periods as Teaching Times

Throughout the day, there are quick moments between classes and activities in which we can reinforce what we've been teaching. These are ideal times to work with:

- ☐ Phonemic awareness.
- ☐ Rhyming words.
- ☐ Vocabulary.
- ☐ Spelling.

Karen Sher teaches much of her phonemic awareness incidentally (but deliberately), often during moments spent cleaning up, walking down the hall, going to lunch, getting ready for the next activity. Daily, depending on the letter and sound she is emphasizing, students transform sentences by substituting the designated sound for the initial consonant of each word. For example, when the emphasis is on the /p/ sound, "Let's go out for recess" becomes "Pet's po out por pecess." All students eventually do this easily.

Brief moments like these are also ideal for reinforcing vocabulary. Use the words you've been discussing in texts students are reading. Encountering new words in everyday conversation helps kids retain and apply the words in other contexts. For example, as we were getting ready to leave the classroom one day, I said "I'm flabbergasted that anyone would want to delay going to lunch."

Introduce "Mystery Words"

Kids love solving words, and doing so heightens their awareness of and interest in learning new words. One quick, daily activity that students savor is to figure out a partially written word or phrase from the letters and context provided. For example, I write *v_s_t_r* on the board and say to kindergartners, "Our mystery word has something to do with what will be happening today in our classroom." Or, I write *d_sposa_ _ _ cam_ _ a* in front of first graders and say, "This is something we're going to use today to help us add pictures to a classroom story we'll be writing" (see page 58). Some primary teachers post a "word of the day" to heighten awareness of important words.

Intermediate-grade students love solving words too. One day's mystery word in fifth-grade teacher Marnie Danielski's class was *ubiquitous*. The clue was "what gum chewing is becoming in our classroom." The word was presented as *ub _ q _ _t_ _ _,* and students rushed to the dictionary to try to figure it out.

Make Work Done While Waiting for the Bell to Ring Sensible and Pleasurable

When I come to work, I don't immediately sit down at my desk to "must-dos" like updating my grade book or writing in my journal. I grab a cup of coffee and talk to colleagues as I get ready for the day. If I had to complete assigned written tasks even before the day officially began, I would hate coming to work. Why, then, do we make the start of the day so dreadful for many of our students?

When I walk into kindergarten classes before school and see kids cutting out circles or drawing circles around letters, I cringe. We only have so much time, and we must make sure that we and our students use it wisely. "Why can't the kids just come in and read and write with a friend? Why can't they just talk to each other?" I ask teachers gently. Some tell me the room would get too noisy. Others say the students need to be in their seats so they as teachers can get work done.

When one faculty I worked with told me that before-school "bell work" was not an option—teachers were required to post a daily assignment in writing—here's what I suggested: "Read by yourself or with a partner. Read anywhere in the room. Or write a note to a friend." Like us, our students love starting the day in a relaxed way.

Once teachers move away from mandatory assignments, they rarely go back to worksheets. First of all, there's no "work" for teachers to check, a big timesaver. Then there are no upset students who couldn't do the work or didn't get it done. There is no time spent talking to students about redoing or correcting work. The teacher is free to walk around, talk with students, perform informal assessments, prepare for the day, enjoy the children.

A peaceful start to the day has to be carefully managed. In one first-grade classroom, I gathered the students around during our morning meeting and said:

> Tomorrow when you come in, we're going to have a different start to
> our day. You will love it. You can read or write anywhere in the room.
> You can talk with your friends. You can move around if you want to.

Then we modeled and practiced exactly what that would look like and sound like. Before the morning bell rings in that classroom now, students are reading books at their desk, reading on the floor, reading with a friend, looking for a book in the classroom library, reading chart poems, singing and chanting big books, reading a class-authored story (posted on a big chart) using the teacher's pointer, and writing, receiving, and responding to notes from peers. There is a happy hum as children move around and make their choices.

What a pleasurable way to begin the day for all students and teachers! Not to mention a big payoff: lots more time for practicing and enjoying real reading and writing.

Make Resources in the Room Useful and Easy to Access

The more students can do independently and the quicker they can do it, the more they can go on learning and have time for learning on their own. Make sure students know how to find and access the words, supplies, and books they need.

Examine How You Are Using Word Walls

Many primary classrooms now have word walls, but too few teachers know *why* they have them or how to use them effectively. You can be an excellent teacher and not have a word wall. The word wall per se is not important; what is important is to have available, easy-to-access resources that foster investigating and solving words on one's own. Unfortunately, in too many classrooms, homogeneous word walls decorate the walls rather than inform the students. Often, word walls are also positioned higher than a comfortable eye level. Clearly, this is a misuse of a potential resource.

Word walls can be a powerful tool for younger students if and when the words are discussed and analyzed with students before they are posted. Teachers also need to demonstrate how to use the word wall to figure out new words. For example, "If you know *all*, then you can also read and write words such as *call, mall, ball*." For older students, charts of content-area words or key vocabulary are effective spelling resources.

Curious whether or not your word walls are effective? Evaluate honestly whether or not students are using them in everyday reading and writing. The students in the photo on page 58 are using an alphabetic name wall in their daily writing.

Minimize Coloring

A blatant example of time not being well spent is the enormous amount of mindless coloring children do. In many schools, students spend most of their time coloring during "reading instruction." Since I became aware of this research, I have carefully monitored the amount of coloring students do. After modeling expectations for quality, I say to students something like this:

> Kids, we're going to be illustrating the books we've written, and you can do one page of your book in school. You'll have up to fifteen minutes to complete that page. Because coloring doesn't help you become a better reader—and it's my job to make sure you become the best reader you can be—you can finish coloring at home.

And when we turn our shared writing into a book, the book is illustrated by students, but no one does more than one page. That illustrated copy becomes our permanent class book, and we make photocopies so each student has his own copy to read and practice and take home.

Reduce Interruptions

In schools where learning is taken very seriously, there are few interruptions. See what you can do to change the culture of your school so that teaching and learning are "sacred."

In one school where I worked, teachers seriously tackled reducing interruptions. As a staff, they took all the daily and yearlong happenings that interrupted teaching and learning and listed them under two headings—"in our control" and "not in our control." Then they took a hard look at such nonessential activities as school assemblies, parties, and fund-raisers and eliminated some of them.

In another school, teachers and the principal decided to limit public address announcements to one morning a week. Now when the secretary needs to reach someone, she sends a brief note to the particular classroom.

Reevaluate Time Blocks

Separating literacy components into blocks of thirty or forty minutes is a useful teaching framework and helps alleviate management issues. A reading, writing, or word work block is often a whole-class activity, so you don't need to worry about or prepare for "what the rest of the class is doing."

Once you have implemented the blocks and worked with them for a while, reevaluate the time allotments. Often, there is too much time devoted to isolated word study and too little time for small-group and individualized instruction. You, as the knowledgeable teacher, ultimately need to determine the blocks and time frames that lend themselves to optimal teaching and learning.

Look at Your Schedule Carefully

Closely examine your daily and weekly schedule. Where can you make changes to create more time for teaching and learning? For example, consider eliminating or reducing recess (particularly when students have other opportunities to move around), whole-class bathroom breaks, and some transitional moments. First graders who have early lunch do not need morning recess if your curriculum is engaging and collaborative. Young children can go the bathroom when they need to if you model expectations and procedures. Do you need to linger over teaching the days of the week quite so long each day? As much as possible, try for long, uninterrupted literacy blocks.

Maximize time spent reading. How are you balancing demonstration and practice? Get together as a staff after school and examine your schedules. How can you "add" more time for students to read? In one school, after fourth-grade teachers got together and discussed what was possible, they were able to change their schedules to give less time to guided reading and more time to independent reading.

Examine Your Reading Schedule

Decide first what your priorities are, and then make sufficient time for these in your schedule rather than slotting in activities to preestablished times.

Take a look at some teachers' "before" and "after" schedules. (See pages 213–215, and see also page 158 for time frame guidelines.) Once teachers recognize the critical significance of shared and independent reading, they "make time" for them.

Make Time for Ongoing Professional Development

When we feel less burdened with busywork, we have time for our own learning. Continue reading and studying about your profession and reflecting on your practice. There is no shortcut. Knowledge gives us more time and energy. Then we are able to be decisive, we have fresh ideas, we can figure out what makes sense, we know how to teach our students and move them forward. Not only that, our own enthusiasm for learning increases student achievement.

Unless we keep our knowledge of content, children, management, and effective teaching current, we remain at the mercy of outsiders to make decisions for us. More and more gets piled on, and we become increasingly exhausted and burned out. Only by being informed about research, programs, and best practice can we begin to speak out, take charge, and shape our reading program. These are our responsibilities and rights as educators. Our students' literacy needs and interests must be our priorities—not prescribed programs and test scores.

Left (handwritten schedule):

Diane Mattern   First Grade

7:45 - 8:15 <u>Journal Writing</u>/morning ideas/writing conf. for publishing
concern: kids worried about   time to reteach what I've noticed
    journal topic   kids about get the day before.

8:15 - 8:45ish <u>Shared Reading</u> - explain seatwork & centers for kids
                                       while I do Guided Reading.
concern: could be doing so much
    more here. Not sure how
    to start.

8:45ish - 10:00 <u>Guided Reading</u> - 4 groups   20-25 min apiece
concern - too many kids in groups.
    dont like "must do's" kids are required to do while I do G.R.

10:15 - 10:45 Journal Reading/library checkout

11:25 - 12:15 Read aloud - 30 min
              Spelling - 20 min.

1:00 - 2:00 Math,
            Science (somehow)
            Writing lesson + guided writing practice.

Regie - I've been teaching 1st grade 2yrs. This schedule feels
like I'm wasting time, yet busy teaching pieces. Help!

Right (typed letter):

May 5, 2002

Dear Diane,

I'm looking at your schedule. Some suggestions:

- unless you're teaching journal writing first thing in the morning, I wouldn't start the day with it. Too often teachers just use it as a "time filler." You won't get quality without the teaching. (Take a look at my chapter on journal writing in *Conversations* for ideas for topics and writing)

- shared reading--make sure you use the whole 30 min. for shared reading and not for explaining seat work. If you're doing simple projects and kids are mostly reading during guided reading, you'll have more time for shared reading. You do need at least 30-40 min. in first grade.

- guided reading--have you tried shortening groups to 10-15 min. like I modeled? Do you have a classroom library now so kids have access to books to read while you have groups?

- read aloud time seems right.

- You are missing a carefully, monitored independent reading time. If you shorten guided reading to 4 groups and allow 50 minutes, you'll have 25 min. for independent reading.

Let me know what you try and how it's going. Good luck!

Love,
Regie

Diane Mattern's first-grade reading schedule and Regie Routman's response

<u>Schedule</u>

Below is my old schedule and my new schedule. I am feeling much better about my ability to get in what matters. No minutes were added to my day—I just think I'm making better use of the existing minutes.

<u>Old Schedule</u>
7:45-8:10 Opening
(This included explaining Centers/Must Dos/Rotation Groups, etc.)
8:10-9:40 Guided Reading
9:40-10:30 Writing
10:30-11:00 Explore
11:00-11:45 Specials
11:50-12:05 Finish Explore or Read Aloud
12:05-12:45 Lunch
12:45-1:05 Independent Reading
1:05-2:00 Math
2:00-2:15 Recess
2:15-2:30 Clean Up/Shared Reading//Dismissal

30 min. of shared reading is added

<u>New Schedule</u>
7:45-8:00 Opening
8:00-8:30 Shared Reading/Writing
8:30-9:30 Guided Reading
9:30-10:20 Writing
10:20-11:00 Explore
11:00-11:45 Specials
11:50-12:05 Begin Read Aloud
12:05-12:45 Lunch
12:45-12:55 Finish Read Aloud
12:55-1:40 Math
1:40-2:10 Independent Reading
2:10-2:25 Recess
2:25-2:30 Clean Up/Dismissal

Guided reading time shortened from 90 min. to 60 min.

Independent reading increases from 20 min. to 30 min.

*Explore refers to social studies/science

Robin Wood's second-grade reading schedules

5th Grade Schedule
Marnie Danielski

Previous Schedule

7:50 – 8:35	Specials
8:40 – 9:00	Math Warm-up
9:00 – 10:15	Math
10:15 – 10:45	Read Aloud (no teaching)
10:45 – 11:25	Independent Reading with Guided Reading Groups or Individual
	Conferences (this is where I taught)
11:25 – 12:05	Lunch and lunch recess
12:05 – 12:15	Writing Warm –up
12:15 – 1:15	Writing
	Mini Lesson
	Independent Writing/Publishing and individual conferences
	Sharing
1:15 – 2:15	Science and Social Studies on alternating days
2:15 – 2:30	Homework Assignments, Classroom Clean Up and Dismissal

Current Schedule

Makes read aloud a teaching time- adds shared read aloud

7:50 – 8:35	Specials
8:40 – 9:00	Read/Write/Math Games/Discussion time with partner or individually
9:00 – 9:30 or so	Shared Read Aloud (genre specific, thinking aloud, whole group teaching
9:30 – 10:15 or so	Independent Choice Reading of 'just right' books and
	Individual Reading Conferences during this 40 minute time period
	OR
	Independent Reading of choice guided reading group book and
	Guided Reading Group Meetings
10:15 – 11:20	Writing
	Mini Lesson
	Independent Writing/Publishing and individual conferences
	Sharing
11:25 – 12:05	Lunch and lunch recess
12:05 – 12:20	Math Warm –up
12:20 – 1:20	Math
1:20 – 2:20	Science and Social Studies on alternating days
2:20 – 2:30	Homework Assignments, Classroom Clean Up and Dismissal

Adds choice to independent reading and guided reading

Marnie Danielski's fifth-grade reading schedules

Take Part in Schoolwide Conversations

The importance of professional conversations and collaboration with our fellow teachers cannot be overstated. Schools that are more collegial and collaborative are happier places and have higher student achievement. The most effective teachers I know are the ones who read about their profession, collaborate with their colleagues, carefully observe their students, and continually question and reflect on their practices.

Based on decades of experience, I believe that significant, lasting school change with accompanying higher achievement is not possible without ongoing professional conversations. Most change is only skin-deep—a new program, a new schedule, new practices, new activities—"put" in place with little knowledge about how or why. I recently published an article about the necessity of having my weeklong school residencies supported by weekly faculty conversations throughout the year. There is no shortcut to becoming a teacher-as-professional.

- ✐ Use faculty meetings for professional development. Let a school committee with grade-level representatives handle the school business that usually dominates staff meetings. Use a morning email to communicate important messages/tasks.

- ✐ Collaborate with colleagues. Establish weekly conversations. Here are some ways to find the time:

    - ✐ Set up before-school support groups.

    - ✐ Institute a late start for students one day a week.

    - ✐ Dismiss students early one day a week.

    - ✐ Hire roving substitutes.

    - ✐ Participate in an ongoing mentoring program.

    - ✐ Videotape your and others' lessons.

    - ✐ Add paid days to the school calendar.

    - ✐ Add more time to the school day.

- ✐ Establish common planning periods at your grade level. Exchange ideas. It's too hard to do it all yourself.

Make Time for Personal and Professional Reading

Every exemplary teacher I know reads a lot. It's not that these teachers have any more time than the rest of us; they just make reading a priority because it's how they enrich their lives and continue to grow as a teacher and a learner. My favorite quote on the subject comes from *Better Than Life* by Daniel Pennac:

> If you have to ask yourself where you'll find the time, it means the desire isn't there. Because, if you look at it more carefully, no one has the time to read. Children don't, teenagers don't, adults don't. Life is a perpetual plot to keep us from reading. . . .
>
> Time spent reading is always time stolen. Like time spent writing, or loving, for that matter.
>
> Stolen from what?
>
> From life's obligations. . . .
>
> Time spent reading, like time spent loving, increases our lifetime.
>
> If we were to consider love from the point of view of our schedule, who would bother? Who among us has time to fall in love? Yet have you ever seen someone in love not take the time to love?
>
> I've never had the time to read. But no one has ever kept me from finishing a novel I loved.
>
> Reading does not belong to the societal organization of time. Like love, it is a way of being.
>
> The issue is not whether or not I have the time to read (after all, no one will give me that time), but whether I will allow myself the joy of being a reader.

So where can this time come from? Many teachers, one or two days a week, read a professional article or book while their students are reading independently. Adult book clubs, in and out of school, can push us to read. I use my monthly reading record (see page 34) to help me find time. When it's the middle of the month and a blank page tells me I haven't completed any books yet, I tell myself to watch less television and stay off the phone, and I pick up a waiting tableside book and read. And, of course, if we're doing less busywork for school, we have more time to read.

Do Less, More Effectively

In schools with a new curriculum focus every year followed by one in-service after another, nothing takes hold. It's been said, "Slow down so you can hurry up." When we teach well and deeply, students engage more and acquire the skills and strategies to go on learning. With a clear and meaningful focus, we can do more instruction, more effectively, in less time. Robin Woods comments:

> I am learning that good teaching doesn't have to mean lots of hours. Instead, it requires lots of thinking—thinking about what matters to kids, thinking about what kids need to know, and thinking about how they can be taken to the next level. My husband will now see me spend less time at school or grading papers and hear me think aloud more about my students and how I'm approaching instruction. I'd never really thought about how being a good teacher could mean having more time at home with my family.

Build in Time to Reflect

I have an ordinary spiral notebook with me all the time. I jot down what I am thinking and observing, what has just happened, questions I have. Teaching is so complex and fast moving that if I don't write it down, I've lost the thought forever. When I share my notebook with teachers and talk about how valuable it is as a way to reflect on my teaching and take action, many inquiring teachers begin to keep their own notebooks. Fifth-grade teacher Marnie Danielski comments:

> I keep my notebook handy at all times. Jotting down ideas while they are fresh has made a big difference in my life. Planning time is reduced, because much of my planning is now recorded in my gray spiral notebook. Because I now spend fewer hours after school planning, I have more time to enjoy other important parts of my life. My students like me better, my family and friends like me better, and I like myself better. The combination of reflecting, recording, and implementing new ideas has improved my effectiveness and reduced my stress level. Who would have thought a simple gray spiral notebook could make such a difference?

Cultivate a Love of Learning

We teachers need to continue to evaluate how we use our time. First and foremost, we must do whatever we can to ensure that our students love learning. We all invest more energy when a task is pleasurable. Focusing on strengths is the best way to learn anything. Kids can't be joyful if we're not. I'm with Jim Popham all the way:

> If I were obliged to choose between students' love of learning and their mastery of any collection of cognitive content standards, I'd choose the former every time.

Amen.

Enjoy!

My vibrant, independent, eighty-five-year-old father, who had continued to report to his office daily and carry a full workload, suffered a severe stroke a month ago. In order to survive, he needed immediate surgery to remove a large blood clot on his brain. We, his family, agreed to the surgery because Dad had come into the emergency room "almost normal," still talking coherently after directing the ambulance driver to his hospital of choice, identifying his preferred doctor, and even relating the doctor's phone number from memory. But after that burst of clarity, his deterioration was rapid, and he appeared to be in a coma, seeming not to hear us as he was being readied for surgery. My husband, two sisters, and I planned to catch a bite to eat while Dad was in surgery. Then we would return and await the results. As we were preparing to leave, I leaned over my father's bed and explained:

> Dad, we're all going out to an Italian restaurant down the street. It's just the kind of place you love—festive and lively, with great food. We're going to have some wine and drink a toast to you.

We turned to leave, and my dear father, who had not spoken a word for more than six hours, said "Enjoy." We were stunned and elated. And I thought, "How so like Dad." That was how he lived his life. He loved people, he traveled, he went dancing, he took great pleasure in his work, he delighted in his family, including all the grandchildren and great grandchildren. He relished life and welcomed each day with enthusiasm and joy.

Without Human Caring, the Best Science Is Minimally Effective

My dad's surgery was successful, but his doctors were puzzled by his lack of response. Four weeks after the stroke and surgery, he was still mostly unresponsive and it was difficult to tell what spark of life remained within his continuous sleep and silence. Sitting right next to him day after day, I talked to him, stroked him, kissed him, read to him, encouraged him to fight to live, and tried to gauge his facial expressions. He appeared to be in a deep depression, not surprising, since he was living his worst nightmare, being totally dependent and helpless. I was convinced his main problem was his mind and spirit. Medical science had taken him to the brink of possibility. But without a determined will to live, I knew he would give up and die. How could we, his family and friends, help him muster up his lifelong optimism and joy for living? How could we stir his heart?

Little by little, with daily encouragement and surrounded by our love, he began to respond—a smile, a wave, a squeeze of the hand, an attempt to mouth words. Each response was a huge victory and sent waves of joy through me. "You can do it, Dad!" We continue to cheer him on. Although he needs to relearn how to talk, feed himself, move, function in so many simple and complex ways, I have little doubt he will continue to progress and live a quality life as long as he feels supported and loved.

In the many hours I have spent with my dad, I have thought a lot about teaching and kids—mostly how quickly we give up on students, how we fail to celebrate the very small gains, how low our expectations are, how critical lovingkindness is, and what it means to have deep, abiding patience. The science of learning that dominates instruction and programs these days means nothing without a teacher who cares deeply about each and every student. It is we teachers who determine whether or not our students succeed.

I keep my father's advice close to my heart. "Enjoy!" Ask yourself, "What am I doing to ensure that kids are joyful about reading and writing? What am I doing for myself to make my own life richer?" There is no joy in assembly-line teaching nor in hours spent on test preparation, seatwork, or grading papers. If we are to create a thirst for knowledge and learning in our students and ourselves, we must put the joy back into our lives, savor the small victories, cheer our students on, and be unwavering advocates for them. Do whatever you need to do to guarantee that each and every student not only can learn but also savors learning.

Enjoy your students, enjoy your teaching, and enjoy your life.

Appendices

Selected Strategies for Struggling Readers

- Creating original texts
    - predictable text from child's language and experience
    - nonfiction text from child's interests or curriculum focus
    - wordless picture book (adding text)
- Shared reading
    - read book aloud as students follow along in own copy
    - choral reading and echo reading
    - big books in small/whole class grouping
    - listening to book on tape while following along in own copy
- Repeated reading
    - rereading of familiar texts
    - read book aloud before student reads it independently
    - dramatize story
    - buddy reading
    - Reader's Theatre
- Introducing the book/providing background and support before reading
    - brainstorm words/semantic mapping
    - read another book aloud on same topic
    - cloze—read aloud, pause, and have student supply word
- Paired reading
    - new text with more capable reader
    - familiar text with struggling reader
- Sustained Silent Reading of just–right books
- Writing aloud
- Journal writing
- Shared writing
- Cross-age tutoring

Reading Essentials by Regie Routman (Heinemann: Portsmouth, NH); © 2003

12 Practices of the Most Effective Teachers

- are committed to high achievement for all students

- use a variety of approaches, resources, and quality texts and do not over rely on programs

- engage students in high level thinking with challenging curriculum and connect the curriculum and standards to lives in and out of school

- demonstrate explicit instruction in skills, strategies, tasks, procedures, and thinking

- bond with their students

- have excellent classroom management that includes and promotes small collaborative groups and conversations

- take charge of their own professional development and continuously work to improve and reflect upon their practices

- collaborate with colleagues—talk about, demonstrate, and share their knowledge and ideas about teaching and learning

- provide sustained time and opportunities for reading, writing, and talking about worthwhile texts

- use informal and formal assessment to continually monitor each student's progress, set goals, and plan instruction for increased student learning

- communicate effectively with students, parents, administrators, and other stakeholders

- are risk takers

Why Independent Reading Is Necessary

Dear Parents/Caregivers,

Decades of internationally based research shows that students who read more read better. They develop more expansive vocabularies and achieve higher levels of reading and writing development. This is particularly true for students who have daily opportunities to read, year after year.

Daily time to read in school is not a frill or waste of classroom time; on the contrary, it is one of the best ways for your child to:

- Learn new vocabulary and information.
- Increase speed and fluency (that is, read smoothly and accurately).
- Improve comprehension.
- Notice authors' writing styles (which in turn helps their own writing).
- Develop a greater interest in reading and learning.
- Develop a love of reading.

Therefore, a major part of our reading program will be daily quiet time during which students read books of their own choosing. During that time, I will be monitoring your child's reading development through individual reading conferences. Your child will also be expected to maintain a reading record and to read at home each evening. Our reading program will also include whole-class and small-group work.

Your child is expected to have a book at school every day, one he or she has selected from our classroom library, the school library, the public library, or your home library. Our main goals are for your child to enjoy reading for pleasure and information and to become a stronger, more flexible reader. Please join me in helping create an environment in which our children can enjoy books for a lifetime.

Sincerely,
Your child's teacher

Reading Essentials by Regie Routman (Heinemann: Portsmouth, NH); © 2003

Help Your Child Choose a "Just-Right" Book and Encourage Home Reading

Dear Parents/Caregivers,

Reading for pleasure will help your child become a good reader. Help your child choose books he can read and wants to read, what we call "just-right" books. This means that your child:

- Is interested in the book.
- Can read and figure out almost all the words.
- Understands what he or she is reading (can tell you what the story is about or what he or she is learning).
- Can read fairly smoothly. If your child is stumbling over many words, she or he will not be able to focus on reading for understanding.

In helping your younger child select a "just-right" book, try the "five-finger rule." As your child reads, have him or her count on one hand any unknown words. If there are five or more different unknown words on a full page, this book is too hard for your child to read alone, although you may still want to read it aloud. Have older children or children who are already good readers read at least several pages before deciding whether a book is too hard. Sometimes, a book that may initially seem too hard is "just right" once the child has read enough for meaning to "kick in."

If your child wants to read aloud to you, that's great. However, it is not necessary for your child to read aloud to you every night. Once students are readers, they do most of their reading silently. Talk with your child about what he is reading, but don't quiz him or her; keep your conversations relaxed and informal.

Be a reading model for your child. If possible, try to set aside time during which the whole family reads. Also, students read more when they have their own libraries. Create a shelf for your child's books and give books as gifts on special occasions.

Thank you for working with me in encouraging your child to become a reader.

Sincerely,
Your child's teacher

Use the Goldilocks Strategy to Choose Books

Good readers spend time with easy, "just-right," and hard books but mostly "just-right" books.

Easy Books

Ask yourself these questions. If you answer yes, *this book is probably an easy book for you. EASY books help you to read more smoothly and are fun to read aloud and silently.*

1. Is it a favorite book you have read before?
2. Do you understand the story (text) very well?
3. Do you know (can you understand and read) just about every word?
4. Can you read it easily and smoothly?

Just-Right Books

Ask yourself these questions. If you answer yes, *this book is probably a "JUST-RIGHT" book for you. "Just-right" books help you learn the most because you can figure out most of the words and you understand what's going on in the text.*

1. Is this an interesting book that you want to read?
2. Are you familiar with the content, author, series, genre?
3. Can you tell another person what is happening in the story and/or what you're learning?
4. Do you sometimes need to reread a part to understand it?
5. Are there just a few words per page you don't know?
6. When you read are most places smooth and some choppy?

Hard Books

Ask yourself these questions. If you answer yes, *this book is probably a HARD book for you. Spend a little time with it now and learn what you can. Perhaps, someone can read the book to you. Give it another try on your own later (perhaps in several months).*

1. Are you interested in reading this book?
2. Are you confused about what is happening in most of this book?
3. Is it hard to understand even when you reread?
4. Do you need lots of help to read this book?

Brainstorm similar criteria with your students. Your own list in "kid friendly" language is always the most meaningful.

Reading Essentials by Regie Routman (Heinemann: Portsmouth, NH); © 2003. Adapted from *Invitations: Changing as Teachers and Learners K–12* by Regie Routman (Portsmouth, NH: Heinemann, 1994, p. 189b), citing "Lessons from Goldilocks: 'Somebody's Been Choosing My Books But I Can Make My Own Choices Now!" by Marilyn M. Ohlhausen & Mary Jepsen, 1992.

Choosing Books for Independent Reading

Easy Books

You can read all the words.

You might have read it before.

You read smoothly—fluently.

It's easy to understand.

You understand everything.

You can just read it.

You can read the book all by yourself.

Just-Right Books

You can learn things.

You like the book.

(You enjoy reading it.)

You can read almost all the words.

(You can look at the cover, read half a page, look at the back cover,
take a picture walk, look at the print)

You understand almost all of it.

You might have read it before.

Hard Books

It has many words you don't understand.

It doesn't make sense to you.

You don't have the background.

You're not that interested in the topic.

If it's confusing, it may be too hard.

Sometimes it's OK to read these, but

Not very often

Not for very long

A shared writing with Robin Wood's grade 2 class

SSR Reading

1. Read at least 30 minutes each day at home.

2. List the books monthly.
   - ☐ the title and author (and illustrator)
   - ☐ the date you completed the book
   - ☐ the genre (type of book)

3. Rate the books you finish.

   Choose the rating method you like best

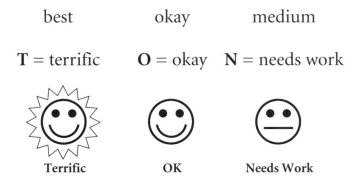

best	okay	medium
T = terrific	**O** = okay	**N** = needs work
Terrific	OK	Needs Work

   - ☐ Make up your own rating system

   - ☐ If you think other students would like this book, put an R (for recommend).

A shared writing with a grade 4 class

Reading Essentials by Regie Routman (Heinemann: Portsmouth, NH); © 2003

Informal Reading Conference

NAME _____ DATE _____

☐ *Bring me a book that you can read pretty well.*

   TITLE OF BOOK _____GENRE _____

☐ *Why did you choose this book?*

☐ *What is the reading level of this book for you?* ____ hard ____ easy ____ just right

☐ *Tell me what the book is about so far.*

☐ *Read this part of the book for me.* (Take notes as the child reads silently or orally.)

☐ *Tell me what you remember about what you just read.*

☐ *Let's discuss your strengths and what you need to work on.*
   Strengths:

   Goals:

☐ *How long do you think it will take to complete this book?*

Reading Log

Title _____

Author _____

Genre _____ Date Finished _____

Rate the Book _____

_____

Title _____

Author _____

Genre _____ Date Finished _____

Rate the Book _____

_____

Title _____

Author _____

Genre _____ Date Finished _____

Rate the Book _____

_____

 Reading Essentials by Regie Routman (Heinemann: Portsmouth, NH); © 2003

Monthly Recording

Month/Year _____

Title	Author	Genre	Rating
1.			
2.			
3.			
4.			
5.			
6.			
7.			
8.			

Favorite authors of the month:

Favorite books (I'll be sure to reread):

Brief Definitions of Terms

Following are definitions for terms that may not be defined in the body of the text or are introduced in the text before they are fully discussed.

assessment

Collecting data and gathering evidence regarding the appropriation of knowledge; not useful unless evaluation is included.

automaticity

Accurate and rapid word recognition, including reading in meaningful phrases; allows reader to focus attention on meaning.

benchmark book

A book that represents typical difficulty or quality; used as a guide for assessment and in leveling books in a collection.

book look

Students look through the text and pictures of a self-chosen book, making meaning and enjoying the book alone or with friends; common practice for preschoolers and kindergartners.

cut-up sentence

A sentence (often connected to a content area) written with students that students then cut apart into individual words in order to focus on features of print; used in word study and word sorts.

differentiated instruction

Challenging and relevant instruction that meets the needs and interests of each learner. In a heterogenous group (often whole class), students receive scaffolded, multi-level instruction across content, processes, and product that enables each student to be successful.

evaluation

Interpreting, analyzing, and reflecting on assessment data in order to make it meaningful; includes making wise instructional decisions based on careful examination of the evidence.

evidence-based research

Another term for *scientific research*; both terms have political overtones, as the federal government defines *scientific* in extremely narrow terms referring to behavioral interventions that can be measured and monitored quantitatively.

guided reading

A teaching technique in which a student or students read—mostly silently—a carefully chosen book at their reading level, and the teacher supports, teaches, and evaluates as necessary.

independent reading

On their own, readers choose and read books they enjoy and understand; usually involves daily sustained silent reading in school along with careful teacher monitoring.

informal reading conference

A one-on-one reading evaluation in which the teacher listens to a student read aloud and retell, or the teacher silently reads a portion of text along with the student and then asks the student to talk about what has been read; includes analyzing progress with the student and setting goals.

interactive reading

The teacher reads out loud and invites students to talk about the text during her reading, not just after she has finished.

literacy centers

Specially designated classroom areas organized for independent, self-managed, student work while teacher is working with one student or a small group; not always meaningful or relevant to curriculum.

literature circles

Small, heterogeneous, often student-directed literature conversations about an excellent text.

miscue

Any departure from a written text a reader makes while reading; for example, omitting, reversing, or substituting a word, phrase, or punctuation. (Based on the research of Ken Goodman.)

modified running records

As a student reads a portion of text out loud, the teacher notes the miscues by drawing a line and recording what the child says above the line and what the text says below the line. The quality of miscue, not the number of miscues, is emphasized. For example, a meaningful substitution may indicate comprehension.

morning message

A brief written message constructed by the teacher (sometimes with student input) about daily activities, upcoming events, and curriculum. Students attempt to read the message, and the teacher makes a few important teaching points.

oral cloze

The teacher reads aloud (while students follow along visually), pausing periodically as a signal for students to say the upcoming word aloud.

partner reading

Taking turns reading aloud a text with a peer, supporting each other, and intermittently stopping to discuss the text; also called paired reading.

phonemic awareness

Sensitivity to and awareness of the fact that sounds make up spoken words; being able to discriminate between different consonants and to sequence each small unit of sound (phoneme) in a word.

predict

To make a smart prediction about an unknown word or phrase or idea based on what is already known about the text; the reader then confirms or disconfirms his prediction after reading on and acquiring additional information.

Readers Theatre

Performing a text or part of a text orally for an audience from a script; often uses well-loved stories; few or no props; excellent for repeated reading.

reading aloud

Teachers (or students) fluently read aloud excellent fiction and nonfiction to the class; hearing the material allows students to listen to ideas and vocabulary they may not yet be ready to read on their own and introduces them to new authors and genres; when it also involves discussion, it is called *interactive reading aloud.*

reading record (or reading log)

A place in which to record titles and authors of books read; what is included in the record may be negotiated with students' daily, weekly, or monthly entries; genre; rating for quality, enjoyment, difficulty; date finished; and so on.

reciprocal teaching

Interactive, scaffolded instruction for strengthening reading comprehension; the teacher (or peer, older student, parent) leads a group of students through a text to understand it; involves an emphasis on four strategies—generating a question, clarifying, predicting, and summarizing. (Developed by Annemarie Sullivan Palinscar and Ann L. Brown.)

retelling

A detailed oral or written recounting of a story that includes major and minor events, setting, characters, problems, and resolution; easier to do than a summary, which involves deleting less important information.

rime/onset

The *rime* is the part of the syllable that begins with the vowel and comes after the onset. The *onset* is the part of the syllable that comes before the vowel; it consists of one or more consonants. For example, in the word *clay, cl* is the onset and *ay* is the rime. Nearly five hundred words can be derived from only thirty-seven rimes.

round-robin reading

Students take turns reading a teacher-chosen text aloud; the teacher interrupts the reading as she deems necessary to supply difficult words and to ask questions.

rubric

Specific criteria used to establish guidelines for quality and/or to evaluate work.

running records

Sitting right next to a student, the teacher listens to the student read a new or familiar text out loud and makes notations for every word, indicating the student's accurate reading as well as the errors and corrections; mostly used for developing readers in K–2 or with older students still learning to read.

scaffolding

Temporary support from a teacher, parent, or accomplished peer that enables the learner to succeed.

self-monitoring

The reader is aware of her own word reading and comprehension or the limits of her comprehension and is able to "fix" gaps in meaning or answer her own questions about a text that arise as she reads.

shared reading

Students and teacher read a text together, the teacher taking the lead and the students following along and actively participating; in the early grades, mostly involves lots of repeated reading of poems, stories, enlarged texts; with younger and older students, shared reading may also involve introduction to and demonstration of new genres and strategies.

shared writing

Students and teacher compose a coherent text collaboratively, the teacher doing the writing while scaffolding children's language and ideas; often these texts become shared reading texts as well as published texts for guided and personal reading.

word sort

Students group words that are written on individual cards into different categories based on a specified criterion or contrast.

Notes

Chapter 1

5   I also discuss professional conversations in "Teacher Talk," *Educational Leadership* (March 2002), pp. 32–35. See *Conversations*, pp. 524–27, *Invitations*, pp. 465–72, in this text for discussions of how to set up weekly professional meetings in your school.

6   I define what it means to be professional as a teacher on pp. 1–12 of *Conversations*.

7   One prominent source questioning voluntary reading in the classroom is *Report of the National Reading Panel. Teaching Children to Read: An Evidence-Based Assessment of the Scientific Research Literature on Reading and Its Implications for Reading Instruction (NRP)* (Washington, DC: National Institute of Child Health and Human Development, 2000).

9   The statement that scientific knowledge and professional experience and judgment must go hand in hand is supported by Louise Spear-Swerling and Robert J. Sternberg, "What Science Offers Teachers of Reading," *Learning Disabilities Research and Practice* 16, no 1, pp. 51–57.

Chapter 2

11   The Don Holdaway epigraph is from "Schools That Work," a symposium held at the annual meeting of the International Reading Association, Indianapolis, Indiana, May 2000.

13   The two paragraphs by Don Holdaway are quoted from an email he sent me in April 2002.

13   Worldwide, the strongest predictors of reading achievement are the quality of student-teacher relations: Organization for Economic Cooperation and Development, *Knowledge and Skills for Life: First Results of PISA 2000* (Paris: OECD, 2001).

15   Techniques to encourage successful writing experiences will be treated in my *Writing Essentials,* forthcoming from Heinemann.

18–20   Our students learn vocabulary, grammar, new information, and how stories and written language work . . .: Jim Trelease, *The Read-Aloud Handbook,* 5th ed. (New York: Penguin Books, 2001).

20   The statement that reading aloud produces successful, interested readers is supported by Richard Anderson et al., *Becoming a Nation of Readers: The Report on the Commission on Reading* (Champaign, IL: University of Illinois Center for the Study of Reading, 1985); Ronald Carver and Robert Leibert, "The Effect of Reading Library Books at Different Levels of Difficulty upon Gain in Reading Ability," *Reading Research Quarterly* (January/February/March 1995), pp. 26–45; Daniel Pennac, *Better Than Life* (Portland, ME: Stenhouse, 1999); and Janet Allen and Kyle Gonzalez, *There's Room for Me Here: Literacy Workshop in the Middle School* (Portland, ME: Stenhouse, 1998). See *Conversations,* pp. 29–33 and 445–47, for discussions of reading aloud nonfiction.

20   Afi Scruggs, *Jump Rope Magic* (New York: Blue Sky Press/Scholastic, 2000).

Chapter 3

26   The principal referred to is Pat Heilbron, in Shaker Heights, Ohio, who says she was inspired by teacher Cindy Campbell.

26   Even students with reading disabilities can become proficient readers . . .: Rosalie Fink, "Successful Dyslexics: A Constructivist Study of Passionate Interest in Reading," in *Reconsidering a Balanced Approach to Reading,* edited by Constance Weaver (Urbana, IL: National Council of Teachers of English, 1998).

27   The fifty-books statistic is from *Phi Delta Kappan* (December 1999), p. 296.

27   The higher-number-of-books-per-student statistic is from United States Department of Education, *NAEP Trends in Academic Progress Report* (Washington, DC; U.S. Department of Education, 1997).

28   *Hateship, Friendship, Courtship, Loveship, Marriage* was reviewed on page 9 of *The New York Times Book Review* of November 25, 2001, by William H. Pritchard.

30   See *Conversations,* pp. 171–204, for guidelines and specifics relative to literature conversations and "The Blue Pages: Resources for Teachers," pp. 26b–28b, for annotated, recommended resources for book groups and effective questioning. Also see Harvey Daniels, *Literature Circles: Voice and Choice in Book Clubs and Reading Groups* (Portland, ME: Stenhouse, 2002) and Katherine Schlick-Noe and Nancy Johnson, *Getting Started with Literature Circles* (Norwood, MA: Christopher Gordon, 1999).

Chapter 4

44   Don Holdaway's principles of developmental and social learning are put forth in his "Affinities and Contradictions: The Dynamics of Social or Acquisition Learning," *Literacy Teaching and Learning: An International Journal of Early Reading and Writing* 5, no. 1 (2000), pp. 7–25; *The Foundations of Literacy* (Sydney: Ashton Scholastic, 1979; also available through Heinemann in

Portsmouth, NH); and "The Structure of Natural Learning as a Basis for Literacy Instruction," in the *Pursuit of Literacy*, edited by Michael Sampson, pp. 56–64 (Dubuque, IA: Kendall/Hunt, 1986). The learning model also derives from and builds upon Brian Cambourne's conditions of learning, Vgotsky's zone of proximal development, Bruner's "handover" theory, Frank Smith's principles of engagement, and P. David Pearson's idea of gradual release of responsibility.

45   "teaching and learning are seen as inseparable components of the same process": Holdaway 1986, pp. 12–13.

45   "In the instructionally rich sharing situations . . .": Holdaway 2000, p. 17.

46   "Because of the cooperative support of class members . . .": Don Holdaway, personal communication, April 2002.

46   "self-improving system" is Marie Clay's term. See her *Becoming Literate: The Construction of Inner Control* (Portsmouth, NH: Heinemann, 1991).

46   "To become dependent on being corrected by someone else . . .": Holdaway 2000, p. 15.

47   "the bonded skill user who has shared and introduced the skill": Holdaway 2000, p. 15.

47   "a powerful, invitational relationship that pulls the learner in": Holdaway 2000, p. 17.

47   "The idea that children achieve mastery of the conventional forms of literacy . . .": Lawrence R. Sipe, "Invention, Convention, and Intervention: Invented Spelling and the Teacher's Role," *The Reading Teacher* (November 2001), p. 265.

48   "with others, with context, with environment, with the world, and with self": Holdaway 2000, pp. 7–25.

50   Students do best . . . economically impoverished areas: Judith Langer et al., *Guidelines for Teaching Middle and High School Students to Read and Write Well: Six Features of Effective Instruction* (Albany, NY: National Research Center on English Learning and Achievement, 2000).

50   "individuals who are performing below their peers. . .: Michael Knapp and Associates, *Teaching for Meaning in High-Poverty Classrooms* (New York: Teachers College Press, 1995), p. 143; italics are the author's.

50   "this advantage does not appear to transfer to everyday reading and writing tasks": Barbara M. Taylor, Richard C. Anderson, Kathryn H. Au, and Taffy E. Raphael, "Discretion in the Translation of Reading Research to Policy" (Ann Arbor, MI: Center for the Improvement of Early Reading Achievement, September 1999).

50   Students who receive meaningful instruction are more likely to show an understanding of advanced skills by the end of the school year: Knapp and Associates 1995, p. 128.

51   If children do not have adequate and rich language to scaffold their reading and writing, their learning often stalls or regresses: Lance M. Gentile, "The Identification and Comparison of Language Structures Used by Reading Recovery Children Who Did or Did Not Discontinue in Twenty Weeks," San Francisco State University, unpublished paper, 2001.

51   Attention to print comes after an understanding of story and written language: Marie Clay, *Change over Time in Children's Literacy Development* (Portsmouth, NH: Heinemann, 2001).

51   "fourth grade slump . . . is caused, at least in part . . .": Rand Education Reading Study Group, Catherine Snow, Chair, *Reading for Understanding: Toward an R & D Program in Reading Comprehension* (Arlington, VA: Science and Technology Policy Institute, 2002), p. 36.

51   "To expect children to become literate . . . where the story ends": Jane Healy, *Failure to Connect: How Computers Affect Our Children's Minds and What We Can Do About It* (New York: Touchsone, 1998), p. 232; quoted in Gentile 2001.

51   In particular, teachers who read with young children . . .: Michael Pressley and Richard Allington, "What Should Reading Instructional Research Be the Research Of?" *Issues in Education: Contributions from Educational Psychology* 5, no. 1 (1999), p. 3, citing multiple sources.

51   Most children easily develop phonemic awareness: Richard Allington, in *Building a Knowledge Base in Reading*, by Jane Braunger and Jan Patricia Lewis (Portland, OR: Northwest Regional Educational Laboratory, Newark, DE: International Reading Association, 1997); Hallie Kay Yopp, "A Test for Assessing Phonemic Awareness in Young Children," *The Reading Teacher* (September 1995), pp. 20–29; Hallie Kay Yopp and Ruth Helen Yopp, "Supporting Phonemic Awareness Development in the Classroom," *The Reading Teacher* (October 2000), pp. 130–43.

52   This explicit attention to oral language development and vocabulary are a crucial part of comprehension instruction: Rand Education Reading Study Group 2002, p. 101.

52   When our instruction increases student engagement, student achievement increases: Rand Education Reading Study Group 2002, p. 42.

52   When students informally . . . their reading understanding: Susan Neuman, Donna Celano, Albert Greco, and Pamela Shue, *Access for All: Closing the Book Gap for Children in Early Education* (Newark, DE: International Reading Association, 2001), p. 10, citing Gordon Wells and Gen Ling Chang-Wells, *Constructing Knowledge Together: Classrooms as Centers of Inquiry and Literacy* (Portsmouth, NH: Heinemann, 1992).

53   Young students often write before they read: Clay 1991; Holdaway 1979.

53   "First, students learn the 'basics' . . .": Linda McNeil, "Creating New Inequalities: Contradictions of Reform," *Phi Delta Kappan* (June 2000), p. 732.

55   I discuss my work with this fourth grader in detail in *Invitations*, pp. 377–85.

62   The statement about financially strapped schools is supported by Kati Haycock, "Closing the Achievement Gap," *Educational Leadership* (March 2001), pp. 6–11.

62   Children in these classrooms must have meaning-oriented instruction in order to succeed at high levels: Knapp and Associates 1995.

Chapter 5

64   Prominent research on libraries and reading achievement includes Jeff McQuillan, *The Literacy Crisis: False Claims, Real Solutions* (Portsmouth, NH: Heinemann, 1998); Stephen Krashen, *Every Person a Reader: An Alternative to the California Task Force Report on Reading* (Culver City, CA: Language Education Associates, 1996); International Association for the Evaluation of

Educational Achievement, *How in the World Do Students Read? IEA Study of Reading Literacy* (The Hague, The Netherlands: IAEEA, 1992); Warwick Elley, "Acquiring Literacy in a Second Language: The Effect of Book-Based Programs," *Language Learning* 41 (1991), 375–411; Stephen Krashen, *The Power of Reading: Insights from the Research* (Englewood, CO: Libraries Unlimited, 1993); Stephen Krashen, "Current Research: The Positive Impact of Libraries (But Have We Tapped the Potential of the School Library?)," *CSLA Journal* 25, no. 1 (Fall 2001), pp. 21–24; Jann S. Fractor et al., "Let's Not Miss Opportunities to Promote Voluntary Reading: Classroom Libraries in the Elementary School," *The Reading Teacher* (March 1993), pp. 476–84; Carol Simon Weinstein and Lesley Mandel Morrow, "Encouraging Voluntary Reading: The Impact of a Literature Program on Children's Use of Library Centers," *Reading Research Quarterly* (Summer 1986), pp. 330–46; Susan Neuman et al., *Access for All: Closing the Book Gap for Children in Early Education.* (Newark, DE: International Reading Association, 2001.)

64   The home-school literacy book pack idea is Gretchen Owocki's. See her *Make Way for Literacy!* (Portsmouth, NH: Heinemann, 2001).

65   Jim Trelease's *The Read-Aloud Handbook*, 5th (New York: Penguin, 2001) contains many book titles and resources to suggest to parents.

65   One recent study found . . .: Jeff McQuillan et al., "If You Build It, They Will Come: A Book Flood Program for Struggling Readers in an Urban High School," in *But I'm an English Teacher! Focusing on Reading in the High School Classroom*, edited by B. Ericson (Urban, IL: NCTE, in press).

65   Too often there are too few books available that struggling readers can actually read: Richard Allington et al., *The First R: Every Child's Right to Read*, edited by Michael F. Graves, Paul van den Broek, and Barbara M. Taylor (New York: Teachers College Press, 1996), p. 84.

65   *Conversations*, pages 75b–78b, lists highly recommended fiction and nonfiction series that provide reliable reader support. (These lists can also be downloaded from the Heinemann website.) Many of these series feature excellent writing and can work well for guided reading.

66   Students' success and confidence with series books . . .: Christine Jenkins, "The Baby-Sitters Club and Cultural Diversity, or Book #X: Jessi and Claudia Get Lost," in *Using Multiethnic Literature in the K–8 Classroom*, edited by Viloet J. Harris (Norwood, MA: Christopher-Gordon, 1997).

67   The daily book sign-out procedures are taken from *Conversations*, pp. 89–90; see those pages for more information.

68   Even middle school and older students will choose to read . . .: Jim Trelease, *The Read-Aloud Handbook*, p. 138; Jo Worthy and Karen Broaddus, "Fluency Beyond the Primary Grades: From Group Performance to Silent, Independent Reading," *The Reading Teacher* (December/January 2001–2002), pp. 334–343.

68–69   The top three choices . . .: Gay Ivey and Karen Broaddus, "'Just Plain Reading': A Survey of What Makes Students Want to Read in Middle School Classrooms," *Reading Research Quarterly* (October/November/December 2001), p. 364.

69   "reading comprehension test scores are more influenced by students' amount of engaged reading than any other single factor": John Guthrie, "Preparing Students for High-Stakes Test Taking in Reading," in *What Research Has to Say About Reading Instruction*, 3d ed., edited by Alan E. Farstrup and S. Jay Samuels, p. 382 (Newark, DE: International Reading Association, 2002).

69   "No grade-level markings . . .": Jeff McQuillan et al., "If You Build It, They Will Come: A Book Flood Program for Struggling Readers in an Urban High School," in *Teaching Reading in the High School English Classroom*, edited by B. Ericson, pp. 69–83 (Urbana, IL: National Council of Teachers of English, 2001).

70   . . . nonfiction books still tend to be scarce in classrooms: Nell Duke, "The Scarcity of Informational Texts in First Grade" (Ann Arbor: CIERA/University of Michigan, 1999); Nell Duke, "3.6 Minutes per Day: The Scarcity of Informational Texts in First Grade," *Reading Research Quarterly* 35 (2000), pp. 202–24.

70   More nonfiction reading is connected to more informational writing, which is related to higher reading achievement: David K. Dickinson and Lori Lyman DiGisi, "The Many Rewards of a Literacy-Rich Classroom," *Educational Leadership* (March 1998), pp. 23–26.

71   See *Conversations*, pp. 451–57, for a whole-class, demonstration reading lesson using a nonfiction magazine article.

78   Mike Oliver credits Jim Trelease's *The Read-Aloud Handbook* for the rain gutter idea. He has written about the project in "The Rain Gutter Literacy Revolution: Enriching the Reading Climate by Advertising Children's Literature" (unpublished paper, 2001).

80   Research tells us that children who do not read regularly throughout the summer months . . .: Richard Allington, talk at a Title 1 conference in Columbus, Ohio, in February 2002.

81   In some California schools . . .: Thomas Newkirk, "Reading and the Limits of Science," *Education Week* (April 24, 2002), p. 39.

81   "What are we feeding our children? . . .": Katherine Paterson, "The Future of Literature: Asking the Question," *The New Advocate* (Winter 2000), p. 5.

Chapter 6

82   The epigraph is taken from Thomas Newkirk, "Reading and the Limits of Science," *Education Week* (April 24, 2002), p. 39.

83   Any reading program that substantially increases the amount of reading students do will impact their reading achievement: Richard Allington, *What Really Matters for Struggling Readers* (New York: Longman, 2001); Stephen Krashen, *The Power of Reading* (Englewood, CO: Libraries Unlimited, 1993); Daniel Fader, *The New Hooked on Books* (New York: Berkley, 1982).

84   Brian's comment is from *Lifers: Learning from At-Risk Adolescent Readers*, by Pamela N. Mueller (Portsmouth, NH: Heinemann, 2001), p. 23.

84   Richard Allington found that . . .: Allington 2001.

85   A longstanding, highly respected body of research definitively shows that students who read more read better and have higher reading achievement: Richard C. Anderson,

Paul T. Wilson, and Linda G. Fielding, "Growth in Reading and How Children Spend Their Time Outside of School," *Reading Research Quarterly* (Summer 1988), pp. 285–303; National Center for Education Statistics, *Executive Summary: NAEP 1998 Reading Report Card for the Nation and the States* (Washington, DC: National Center for Education Statistics, 1999), p. 134; Jim Trelease, *The Read-Aloud Handbook*, 5th ed. (New York: Penguin, 2001); U.S. Department of Education, *National Assessment of Educational Progress (NAEP) Trends in Academic Progress Report* (Washington, DC: U.S. Department of Education, 1997); Stephen Krashen, "Free Voluntary Reading: Still a Very Good Idea," in *Selected Papers from the Tenth International Symposium on English Teaching*, held by the English Teachers' Association in the Republic of China, November 16–18, 2001; Barbara M. Taylor, P. David Pearson, Kathleen F. Clark, and Sharon Walpole, *Beating the Odds in Teaching All Children to Read* (Ann Arbor, MI: Center for the Improvement of Early Reading Achievement, CIERA Report #2-006, September 1999) (one of the findings of this report is that the most effective teachers of students in grades 1–3 devote more time to independent reading).

85   . . . the value of free voluntary reading in classrooms has recently been called into question: *Report of the National Reading Panel. Teaching Children to Read: An Evidence-Based Assessment of the Scientific Research Literature on Reading and Its Implications for Reading Instruction (NRP)* (Washington, DC: National Institute of Child Health and Human Development, 2000); S. Jay Samuels, "Reading Fluency: Its Development and Assessment," in *What Research Has to Say About Reading Instruction*, 3d ed., edited by Alan E. Farstrup and S. Jay Samuels, p. 174 (Newark, DE: International Reading Association, 2002).

85   . . . research linking independent reading with achievement and to share this information with administrators and parents: In particular, see Stephen Krashen, "More Smoke and Mirrors: A Critique of the National Reading Panel Report," *Phi Delta Kappan* (October 2001), pp. 118–21. Krashen reports that in his review of the research on voluntary reading programs in school, in 51 out of 54 comparisons, students (both traditional language arts students and second language learners) participating in voluntary reading programs did as well or better on tests of reading comprehension as students who did not participate in such programs. The longer the program lasted, the better the results. Krashen explains, "The National Reading Panel report included only studies of sustained silent reading, included no long-term programs, contained only a dozen comparisons, and misinterpreted and misreported some of the studies they did include."

89   "Chatterbox" is an idea by fifth-grade teacher Marnie Danielski, of Westminster, Colorado. Her students chose the name.

91   "become more self-sufficient and less reliant on the teacher for assistance": Mary Lee Griffin, "Why Don't You Use Your Finger? Paired Reading in First Grade," *The Reading Teacher* (May 2002), p. 766; Lynn Rhodes and Nancy Shanklin, *Windows into Literacy: Assessing Learners K–8* (Portsmouth, NH: Heinemann, 1993).

91   What's more, research shows that taking turns reading increases reader involvement, attention, and collaboration: Griffin 2002, p. 772.

93–94   The statement that if you read a steady diet of books that are too hard for you, your reading gets worse, is supported by Marie Clay, *Becoming Literate* (Portsmouth, NH: Heinemann, 1991).

97   A study of middle school students found that . . . : Gay Ivey and Karen Broaddhus,
            "'Just Plain Reading': A Survey of What Makes Students Want to Read in Middle
            School Classrooms," *Reading Research Quarterly* (October/November/December
            2001), pp. 350–77.

Chapter 7

98   The epigraph is taken from Lorrie A. Shepard, "The Challenges of Assessing
            Young Children Appropriately," *Phi Delta Kappan* (November 1994), p. 208.

101   For information on running records, modified running records, and miscue
            analysis, see *Conversations*, pp. 112–14; Marie Clay, *An Observation Survey of Early
            Literacy Achievement* (Portsmouth, NH: Heinemann, 1993); Peter Johnston,
            Knowing Literacy: Constructive Literacy Assessment (Portland, ME: Stenhouse,
            1997); Irene C. Fountas and Gay Su Pinnell, *Guided Reading: Good First Teaching
            for All Students* (Porstmouth, NH: Heinmann, 1996); Sharon Taberski, *On Solid
            Ground* (Portsmouth, NH: Heinemann, 2000).

101   Common assessment tools that can be used to meet state guidelines are discussed
            in *Conversations*, pp. 576–78 and 195b–204b.

106   Guidelines for goals for younger students are further discussed in Marie Clay 1991.

107   See *Conversations*, pages 115–21, for additional teaching methods and procedures
            for and examples of informal reading conferences.

108   Students do well on high-stakes tests . . . : Judith Langer et al., *Guidelines for
            Teaching Middle and High School Students to Read and Write Well: Six Features of
            Effective Instruction* (Albany, NY: National Research Center on English Learning
            and Achievement, 2000); Michael S. Knapp, Patrick M. Shields, and Brenda J.
            Turnbull, "Academic Challenge in High-Poverty Classrooms," *Phi Delta Kappan*
            (June 1995); Richard Allington, "Research on Reading/Learning Disability
            Interventions," in *What Research Has to Say About Reading Instruction*, 3d ed.,
            edited by Alan E. Farstrup and S. Jay Samuels (Newark, DE: International
            Reading Association, 2002).

108   If we teach well and deeply . . .: Langer et al. 2000.

Chapter 8

117   The epigraph is from Susan Kidd Villaume and Edna Greene Brabham,
            "Comprehension Instruction: Beyond Strategies," Questions and Answers, *The
            Reading Teacher* (April 2002), p. 674.

118   . . . the most recent NAEP results: *National Assessment of Educational Progress*
            (Washington, DC: National Center for Education Statistics, Office of Educational
            Research and Improvement, U.S. Department of Education, 2001).

118   Key reading strategies are discussed in P. D. Pearson, L. R. Roehler, J. A. Dole, and
            G. G. Duffy, "Developing Expertise in Reading Comprehension," in *What Research
            Has to Say About Reading Instruction*, edited by J. Samuels and A. Farstrup (Newark,
            DE: International Reading Association, 1992); Stephanie Harvey, *Nonfiction Matters*
            (Portland, ME: Stenhouse, 1998); Ellin Keene and Susan Zimmerman, *Mosaic of
            Thought* (Portsmouth, NH: Heinemann, 1997); *Report of the National Reading*

Panel. Teaching Children to Read: An Evidence-Based Assessment of the Scientific Research Literature on Reading and Its Implications for Reading Instruction (NRP) (Washington, DC: National Institute of Child Health and Human Development, 2000); Stephanie Harvey and Anne Goudvis, *Strategies That Work* (Portland, ME: Stenhouse, 2000); Jane Braunger and Jan Patricia Lewis, *Building a Knowledge Base in Reading* (Portland, OR: Northwest Regional Educational Laboratory, 1997).

119   The good news is that comprehension has become a long overdue reading focus: NRP 2000.

119–120 "We learned that on average, dedicating about one fifth of each period . . .": James Baumann, Helene Hooten, and Patricia White, "Teaching Comprehension Through Literature: A Teacher-Research Project to Develop Fifth Graders' Reading Strategies and Motivation," *The Reading Teacher* (September 1999), p. 50.

120   The list of key processes is taken from Michael Pressley and Richard Allington, "What Should Reading Instructional Research Be the Research Of?" *Issues in Education* 5, no. 1 (1999), p. 18.

121   Without our direct modeling and intervention . . . our low-achieving students need to be taught comprehension strategies explicitly: Snow 2002, p. 33.

122   Students are more likely to show increased reading comprehension . . .: *NRP 2000*, pp. 4-42, 4-46, and 4-83.

122   "Being strategic is much more than knowing . . .": *NRP 2000*, p. 4-47, citing Gerald G. Duffy, "Rethinking Strategy Instruction: Four Teachers' Development and Their Low Achievers' Understanding," *The Elementary School Journal* (January 1993), p. 244.

122   When given opportunities to reread material, readers' comprehension always goes up: Kylene Beers, "Reading and Writing: Moving Struggling Students Toward Success," presentation at the National Council of Teachers of English, Baltimore, MD, November 17, 2001.

122   And research consistently shows . . .: John Pikulski, "Five Successful Reading Programs for At-Risk Students," *The Reading Teacher* (September 1994), pp. 30–39.

123   See *Conversations*, pp. 451–55, for demonstration lessons on using writing to aid understanding.

124   . . . text-to-text, text-to-self, and text-to-world connections: Stephanie Harvey and Anne Goudvis, *Strategies That Work*, 2000, p. 21.

124   Many studies have been done that show that readers are unaware of how they comprehend: *NRP 2000*, p. 4-43.

126   The role of talk and collaboration in making meaning is discussed in Annemarie Sullivan Palinscar, "The Role of Dialogue in Providing Scaffolded Instruction," *Educational Psychologist* 21, nos. 1 and 2 (1986), pp. 73–98; *NRP 2000*, pp. 4-45 and 4-46; Gordon Wells and Gen Ling Chang-Wells, *Constructing Knowledge Together: Classrooms as Centers of Literacy and Inquiry* (Portsmouth, NH: Heinemann, 1992); Richard Allington, "What I've Learned About Effective Reading Instruction from a Decade of Studying Exemplary Elementary Teachers," *Phi Delta Kappan* 83, no. 10 (June 2002); Jeanne R. Paratore and Rachel L. McCormack, eds., *Peer Talk in the Classroom: Learning from Research* (Newark, DE: International Reading Association, 2000).

127   Examine how texts are leveled, especially at beginning levels where word recognition is critical: E. Hiebert, "Standards, Assessments, and Text Difficulty," in *What Research Has to Say About Reading Instruction*, 3d ed., edited by Alan E. Farstrup and S. Jay Samuels, pp. 337–70 (Newark, DE: International Reading Association, 2002). See *Conversations*, pp. 82–84, for leveling guidelines and resources.

128   "the ability to read a text quickly, accurately, and with proper expression": *NRP 2000*, pp. 3–5.

128   Fluency as an important reading goal is supported by Catherine E. Snow, Susan Burns, and Peg Griffin, eds., *Preventing Reading Difficulties in Young Children* (Washington DC: National Academy Press, 1998), p. 233: "Adequate progress in learning to read English (or any alphabetic language) depends on sufficient practice in reading to achieve fluency in different texts."

128   For information on asking better questions, see *Conversations*, pp. 183–86, 460–61, and 27b–28b.

129   Strategies must be "invoked" by the learner: Richard L. Allington and Peter Johnston, "Characteristics of Exemplary Fourth-Grade Instruction," in *Research on Effective Teaching*, edited by C. Roller (Newark, DE :International Reading Association, 2000).

Chapter 9

130   For specific shared reading procedures, see Don Holdaway, *Foundations of Literacy* (Sydney: Ashton Scholastic, 1979; also available through Heinemann in Portsmouth, NH); *Invitations*, pp. 33–38; *Conversations*, pp. 33–37.

130   Furthermore, research indicates that shared reading typically improves reading achievement: Eldredge, D. Ray Reutzel, and P. M. Hollingsworth, "Comparing the Effectiveness of Two Oral Reading Practices: Round-Robin Reading and the Shared Book Experience," *Journal of Literacy Research* 28, no. 2 (1996), pp. 201–25; Warwick Elley, *Raising Literacy Levels in Third World Countries: A Method That Works* (Culver City, CA: Language Education Associates, 1998), p. 140.

131   See *Invitations*, pp. 110–11, 392, and *Conversations*, pp. 429–31, for word work suggestions and examples.

132   Many unmotivated middle school readers . . .: Kylene Beers, "Choosing Not to Read: Understanding Why Some Middle Schoolers Just Say No," in *Into Focus: Understanding and Creating Middle School Readers*, edited by Kylene Beers and Barbara Samuels, pp. 55–57 (Norwood, MA: Christopher-Gordon, 1998).

133   Such talk is not just enjoyable and enriching . . .: Michael Knapp and Associates, *Teaching for Meaning in High-Poverty Classrooms* (New York: Teachers College Press, 1995); R. Fall, N. M. Webb, and N. Chudowsky, "Group Discussion and Large-Scale Language Arts Assessment: Effects on Students' Comprehension," *American Educational Research Journal* 37, no. 4 (2000), 911–41.

139   Jeri Hanel Watts and Felicia Marshall, *Keepers* (New York: Lee & Low, 1997).

139   Procedures for writing "keeper" essays are found in *Conversations*, pp. 382–83.

143   David Adler, *America's Champion Swimmer: Gertrude Ederle*, illustrations by Terry Widener (San Diego: Harcourt, 2000).

147   Elizabeth George Speare, *The Witch of Blackbird Pond* (New York: Bantam Doubleday, 1986).

Chapter 10

150   Guided reading came to prominence when Irene C. Fountas and Gay Su Pinnell published *Guided Reading: Good First Teaching for All Children* (Portsmouth, NH: Heinemann, 1996).

150   The definition of guided reading is based on Margaret Mooney, "Guided Reading—The Reader in Control," *Teaching, K–8* (February 1995), pp. 54–57, and Fountas and Pinnell 1996, pp. 2–4.

151   I view guided reading more broadly . . .: I also define guided reading on p. 140 of *Conversations*.

152   Once students are already reading . . . students want and need to be in mixed-ability groups: Batya E. Elbaum, Jeanne Shay Schumm, and Sharon Vaughn, "Urban Middle-Elementary Students' Perceptions of Grouping Formats for Reading Instruction," *Elementary School Journal* (May 1997), p. 487; Richard M. Jaeger and John A. Hattie, "Detracking America's Schools: Should We Really Care?" *Phi Delta Kappan* (November 1995), p. 219; also see *Conversations*, pp. 145–46.

153   For sample reciprocal teaching lessons, see *Conversations*, pp. 137–40.

153   See *Conversations*, pp. 82–84 and 18b–19b for recommended resources that provide leveling guidelines and lists of leveled books. Recent excellent resources to check when purchasing and choosing books for guided reading and discussion include Nancy Johnson, Bonnie Campbell Hill, and Katherine Schlick Noe, *Literature Circles Resource Guide* (Norwood, MA: Christopher-Gordon, 2000); Charlotte Huck, S. Hepler, J. Hickman, and B. Ziefer, *Children's Literature in the Elementary School* (Columbus, OH: McGraw-Hill, 2000); Teri S. Lesesne, editor, "What Books Should Anyone Working with Teens Know?" *Voices from the Middle* (March 2002), pp. 47–53 (annotated YA titles highly recommended by more than a hundred teachers and librarians); and Jim Trelease, *The Read-Aloud Handbook*, 5th ed. (New York: Penguin, 2001).

154   Kate DiCamillo, *Because of Winn-Dixie* (Cambridge, MA: Candlewick Press, 2000); Cynthia Rylant, *Every Living Thing* (NY: Aladdin, 1985); Louis Sachar, *Holes* (New York: Farrar Strauss & Giroux, 1998); Christopher Paul Curtis, *Bud, Not Buddy* (New York: Delacorte, 1999); Pam Munoz Ryan, *Esperanza Rising* (New York: Scholastic, 2000).

155   For more information, guidelines, and resources regarding leveling and selecting texts for developing readers, see *Transitions*, pp. 299–309, *Invitations*, pp. 43–44, and *Conversations*, pp. 82b–88b.

160   . . . students—especially low-performing readers—need to process massive amounts of comprehensible texts in order to read well: Richard Allington, *What Really Matters for Struggling Readers* (New York: Longman, 2001).

162   For more on written response, see my *Writing Essentials*, forthcoming from Heinemann.

167   The guidelines and details of a guided reading lesson have been spelled out by many: Fountas and Pinnell 1996; Michael F. Opitz and Michael P. Ford, *Reaching Readers* (Portsmouth, NH: Heinemann, 2001).

167   Sharon Taberski, *On Solid Ground* (Portsmouth, NH: Heinemann, 2000); Regie Routman, *Conversations* (Portsmouth, NH: Heinemann, 2000).

170   See also *Conversations*, pp. 149–52, "Framework for a Guided Silent Reading Lesson."

175   Kate McGough, *Making a Hat* (Washington, DC: National Geographic, Windows on Literacy, 2001).

178   Arnold Lobel, "The Garden," *Frog and Toad Together*, pp. 18–29 (New York: HarperCollins, 1971).

180   Janice Shefelman, *Young Wolf's First Hunt*, illustrated by Tom Shefelman (a Step into Reading book, grades 2–3) (New York: Random House, 1993).

182   Kate DiCamillo, *Because of Winn-Dixie* (Cambridge, MA: Candlewick Press, 2000).

Chapter 11

185   The epigraph is from Richard Allington's presentation "What Really Matters for Struggling Readers" at the Florida Reading Association meeting in Orlando, Florida, on October 14, 2000.

186   The new education directive is promulgated in G. W. Bush, *No Child Left Behind* (Washington, DC: U. S. Department of Education, 2002). The website for the Bush Education Plan as well as for information on "Early Reading First" initiatives is www.ed.gov.

186   There is no best program or perfect model of teaching reading: S. J. Samuels, Editorial, *Reading Research Quarterly* 19 (1984) pp. 390–92. Samuels is a member of the National Reading Panel, and his statement is therefore significant.

187   Students need caring teachers: Don Holdaway, *The Foundations of Literacy* (Sydney: Ashton Scholastic, 1979; also available through Heinemann in Portsmouth, NH).

187   Readers need to have a large bank of words that they can read automatically: Marilyn Jager Adams, *Beginning to Read: Thinking and Learning About Print* (Cambridge, MA: MIT Press, 1990); S. J. Samuels, N. Shermer, and D. Reinking, "Reading Fluency: Techniques for Making Decoding Automatic," in *What Research Has to Say About Reading Instruction*, 3d ed., edited by Alan E. Farstrup and S. Jay Samuels, pp. 124–44 (Newark, DE: International Reading Association, 2002); J. Mason and K. Au, *Reading Instruction for Today* (Glenview, IL: Scott Foresman, 1990).

187   Phonics instruction is most effective when largely completed by the end of first grade: *The Report of the National Reading Panel. Teaching Children to Read: An Evidence-Based Assessment of the Scientific Research Literature on Reading and Its Implications for Reading Instruction (NRP)* (Washington, DC: National Institute of Child Health and Human Development, 2000).

187   Phonemic awareness is necessary for students to become readers and is acquired by most children through rhyming and word play in rich, literacy contexts: H. Yopp, "Developing Phonemic Awareness in Young Children," *The Reading Teacher* 45 (1992), pp. 696–703.

187   All good readers miscue (make errors), correct themselves (when necessary for meaning), and problem solve as they read: Kenneth Goodman, *On Reading: A Common-Sense Look at the Nature of Language and the Science of Reading* (Portsmouth, NH: Heinemann, 1996); Marie Clay, *An Observational Survey of Early Literacy Achievement* (Portsmouth, NH: Heinemann, 2002).

187   Students need to be matched with books they can read: Marie Clay, *Becoming Literate: The Construction of Inner Control.* (Portsmouth, NH: Heinemann, 1991); Elfrieda Hiebert, "Selecting Texts for Beginning Reading Instruction," in *Literature-Based Instruction: Reshaping the Curriculum,* edited by Taffy E. Raphael and Kathryn H. Au, pp. 195–218 (Norwood, MA: Christopher-Gordon, 1998); Barbara Peterson, "Selecting Books for Beginning Readers," in *Bridges to Literacy: Learning from Reading Recovery,* edited by Diane DeFord, Carol Lyons, and Gay Su Pinnell, pp. 119–47 (Portsmouth, NH: Heinemann, 1991); Irene C. Fountas and Gay Su Pinnell, *Matching Books to Readers: Using Leveled Books in Guided Reading, K–3* (Portsmouth, NH: Heinemann, 1999).

187   Struggling readers need to spend more time reading, not doing activities about reading: Richard Allington, "If They Don't Read Much, How They Ever Gonna Get Good at It?" *Journal of Reading* 21 (1977), pp. 57–61; Richard Allington, *What Really Matters for Struggling Readers: Designing Research-Based Programs* (New York: Longman, 2001); Stephen Krashen, *The Power of Reading* (Englewood, CO: Libraries Unlimited, 1993).

187   Avid readers can talk about favorite books and authors: Kathy Short and Kathyrn Mitchell Pierce, *Talking About Books: Literature Discussion Groups in K–8 Classrooms* (Portsmouth, NH: Heinemann, 1998); Shelley Harwayne, *Lifetime Guarantees: Toward Ambitious Literacy Teaching* (Portsmouth, NH: Heinemann, 2000).

187   Effective readers integrate many strategies to comprehend text: P. David Pearson, L. R. Roheler, J. A. Dole, and G. G. Duffy, "Developing Expertise in Reading Comprehension," in *What Research Says to Teachers,* 2nd ed., pp. 145–99, edited by S. J. Samuels and A. E. Farstrup (Newark, DE: International Reading Association, 1992); National Reading Panel Report: Reports of the Subgroups. "Chapter 4: Text Comprehension Instruction" pp. 4-39–4-52; Nell K. Duke and P. David Pearson, "Effective Practices for Developing Reading Comprehension," in *What Research Has to Say About Reading Instruction,* 3d ed., edited by Alan E. Farstrup and S. Jay Samuels, pp. 205–42 (Newark, DE: International Reading Association, 2002).

187   Access to books and libraries positively impacts reading achievement: S. Krashen, "School Libraries, Public Libraries, and the NAEP Reading Scores," *School Library Media Quarterly* 23 (1995), pp. 235–36; S. Neuman and D. Celano, "Access to Print in Low-Income and Middle Income Communities," *Reading Research Quarterly* 36 (January/February/March 2001), pp. 8–26; Anne McGill-Franzen and Richard L. Allington, "What Are They to Read? Not All Kids, Mr. Riley, Have Easy Access to Books," *Education Week* 26 (October 13, 1993); Leslie Morrow 1983, as cited in Krashen 1993 (see *Conversations,* p. 549).

187   More nonfiction texts need to be housed and read in classrooms: Nell Duke, "3.6 Minutes Per Day: The scarcity of Information Texts in First Grade," *Reading Research Quarterly,* 35 no. 2 (April/June 2000), pp. 202–224. Susan Neuman et al., *Access for All: Closing the Book Gap for Children in Early Education* (Newark, DE: International Reading Association, 2001).

187   Interest plays an important role in engaging readers: Jo Worthy and Karen Broaddus, "Fluency Beyond the Primary Grades: From Group Performance to Silent, Independent Reading," *The Reading Teacher* (2002); Daniel Fader, *The New Hooked on Books* (New York: Berkley, 1982); Rosalie Fink, "Successful Adults With Dyslexia Develop High Literacy," *The Annals of Dyslexia* 48 (December 1998).

187   Readers who enjoy reading and are motivated to read do read more: Jan Pilgreen, *The SSR Handbook: How to Organize and Manage a Sustained Silent Reading Program* (Portsmouth, NH: Heinemann, 2000); John Guthrie, "Preparing Students for High-Stakes Test Taking in Reading," in *What Research Has to Say About Reading Instruction*, 3d ed., edited by Alan E. Farstrup and S. Jay Samuels, p. 382 (Newark, DE: International Reading Association, 2002).

187   Students learn more when basic skills are integrated and connected to relevant and challenging curriculum: Ellen Langer, *Mindfulness* (New York: Addison-Wesley, 1989); Ellen Langer, *The Power of Mindful Learning* (New York: Addison-Wesley, 1997); Judith Langer, "Guidelines for Teaching Middle and High School Students to Read and Write Well" (Albany, NY: The Center on English Learning and Achievement, September 2000). Ellen Langer's work shows that skills are linked to the context in which they are taught. If they are taught in isolation, they are invariant and do not transfer to authentic contexts.

187   . . . "research-based" practice is viewed as one of the hottest topics in education: Jack Cassidy and Drew Cassidy, "What's Hot, What's Not for 2002," *Reading Today* (December 2001/January 2002), p. 18.

188   However, when respected scholars and educators question research . . .: Those scholars and educators include Richard Allington, *Big Brother and the National Reading Curriculum* (Portsmouth, NH: Heinemann, 2002); Gerald Coles, *Misreading Reading* (Portsmouth, NH: Heinemann, 2000) and *Reading the Naked Truth: Literacy, Legislation, and Lies* (Portsmouth, NH: Heinemann, 2003); J. Cunningham, "Essay Book Review: The National Reading Panel Report," *Reading Research Quarterly* 36, no. 3 (2001), pp. 326–335; Elaine Garan, "Beyond the Smoke and Mirrors: A Critique of the National Reading Panel Report on Phonics," *Phi Delta Kappan* 82, no. 7 (2001), pp. 500–506; Elaine Garan, *Resisting Reading Mandates* (Portsmouth, NH: Heinemann, 2002); Stephen Krashen, "More Smoke and Mirrors: A Critique of the National Reading Panel Report on Fluency," *Phi Delta Kappan* 83, no. 2 (2001), pp. 119–23; J. Yatvin, "Babes in the Woods: The Wanderings of the National Reading Panel," *Phi Delta Kappan* 83, no. 5 (2002), pp. 364–69; Jeff McQuillan, *The Literacy Crisis: False Claims, Real Solutions* (Portsmouth, NH: Heinemann, 1998).

188   For more on teaching phonics see *Literacy at the Crossroads*, pp. 93–96.

188   There is no one best way to teach phonics: Steven Stahl, Ann Duffy-Hester, and Katherine Dougherty Stahl, "Everything You Wanted to Know About Phonics (But Were Afraid to Ask)," *Reading Research Quarterly* 33, no. 3 (1998), pp. 338–55.

188   Effective teachers use a combination of approaches: Richard L. Allington, "What I've Learned About Effective Reading Instruction from a Decade of Studying Exemplary Elementary Classroom Teachers," *Phi Delta Kappan* 83, no.10 (June 2002), pp. 740–47. Lesley M. Morrow, Diane Tracey, Deborah G. Woo, and Michael Pressley, "Characteristics of Exemplary First Grade Literacy Instruction." *The Reading Teacher*, February 1999, pp. 462–476; Michael Pressley, Joan Rankin, and Linda Yokoi, "A Survey of Instructional Practices of Primary Teachers Nominated as Effective in Promoting Literacy," *The Elementary School Journal*, 96, No. 4 (1996), pp. 363–384.

188   Phonics instruction is most effective if it is mostly completed by the end of first grade: *NRP* 2000.

188   Intensive phonics instruction is not effective for older, struggling readers: *NRP* 2000.

188   Students need both systematic, explicit phonics and phonics taught in the learning context, at the point of need: Pressley et al. 2002.

188   Children learn a lot about phonics through invented spelling in their writing: Richard Gentry and Jean Wallace Gillet, *Teaching Kids to Spell* (Portsmouth, NH: Heinemann, 1993); Sandra Wilde, *You Kan Red This! Spelling and Punctuation for Whole Language Classrooms, K–6* (Portsmouth, NH: Heinemann, 1991); Edmund Henderson, *Teaching Spelling* (New York: Houghton Mifflin, 1990).

188   Excellent phonics instruction is necessary but not sufficient for becoming a reader: *NRP* 2000.

188   An early phonics emphasis does not necessarily translate to increased comprehension: Richard C. Anderson et al., *Becoming a Nation of Readers* (Champagne, IL: University of IL, 1985); Coles 2000.

188   "Phonics instruction should aim to teach only . . .": Anderson et al. 1985, p. 38.

189   The National Reading Panel report, reports of the subgroups, and the video are available at no charge through *www.nationalreadingpanel.org* or by calling 800-370-2943.

189   And keep in mind that some claims in the news media for the study's findings were not supported by a close, careful look at the full report: Garan 2002.

191   Students in classrooms with effective teachers are better readers regardless of the approach, program, or materials the teachers use: Richard Allington, "What I've Learned About Effective Reading Instruction from a Decade of Studying Exemplary Elementary Classroom Teachers," *Phi Delta Kappan* 83, no. 10 (June 2002), pp. 740–47. Allington's article is based on the National Research Center on English Learning and Achievement's decade of careful observation, interviews, study, and analysis of exemplary first- and fourth-grade teachers in "schools that enrolled substantial numbers of poor children and schools that reflected the racial, ethnic, and linguistic diversity of the nation."

191   . . . the lowest achievers make the most gains: Allington 2002; Karla Scoon Reid, "Study Tracks Cincinnati's New Teacher Ratings, Tests Scores," *Education Week*, April 3, 2002, p. 9.

194   A small percentage of students may benefit from such a program . . . : See *Literacy at the Crossroads*, pp. 99–100.

194   The use of direct instruction programs is increasing and, in many cases, is being mandated: Suzanne Pardington, "Driven to Perform: A School Struggles to Improve," *Contra Costa [CA] Times*, December 3, 2000.

194   One problem is that the majority of direct instruction research has been done by the program developers themselves: Richard Allington, *What Really Matters for Struggling Readers: Designing Research-Based Programs* (New York: Longman, 2001) p. 10; Garan 2002; Coles 2000 and forthcoming; Stahl et al., 1998.

194   . . . the promise of higher test scores has not materialized in a number of schools: "Some Test Scores Falling Despite Reading Programs," *Columbus [OH] Dispatch*, October 17, 2000.

194   ... after several years of direct instruction, the reading test scores can decline sharply, particularly once students hit the greater reading demands in the intermediate grades: Margaret Moustafa and Robert Land, "The Research Base of Open Court and Its Translation into Instructional Policy in California" (Los Angeles: California State University, 2000); Pardington 2000.

195   "The evidence suggests that highly prescriptive curricular mandates do not improve student learning, especially if they effectively control teaching": Linda Darling-Hammond, *The Right to Learn: A Blueprint for Creating Schools That Work* (San Francisco: Jossey-Bass, 1997), p. 53.

195   "In other words, virtually every proponent . . .": Allington 2001, p. 11.

196   *Preventing Reading Difficulties in Young Children* (Washington, D.C.: National Research Council, 1998).

197   Some direct instruction programs rely on outdated research to make current claims for success: Richard Allington, "What Do We Know About the Effects of Direct Instruction on Student Reading Achievement?" (Gainsville: University of Florida, 2001).

197   Sometimes the researchers or those paying for the study are the very people who created the program or who analyze the results or write the conclusions: Garan 2002.

197   "Voucher Study Indicates No Steady Gains in Learning," *The New York Times*, December 9, 2001, National News, A33.

197   In order to be considered truly "scientific," the evidence from a study must be so convincing that someone with an open mind would be persuaded to reconsider his views: J. Cunningham, *Reading Research Quarterly*, 2001.

198   In the short run, students get better on the discrete skills we teach them but do not necessarily transfer these skills to reading: Gerry Coles, *Misreading Reading* (Portsmouth, NH: Heinemann, 2000).

198   Program developers tout the fact that students are motivated to read more and better books, but few peer-reviewed journal articles support these claims: Linda Pavonetti, Kathryn Brimmer, and James Cipeilewsk, "Accelerated Reader: What Are the Lasting Effects on the Reading Habits of Middle School Students Exposed to Accelerated Reader in Elementary Grades?" presentation at the 50th annual meeting of the National Reading Conference, Scottsdale, AZ, November 30, 2000; Linda Lamme, Danling Fu, and Richard Allington, "Is This an Accelerated Reader Book? A closer examination of a popular reading program." *Florida Reading Quarterly* 38, 3 (2002) pp. 27–32.

198   ... any program that greatly increases the amount of reading students do is likely to positively impact achievement: Allington 2001.

198   ... most AR books are fiction. New titles, informational books, and poetry are underrepresented: Betty Carter, "Hold the Applause! Do Accelerated Reader and Electronic Bookshelf Send the Right Message?" *School Library Journal* (October 1996), pp. 22–25.

199   "Many of the lower-level AR books . . .": L. Lamme, D. Fu, and R Allington, "'Is This Book an AR Book?' A Closer Examination of a Popular Reading Program," *Florida Reading Quarterly* 38, no. 3 (2002) pp. 27–32.

199 . . . extrinsic motivation . . . undermines voluntary reading for pleasure in the long run: Alfie Kohn, *Punished by Rewards: The Trouble with Gold Stars, Incentive Plans, A's, Praise, and Other Incentives* (Boston: Houghton Mifflin, 1999).

Chapter 12

204 Authentic reading and writing in which students have some challenge, choice, control, and opportunity to collaborate motivate students most: Julianne Turner and Scott G. Paris, "How Literacy Tasks Influence Children's Motivation for Literacy," *The Reading Teacher* (May 1995), pp. 662–73.

204 Create your own texts for reading and writing "on the spot": see *Conversations*, pp. 38–44 and pp. 123–24 for lots of possibilities.

205 For examples of word work "seat work," see *Conversations*, pp. 423–33. For suggestions on reading responses, see *Conversations*, pp. 75–78 and 167–68, and *Invitations*, pp. 103–17.

206 I discuss reciprocal teaching procedures in detail on pages 137–40 of *Conversations*.

206 Recent brain research indicates that we have kids' attention for less than ten minutes before they need a "cognitive rest": Eric Jensen, *Teaching with the Brain in Mind* (Alexandria, VA: ASCD, 1998), pp. 41–51.

208 Being aware of and learning new words is the subject of Michael F. Graves and Susan M. Watts-Taffe, "The Place of Word Consciousness in a Research-Based Vocabulary Program," in *What Research Has to Say About Reading Instruction*, 3d ed., edited by Alan E. Farstrup and S. Jay Samuels, pp. 144–47 (Newark, DE: International Reading Association, 2002).

210–211 In many schools, students spend most of their time coloring during "reading instruction": Mike Schmoker, "The Crayola Curriculum," *Education Week*, October 24, 2001.

216 Schools that are more collegial and collaborative are happier places and have higher student achievement: Roland Barth, *Improving Schools from Within: Teachers, Parents, and Principals Can Make the Difference* (Jossey-Bass Education series) (San Francisco: Jossey-Bass, 1991).

216 The article mentioned is "Teacher Talk," *Educational Leadership* (March 2002), pp. 32–35.

217 If you have to ask yourself where you'll find the time . . . : Daniel Pennac, *Better Than Life* (Portland, ME: Stenhouse, 1999), pp. 145–47.

219 "If I were obliged to choose between students' love of learning . . .": W. James Popham, *The Truth About Testing: An Educator's Call to Action* (Alexandria, VA: ASCD, 2001), p. 120.

Index